# ROBERT STERN

# ROBERT STERN

## Introductory Essay by Vincent Scully

ACKNOWLEDGEMENTS
Our thanks are due to Robert Stern for his much appreciated collaboration, and to David Dunster for invaluable editorial assistance and advice.

The following people have made a significant contribution to the graphic expression of the architectural ideas represented by the drawings in this exhibition and catalogue: Mark Albert, Terry Brown, Daniel Colbert, Randy Correll, John Ike, Benjamin Kracauer, Gavin Macrae-Gibson, Mark Miriscal, Fabrizio Medosi, Peter Pennoyer, Piroska Savani, Roger Seifter, Edmund Stoeklein, Charles Warren

Edited and designed by Ian Latham and Penelope Farrant with Richard Cheatle

Cover design: Dennis Crompton

*Front cover* 'Human scale at the end of the age of modernism' (● 122) 1980

*Back cover* Residence, Armonk, New York (● 053) 1976 (photo: Norman McGrath)

*Frontispiece* New York Townhouse (● 055) 1975 (photo: Ed Stoecklein)

*Page three* Best Products Facade, detail (● 096) 1979 (photo: Ed Stoecklein)

Photographs on pages 2, 3, 6, 7, 10, 15 by Ed Stoecklein

This publication and the accompanying exhibition of architectural drawings by Robert Stern are sponsored by *Architectural Design* magazine.

Robert Stern's essay 'The Doubles of Post-Modern' was reprinted from *Harvard Architecture* 1 by permission of the MIT Press and of the author.

**Robert A.M. Stern**, architect, writer and teacher, was born in New York in 1939. Educated at Columbia University (B.A. 1960) and at Yale (M.Arch 1965), Stern became a partner in the firm John S. Hagmann, architects and planners, in 1969, having, among other activities, worked as a designer in Richard Meier's New York office, and as a consultant to Philip Johnson for a television documentary on New York. Since 1977 he has been principal of Robert A.M. Stern Architects, New York. Stern is a professor at Columbia University, and was William Henry Bishop Visiting Professor at Yale in 1978. He has been a member of a number of architectural and pedagogical committees and was President of the Architectural league of New York from 1973 to 1977, and Director of the New York Chapter of the American Institute of Architects from 1976 to 1978. Author of numerous books and articles, and both subject and organiser of a wide range of exhibitions on architecture, art and design, Stern's considerable influence in architectural practice and his outstanding contributions to architectural debate must be seen as a reflection of the man's versatility and vitality.



Published in Great Britain by Architectural Design
7 Holland Street London W8
Printed in Great Britain by Balding and Mansell, Wisbech, Cambridgeshire

To subscribe to *Architectural Design* write to:
Subscriptions Department
7/8 Holland Street, London W8

# Foreword

The name and work of Robert A.M. Stern are ineradicably entwined with the polemics of Post-Modernism. That deals with what he is, though not with how and why he came to be. Stern is a building architect first and foremost, not overmuch given to paper utopias, and second, a spokesman for eclectic freedom. His work justifies his words, and the eclecticism of that is surely comparable in richness to that of the Edwardian country house or the Garden City movement; England, in other words, at the turn of the century. It is appropriate, to say the least, that Stern's first major retrospective should be mounted in London, a city he knows well and one from which he seems to have learnt more than his English contemporaries.

The link with England invites a telling analogy. Looking back to that honeymoon period before the 1914-18 war, the professional family, not yet aware of the discoveries of Freud's *The Interpretation of Dreams*, first published in German in 1900, seems to have looked inward to the home as more than a castle. Their dream — music, books, art, clean living and tolerance — was given form by the architects of that period in eclectic buildings. Forget however the tension between the dream and the reality, and take only the ideas of the plans; transpose these wandering spaces onto the home stock of an indigenous American architecture; re-draw them in forms that do not forget the planning discoveries of the Modern Movement; build them with confidence and craft — such could be the scenario for Stern's work. He offers a definition of the good life at once comfortable and provocative, varied yet clear.

Within the work produced however there is a strong move away from that open-plan, dominant in the earlier works, towards a kind of room planning which takes off from axes and views in the later work. Always each space has been differentiated from its neighbours. A study could never be confused with the bedroom in one of his houses, nor does any principle of zoning exclusively dominate the building. This derives, it seems, from an experimental energy, consistently applied through the work that makes one suspect that the maxim of the office, in neon Times Roman, is *'Do It'*.

This technique of planning, or better perhaps of composing the plan, resembles collage, but only in the sense of juxtaposition. A house by Stern is never that stern, and what unites is something like his personality, impish, mercurial and, above all, witty. An architecture of character perhaps? Certainly these schemes are not universal solutions, though certain characteristic solution-types appear — the staircase for example, wide at the bottom, a landing one third of the way up, the middle flight presented as an elevation as it were, and the third and final flight disappearing over the first flight. If it is character which comes off the page, it is firmly placed within a tradition of pragmatism mixed with a sound sense of economy.

So his work appeals to more than just the word-games of post-modernists. That dream of the good life lives on. Tomorrow the shining sun will greet the orange juice freshly squeezed for breakfast. In his buildings there seems a place for that sentiment. It may be arguable that this is no great vision but that would be to blot out the sun and substitute rancid coffee for the orange. Pleasure, a feeling of luxury, delight; these qualities are offered by the work, not thrust upon the world. To provide such a choice is no small matter. Without architects like Stern around, the joy in architecture might be forgotten.

*David Dunster*

*Top, and bottom left* Rooftop apartment, New York City, 1972-73 (033)
'This three bedroom rooftop apartment has been remodelled with three aims in mind: first of all, to maximise the impact of a spectacular view south toward mid-town; secondly, to relieve the oppressive nature of the low ceilings by breaking through the room to gain light from above; and thirdly, to clarify the organisation of space thus giving the illusion of greater size. Standard pre-fabricated units (sliding doors, greenhouse, ceramic tile) are used in combination with refined materials (brass, lacquered wood cabinets, antique furniture) to provide an atmosphere that is at once a response to the established lifestyle of the owners and to the contextual demands of a unique rooftop location.' *(RS)*

*Bottom right* New York Townhouse, 1975 (055)
'Rich polychromy characterises the interior design. Bold saturations of colour are employed in individual spaces such as the children's bedrooms, the circular stair and the spaces of arrival, while delicate shades such as lavender and peach are used to emphasise the sensuous curves of cabinetry. In addition, wall planes are themselves used as decoration: the South wall which functions as an inner lining of the building, concealing storage and mechanical equipment, is articulated with deep reveals set between panelled areas, thus giving the wall a sense of materiality while also modulating its scale in relation to the sizes and proportions of the rooms and spaces that it abuts.' *(RS)*

*Top* Poolhouse, Greenwich, Connecticut, 1973-74 (048)
'Inside, the bounding surfaces of the various spaces combine with the natural light that is introduced from overhead sources and the use of dazzling colour to produce a freewheeling series of spaces that seem virtually free of contextual constraint. Not only are these spaces unpredictable from the outside, but they also suggest the freshness of summer all year round and thereby invite the suspension of belief so necessary to a good-time place. The pavilion is conceived of as a billowing shingled tent, washed with light from above, cooled by natural breezes (in the appropriate seasons), and inflected toward principal views. With the exception of the screened porch at the east end, the pavilion is heated in winter.

*Bottom* Westchester Residence, Armonk, New York, 1976 (053)
'This house is reached by a new one-half-mile-long road. The site is at the top of a steep hill; a magnificent hemlock grove and superb views of the neighbouring countryside are its principal features. A curving screen wall is introduced at the entrance which provides for a covered entry, allows for the development of a private outdoor space for the servants, and facilitates the resolution of the diagonal driveway axis with the orthogonal planning of the house itself. On the rear or garden facade, a bowed screen wall in combination with landscaping serves to reduce the apparent length of the garden elevation, provide integral sun protection, and focus views from the principal interior spaces.' *(RS)*

## Vincent Scully

# The Star in Stern: Sightings and Orientation

When George Howe took command as Dean of the Yale School of Architecture in 1950 he prepared an elaborate address which was intended to convey the general conceptual structure of his thoughts about architecture to the school as a whole. The lecture was entitiled 'The Path of the Feet and the Eyes' and was in substance exactly as its title described it. Dean Howe went on for forty-five minutes or so following his feet through history when all at once a peculiar expression crossed his face and he terminated the lecture. As a young instructor I took that look to mean that he had come to the end of his thoughts for that day. Only later did I grow to realise that it meant that he had come to an end of his thoughts for all time. The conceptual reservoir was exhausted. That phenomenon is not unknown among deans and has never been regarded as a handicap to them in the pursuit of their duties. Dean Howe went on to serve in an unexceptionably dean-like manner for five years, delegating authority to various eccentric persons and leaving the school a Byzantine shambles at his retirement. From this it was eventually saved by Paul Rudolph who took over with admirable directness in 1958 and acted as the proverbial breath of fresh air for several fine and highly creative years. One of his most valuable acts was to import a number of young English architects, among them James Stirling, Norman Foster and Sue and Richard Rogers, who immeasurably enriched the intellectual life of the school. Rudolph slowly wilted under the strain, however, as all deans seem sooner or later to do, and he, too, employed several curious individuals who soon reduced the place once again to what was beginning to seem to be its normal paranoiac state.

It was at the height of the Rudolph era, in 1960, just before the first rich odours of putrefaction began to announce themselves, that Robert A.M. Stern entered the school as a first year student. He almost immediately did what most students of architecture resolutely avoided doing, in which they were amply encouraged by the architecture faculty: he enrolled himself in a graduate seminar on modern architecture in the History of Art Department. Curiously enough, in view of Stern's later interests, the first semesters were given over to a consideration of twentieth-century architecture outside the canonical Modern Movement. Stern's intention as a scholar, one which struck horror in every breast which remembered the old days, was to write a critical biography of George Howe's life and work. From this he could never be dissuaded, and he eventually produced, as an M.A. thesis (a degree that he never bothered to take up), the admirably complete and authoritative book which eventually found publication in 1975. It revealed a George Howe much greater in every way than those who had known him only in his last years could have guessed. It also established his central role in the development of a new, American phase in modern architecture, one which was to come to fruition in the work of Louis I. Kahn, Robert Venturi and — Stern would be the first to say to a secondary degree — in that of Stern himself.

There were some outstanding graduate students in the History of Art at Yale during Stern's years there: among them were Helen Searing, now of Smith College, who was just beginning her investigation of the Amsterdam School, on which she wrote her doctoral dissertation in 1972, and Norma Evenson, now of Berkeley, who was well along on the dissertation which resulted in her books on Chandigarh, Le Corbusier, and Brasilia. Sheldon Nodelman and Spiro Kostof, both of the University of California, were also in residence. Neil Levine of Harvard joined them in 1965, just after Stern's graduation. The group as a whole was probably the best ever assembled at Yale, and Stern was an integral part of it as well as an outstanding student in the architecture school itself. There he was by no means a universal favourite. The Bauhaus bloc had marked him down as a natural enemy from the very beginning (all that history) and, in this case wholly without prejudice, the much respected Henry Pfisterer eventually passed him in Structures only after exacting his solemn oath, so Stern tells it, that he would never thereafter design so much as a doghouse without the advice of an engineer.

Stern's interest in history and criticism continued to grow, and in 1965, the year of his graduation, he produced by far the most important issue ever put together of *Perspecta, the Yale Architectural Journal*. *Perspecta* had been founded during the Howe era, with much intellectual and financial encouragement from Philip Johnson (who has remained one of Stern's most loyal backers and friends), and while it had published some good material over the years, it had always tended to suffer from an over-elaborate format and too much design. Stern pretty much cut through all that and brought out a double issue which was immediately recognised as a major document of modern architecture in the sixties. Indeed, it was already prophetic of what Stern might now call Post-Modern architecture, and it can now be recognised as one of the first guns of that movement. Kahn, the young Charles Moore, and many lesser known, but soon to be important, architects were included in it, all entirely through Stern's judgment. Most important of all was the central position given to Robert Venturi and to the opening chapter of his

Robert Venturi's Mother's House, 1962

Wiseman House, Montauk, 1966-68

*Complexity and Contradiction in Architecture*, which was published as a book the following year. It is fair to say that although Venturi already enjoyed a strong local following in Philadelphia at that time and had been published in bits by some of us, it was Stern who first recognised his absolute worth and forced the rest of us to begin to accord him the consideration he deserved. Stern's issue of *Perspecta* (number 9/10) was extensively distributed in the Soviet Union during 1965, in connection with a show of American architecture there, and Venturi's work was an astonishing favourite among Russian architectural students. (One of them, though, during a seminar in Leningrad, referred to Venturi's house for his mother and, having in mind the Soviet Union's desperate need for mass public housing, asked 'Who needs it?' Instantly another student, speaking so much out of the great Russian tradition of intellectual generosity that it brought a catch to the throat, replied, 'Everyone needs everything'.)

Stern carried the critical judgment and energy which had created *Perspecta* number 9/10 with him to New York, and he has continued to function since that time as architect, historian, and critic all at once. The list of his publications speaks for itself. The general direction has remained the same: toward the critical identification and the artistic implementation of what Stern singles out as the most advanced and viable architectural ideas. The tone is pragmatic and realistic and is firmly locked into the history of American culture, especially into that of New York. On that subject Stern is an expert, and he has continually involved himself in civic, social, and professional projects of every kind. He worked hard for Lindsay in his first campaign and played an important role in formulating the Lindsay administration's progressive policies in planning and preservation. In that vein Stern worked in the Housing and Development Administration for three years, and he remains without question an outstanding authority on public housing. He revitalised the Architectural League of New York, restoring its ancient glories and transforming it into a major centre for the discussion of architectural history, theory, and practice. Perhaps his major achievement in the cause of rational discourse was his *rapprochement* with Peter Eisenman and the Institute for Architecture and Urban Studies. Through that intellectual alliance a good deal of the unpleasant partisanship which once characterised disagreements about architecture has disappeared from the New York scene, and the Institute, though originally founded upon a rather narrow ideological base has enormously broadened and enriched its methods and goals. The rise of Post-Modernism as a whole is not unconnected with that development, since diversity of points of view is central to the movement, and it was against the hermetic purism of modern architecture, with its concomitant shouting of intolerant slogans that Charles Jencks, and Stern himself, first consciously rebelled. The alliance between Jencks and Stern is based upon their common belief in pluralism and their dismay at the dogmatic and rather ignorant exclusivism which once characterised so much of modern architectural theory and practice. Stern had indeed seen enough of Yale to show him how deadly it could be, and he deserves perhaps more credit than he has yet been given for walking into the lion's den and making friends with the inhabitants. That act and some of the others noted above have indeed changed the whole tone of architectural practice for the younger generation of New York. That city is once again, as it was in the twenties, the very best place to be, not even primarily for the work but for the mind. It is where the life is, and it is likely that future generations will regard its present state as a kind of architectural golden age. It is at least one in which architects can learn from each other, and in this Stern leads the rest: his open admiration for the work of architects such as Michael Graves, for example, is one of his most sympathetic characteristics.

Stern has indeed said many times that he does not regard himself as a maker of original forms, like the great hero-architects of the Modern Movement or their immediate successors, but as an adaptor of forms who tries to design out of what exists. This is of course the way in which styles are fleshed out and useful vernaculars created. Stern's view of himself as an informed eclectic is therefore a realistic and culturally very useful one, and his work does seem from the very beginning to bear out that self-assessment. The Wiseman House at Montauk, of 1966-68, takes the rear of Venturi's own house, of 1960-63, and turns it around to face the view westward from the height on which it is placed. In accordance with that new topographical position, the main arch motif expands and opens up, and a narrow slit in the wall of the original building is excavated into a deep crevasse in the centre of the new one. Adaptation as exaggeration is suggested; the house is that of a very young man, one year out of school, who is clear enough about what he wants to do but is as yet rather heavy-handed in the execution of it. The Beebe House of only a few years later shows a considerable advance. The distortions in plan, which seemed the result of adjustment to facade cond-

*Left* New York Townhouse, 1975 (055)

Details of model, Residence, Llewellyn Park, New Jersey, 1981 (094)

Lang House, Washington, Connecticut, 1972-73, interior and exterior
Pool House, Greenwich, Connecticut, 1973-74

itions in the Wiseman House, now appear to be generated by essential environmental considerations. Ventilation plays its part in high open volumes of space running up through the body of the house and forcing its walls to expand. Kahn's principle of formal deformation, so exploited by Moore at that period, is certainly involved, as is Stern's knowledge of the Shingle Style of the 1880s. The exterior, like that of the Wiseman House, is indeed shingled, but now the flat-roofed planes suggest a more Regency set of shapes, much less rustic, leaning instead toward some remote descendant of classical design.

All these qualities finally find their way forward to shape the building as a whole in the Lang House of 1974. In my opinion, the criticisms as 'purely visual' and 'effete', which this house seems superficially to invite, miss the point entirely. It is true that the present appearance of the building is highly disconcerting. It has been repainted a Day-Glo orange by a later owner who was apparently of the unshakable conviction that yellow paint induced cancer. A fairly inept pool house by another architect has also been added to it. But the original house is beautifully set on a terrace of hill facing across a sweeping valley, and its curving garden facade functions reciprocally with that view. That facade is the culmination of a physical experience in three dimensions which has been designed in processional terms — indeed as George Howe's 'Path of the Feet and the Eyes'. If Howe's flow diagram to illustrate that method were lifted off the actually quite rigid plan of his Wasserman House, to which he applied it, it would be found to fit much more appropriately over the sequence of spaces in the Lang House. Everything works toward that movement. The entrance facade is a weirdly scaled flat plane. It avoids, through plywood painted to imitate stucco, the structural scale suggested by shingles. It is a stage flat, and that character is reinforced by the continuous band of composite moulding which shoots across it. That moulding is also set to pull the eye of the visitor away from the ill-considered massing of the garage end of the building which faces the driveway, the only path of approach to the house. It obtrudes at the corner and attracts attention to the long flat plane of the entrance front. Its shape encourages grasping, and it is set just at hand height. The moulding is thus the single element of the facade to fix a positive scale; in so doing it draws us with it across the open stage of space that the facade defines. Its use on the upper floor is more problematical. Here it must be taken for what it is: a primitive attempt, following the pioneer suggestions by Venturi on his Visiting Nurses' Building, to make ornament function on architecture once again.

There is no visible door. Lutyens' trick of hiding the door behind an ovoid cavern (and it seems fair to state that Stern came to Lutyens through Venturi and Greenberg) has a very positive point in this place. Doors of the usual size or of the height of the opening would have looked equally ridiculous. As it stands we penetrate a disorienting plane, involving the dramatic effect of the supension of disbelief, and are thus prepared for a new, special unfolding of spaces before us. That unfolding is both generous and gentle. It culminates on axis at the door to the garden, centrally placed in the outward curving wall and framing the soft green of the hill slope beyond it. Hence a firmly symmetrical principle, locked into the landscape, controls what may at first glance seem, especially when read only in plan, to be a perversely distorted set of spaces. In a similar way, while recollections of other architects, especially of Venturi, are to be found in almost every detail of the house from the entrance to the stair, the guest room, and even to the ensemble of living room, dining room, and climactic curving wall, those recollections are adapted, exactly as Stern hoped, to the particular construction of a special environment. The same thought occurs when we look at the house from the garden side. In the end the curved wall, behind which stand Venturi's Brant House and other projects, must be traced back to Kahn and his wrapping of 'ruins around buildings' to protect them from glare and to provide volumetric effects of light and spatial volume. This is exactly the way Stern uses his wall, not only as an iconic image in Venturi's manner, but as a wholly space-making element, and he is prepared to let it stand very separate from the blocky masses of the house behind it in order to permit it to fulfil that role.

It therefore seems to me that the Lang House is a good deal better than I and others used to think it was, and it found a worthy successor in the house Stern built shortly thereafter in Armonk. Here again the sequence of processional movement controls everything and is in fact gentle, flowing and expansive. It starts with a large column, again reminiscent of Venturi, which is fixed on the axis of an interminable entrance road, so that the first effect is of moderate formality, after which the releasing vistas open up, to culminate in a sensitively conceived garden and a splendid pool, reminiscent of Lutyens and Gertrude Jekyll. But here, too, very little of that quality comes through in drawings. The elaborate axonometrics which Stern and Hagmann published make the building look like an incoherent bundle of junk. This emphasises a point which can hardly be made often enough, which is that isometric and axonometric drawings are not right for horizontality extended, asymmetrical buildings of this kind. They should be suspect anyway — as Stern himself soon came to realise — since they are pure abstractions having nothing whatever to do with our actual experience of buildings. But precisely because they were abstractions they had, by the seventies, become the favourite tool of a neo-Corbusian school which was concerned primarily with vertical boxes of space into which objects could intrude and out of which holes could be cut. They also served other academic purposes very well because they were not only easy to draw, much easier than perspectives for example, but also because the draftsmen could use them to lift off the roof and to phantomise other elements in order to show many different features of a building at once. Stern uses them in all these ways to try not merely to illustrate but literally to generate the layered and cut-away forms of his spatially ambitious Pool House at Greenwich. Even here, in a complex building of much interest, one has the feeling that the isometric is in fact deadly for Stern's work. One might go further and suggest that since Post-Modernism is concerned, so it claims, with the direct experience of multiple realities, it might do well to return to perspective drawing in general.

Much has been made of the 'Palladian' character of the Lang and Ehrman Houses, but their major stylistic recollection seems to me to be of Art Deco. This is especially true in the fittings of the interior, where Stern began to show his special talents as a decorator. That word, anathema to the Modern Movement, should, in part for that reason, be emphasised here. 'Decoration' is a lively word at this moment in time, just as the Modern Movement's darling 'Design' is a dusty one. (Over the past fifteen years the

Best Products Facade project, 1979, perspective (096)

Seaside Suburb', Riviera Beach Competition, Singer Island, Florida, 1976 (065)

Drawn by Gavin Macrae-Gibson and Charles Warren

Model, Best Products Facade, project 1979 (096)

Roosevelt Island Competition, 1975
Venturi's Brighton Beach project, 1968
Venturi's Yale Mathematics Building, 1970

St Joseph's Village, model, 1976
Subway Suburb, 1976

Cooper-Hewitt has changed its name from 'Museum for the Arts of Decoration', to 'Museum of Decorative Arts and Design', to 'Museum of Design'. Fifteen years from now it will wish it hadn't.) Stern *is* an interior decorator as well as an architect, and as such he expects to deal with complex assemblages of mouldings, colours, and furniture — just as, outside, he has set himself to learn more of the gardener's craft than most architects seem to feel necessary. There, too, as noted above, Lutyens and Gertrude Jekyll have been important to him, and his gardens have taken on body and decision under their influence.

Inside, all, perhaps inevitably, tended for a time to take on a rather jazzily Art Deco turn of hue and profile, though once again the jazzy quality is much more apparent in the photographs than in actuality. It continued in Stern's sleek remodelling of a town house on Park Avenue. There, too, can be found the semi-Art Deco undulating wall which appeared in the guest room of the Ehrman House and which seems to represent an influence from the work of John Hejduk. Stern's general preoccupation with stylish effects, while surely sympathetic to his rather compulsively perfectionist cast of mind, should also be seen as a positive Post-Modern characteristic, since it is intended to reverse that reduction to pseudo-primitive simplicity which was one of modern architecture's most pervasive characteristics. We should remember, further, that Wright was not reductionist, nor was Aalto, and the former especially designed every detail of his interiors with a visual density and complexity unmatched by that of classical architecture itself.

But Stern, as an adaptor of forms, has shown himself to be much more than a decorator. His winning entry for the Roosevelt Island Housing Competition of 1975, organised by the UDC, refers in part to famous projects from two previous competitions. The first is Venturi's Brighton Beach entry of 1968, and the other is the same architect's winner of the competition for the Yale Mathematics Building, of 1970. There is some pathos in these connections: Venturi's Brighton Beach scheme was a stunning masterpiece which failed to win because it looked not merely ordinary but frighteningly familiar and American to some of the jurors. It cut close to the bone. 'I've been trying to get away from Hoboken all my life', said one of its unsympathetic judges. Another, Philip Johnson, felt that it looked like any old set of apartment buildings around New York. (A year or two later he was claiming just such a virtue for a scheme of his own.) Venturi's proposal for Yale, on the other hand, won a unanimous decision of the jury but has never been built because of the university's parlous financial condition. Stern essentially took the Brighton Beach apartments and slung the curving walls of Venturi's Mathematics Building across them like great shields, vastly blown up in scale. Each tall unit was thus turned into a kind of eager giant looking down and across the river, with the group as a whole deployed into a spectacular column of figures marching along the bank in one vast parade of urban splendour. The architect's statement of purpose was no less bold than the buildings: 'Our decision to enter the Roosevelt Island competition was based on our belief that the recent, revisionist housing theory of Jane Jacobs, Oscar Newman and others remains unfulfilled in formal terms, and that urban multi-family housing design, at least in this country, remains largely alienated from its American antecedents, mired in pseudo-technological pipe dreams and trapped in either the last gasps of the CIAM ... or in a revival of the diagrammatic planning and dry formalism of the *Neue Sachlichkeit* ...' It is no wonder that among the jurors José Luis Sert preferred timid schemes by his own students to this one; he could hardly have done otherwise. The unremitting hostility of Paul Rudolph, Stern's teacher, whose best schemes are recalled in the character of this project, is more difficult to pass over. The UDC collapsed and nothing came of the whole thing, with little harm done except that by far Stern's best and noblest project, like Venturi's for Yale, remains unbuilt.

Two other housing projects by Stern are of considerable interest in terms of fundamental urban problems. One, a competition entry for St Joseph's Village for Senior Citizens, of 1976, was Stern's first attempt to develop a more or less traditional housing type and to organise it in terms of traditional suburban groupings. The research involved was suggested in part by the Venturis' seminar at Yale, 'Learning from Levittown', of 1970. The suburb, like Main Street, had been the target of some of the Modern Movement's most unforgiving polemics, and the Venturis had set out to find out what it was really like, why people liked to live in it, and what its major symbolic structures were. That study has exerted an enormous effect on the Post-Modern movement as a whole, and has been especially influential on the work of Jencks. Stern may be said to have brought it to its major theoretical achievement when he proposed his Subway Suburb as 'an official entry representing the United States' in the Venice Biennale of 1976. Stern's reasoning, which grew out of his research for a general book on the development of the suburb as well as from his special study of the devastated areas of the South Bronx, was that there is plenty of room at the heart of most American cities today for the kind of housing most Americans of all economic groups seem to want: that is, single family houses. Stern proposed such types, along with some double houses masquerading as singles, and grouped them in the kinds of traditional street arrangements that Americans are used to. The rest of the analysis of those features, which seem to have symbolic values for the inhabitants (gables, front and back doors, front and back yards, garages, and so on), is in direct line with the Venturis' conclusions of 1970, but goes beyond them in its serious application. Again, Stern's attempt is to look beyond the prejudices of the Modern Movement in order to revive a vernacular American type. His decision to introduce it into the empty centre of the city and to plug it into the existing transit lines seems his most brilliant and socially promising 'adaptation' so far.

It surely helped him on toward the kinds of decisions he then began to make in his commissions for houses. Those too moved more and more toward a direct revival of the Shingle Style vernacular of the late nineteenth century. That had surely been the richest vernacular tradition that America had developed. It exemplified the kind of adjustment to place, climate, function and materials that was in effect just before consumerism took over and reduced the average house to a stripped-down, air-conditioned box for the containment of gadgets. To revive the Shingle Style was therefore a fundamental act, having little to do with stylistic revivalism *per se*, and much to do with basic considerations of natural suitability, into which questions of energy soon came to play a part. But considerations of style are always latent in any architectural enthusiasm, and they soon came to the fore as well. Stern's own former house in East

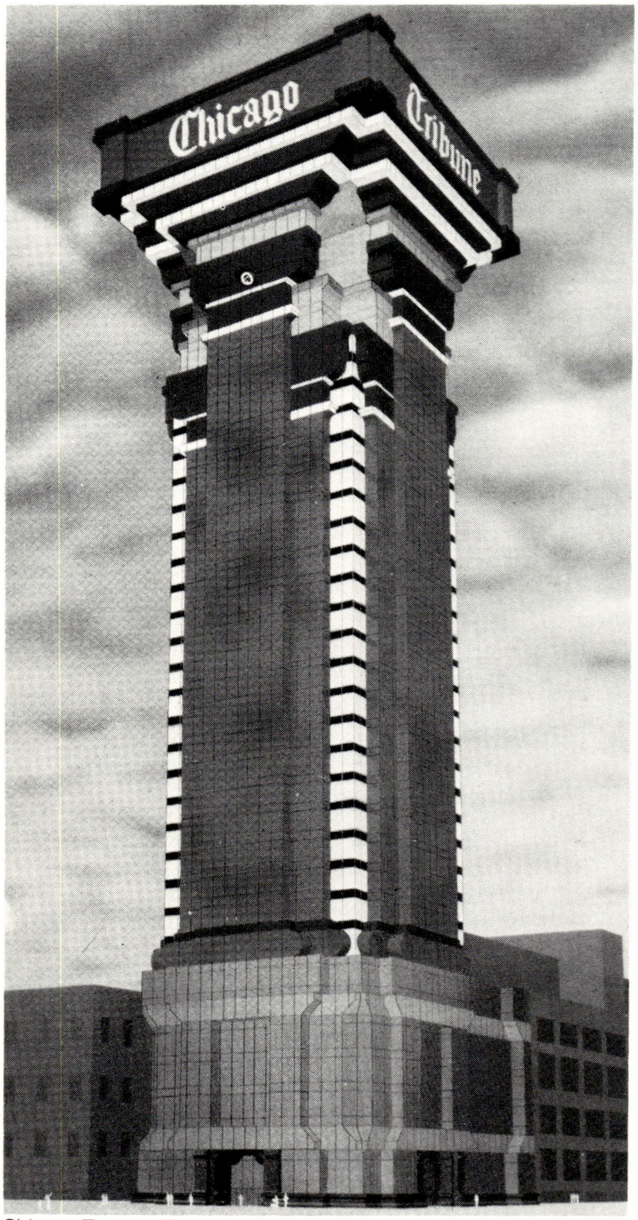


Chicago Tribune Tower entry, 1980

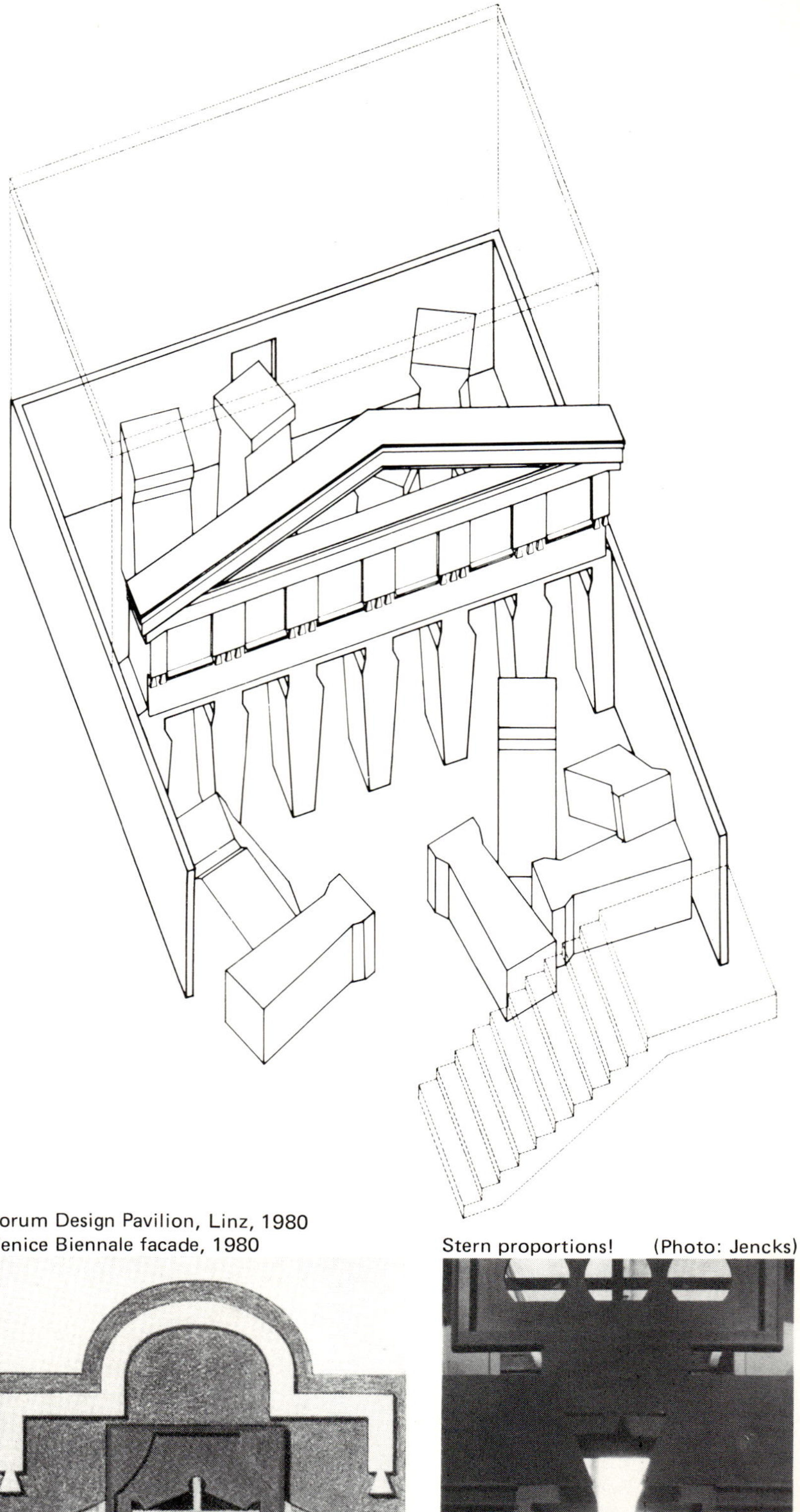

Forum Design Pavilion, Linz, 1980

Best Products Facade, model, 1980

Venice Biennale facade, 1980

Stern proportions! (Photo: Jencks)

Hampton represents an early stage in that development. It was an old Shingle Style house to which Stern added a porch, abstracted in the modern manner but sympathetic to the volumes and materials of the original building. It carefully avoided, however, the other's classical and Queen Anne details. Now Stern's work is beginning to resemble the original house more than his addition to it. Any number of his present commissions show the trend. Among them is the small vernacular house in which he now lives in East Hampton; he monumentalises its modest terrace with a white-painted door surround of his own devising. In a fine Post-Modern gesture he has embraced the tradition, including its details, and is designing along with it — not, however, without adjustments and comments of his own. The plans are becoming simpler, resembling those of the original Shingle Style. Variety is increasingly to be found not in space or massing but in the details. This is of course the way in which architecture has usually worked in the past and in which the most solid growth has occurred over the ages.

In those terms the Modern Movement comes to be seen as an unusually revolutionary reaction against the past — perhaps a necessary and salutary one, but deeply destructive and seductive at the same time. Stern's attitude, and that of the other Post-Modernists, seems in fact more historically normal in every way. Nor does it represent any shade of political opinion; it is not in that sense necessarily conservative. It tries to deal realistically with architecture, and from that point of view Stern, like most architects, will accept any commission that comes along. He is very clear about where the money comes from. He has said, 'The big corporations and those who benefit from them have the money to build. They employ architects'. The European Marxist critics who assert that the architect should not design buildings under such conditions are like the nagging voice of a conscience which, while not exactly bad and which certainly does not accept the European accusations without some irony, is still an uneasy one. The fault is hardly the architect's, however, since the International Style view that the architect controls social policies has shown itself to be without basis in fact. In a saner society, for example, Stern would be building the mass housing for which he has shown himself to be especially qualified. There are surely incongruities. The earnest, liberal client gazing out with the architect over the excavation for a swimming pool of truly Assyrian proportions and threat seems something of a contradiction. Is it a Mannerist one? That is to say, leaving the social question aside to be answered as one sees fit, can we identify the situation as helping to create a more or less Renaissance style with formal characteristics similar to those of historical Mannerism? Certinly most of the formal elements of such a style have already reappeared. The classical columns were the first to come marching back into Stern's work. He employs them to considerable effect in a newly redecorated loft — fully in the round and as Venturi-type cutouts. Indeed they first came, though as yet without capitals, to terminate the admirably formal — thus classical — axis of a swimming pool on Long Island. Now the rustication moves in. Here the generating example for Stern is not only the work of Venturi but also that of Michael Graves. The sombre, sorrowful, Mannerist-primitive rustication that Graves had developed in his incomparable drawings of recent years has had a massive effect on Stern's imagination and has been openly and generously acknowledged by him. Now his remodelling of a house in Llewellyn Park slices a marvellously rusticated bookcase wall diagonally across the second floor while, sinking down below the living room, a fantastic grotto opens out from the depths of the earth. Beside its pool, John Nash's palm columns from Brighton are somewhat squashed down, by way of a design by Hans Hollein. (The palm leaves are being beautifully fabricated in steel by a little machine shop in the Bronx.) Directly ahead, squat columns, suggestive in this case of a famous drawing by Venturi, hold up a massive lintel which spans the broad opening in a spectacularly rusticated wall. Above, a greenhouse roof cascades downward, and the whole massive ensemble turns the garden side of the remodelled house into something suggestive of a ziggurat, or of Caprarola. What do we read here? Decadence? Perhaps not really, but Mannerist contradiction surely, appropriate at once to our power and to our uneasiness, and a splendid Mannerist attack, like those of Giulio Romano, of the sculptural details upon the environmental frame. It records a world rich, restless, and embattled. Municipal and private police guard the gates, and have been doing so since 1850. Yet there is something profoundly innocent in it all, like the movies. D.W. Griffith's Babylonian set for *Intolerance* is recalled.

That famous, fevered vision is also suggested in Stern's project for a store front facade for Best Products, Inc. Like the other entries in that exhibition, with the exception of Venturi's, which had already been built, Stern's pulls out all the stops. In his case these consist of a complex iconography, mother-goddess columns split apart, an enormous pediment, and so on. The energy seems excessive for the programme. Much the same is true of Stern's facade for the street of facades in his and Paolo Portoghesi's architectural exhibition, 'The Presence of the Past', for the Venice Biennale of 1980. Everything is in it in layers, mamma most of all. There is another exhibition for Linz: a temple front with the columns gone positive-negative, and history lies as fallen blocks in front; the likenesses of Post-Modernists appear in the metopes, and the whole thing is explained a bit more behind. All these projects, along with Stern's entry in the Tigerman-Cohen Tribune Competition of 1980, show an ebullience of the first order. The vitality of the young architects in Stern's small but lively office is reflectd in them. Each one of Stern's staff, many of whom were students of his at Columbia, is responsible for a job and receives credit in its publication. Together, they project a sense of common purpose and easy confidence. The feeling is that it is a good place to work, where a lot can be learned and where everybody, including Stern, is on the job most waking hours.

Now they are working hard together to explore all the traditional detailing of classical architecture which the Modern Movement had cast aside. They do not feel that they either parody or reproduce these details; they believe that they are relearning a language and are trying to speak it in an articulate and original way. The suggestion is of discovery, little by little and day by day. One realises that they are all very young. What they are attempting to do would have been inconceivable a few years ago. Watching them, one has the feeling that their generation lives familiarly with the past as friend and tutor in ways that the older generation can never know. As a guide to all this Stern is at his best. Like his life-long friend, Philip Johnson, he is superficially dogmatic but is in fact an ally to new ideas and fresh talents, which he loves to champion and to recognise and support in the young.

# On Drawing

*Drawing is a means of communication about architecture: it is at once an imitation of previous realities and an intimation of realities to come. Perhaps even more than an actual building, the architectural drawing is a record of one's intentions at the moment of design. While I record my architectural ideas at the level of conceptualisation by means of a quick sketch scrawled on tracing paper, on the back of an envelope, on a napkin, on whatever is handy, I do not make the drawings which frequently communicate to the public my architectural intentions and the intentions of my collaborators in the office. Quite frankly, I don't draw all that well; but then, neither am I a master carpenter or stone-mason. Nonetheless, I have lots of ideas about drawings, just as I do about the properties and possibilities of wood and stone. I am also a good listener; so I listen to the carpenter's or mason's idea about how to do one thing or another. So too, do I work with those among my collaborators in the office who have prepared various drawings of our work. These drawings, then, like the architectural ideas they represent, are the products of collaboration — not the collaboration of Gropius's ideal team, but a give and take over empty coffee cups and paper-strewn desks at late hours when the phone has at last stopped its ringing.*

*I believe that techniques of drawing relate not only to the delineator's individual talent, but also to the ideas being delineated and to the role the drawing is expected to play. Thus, seemingly dissimilar projects are drawn in a similar way to make explicit my feelings about their interconnectedness. For example, projects that deal with archetypal images, such as the houses for Subway Suburb or the prototypical facade for Best Products are depicted in a flat highly stylised way to emphasise the explicitly imagistic character of the work.*

*Similarly, other projects which explore subtler issues of decoration and composition are drawn with fine lines and delicate washes of colour in accord with the values intended in the final product. Of course, some projects combine both or more sets of considerations, are at once intended as icons and vessels, so frequently many different ways of drawing will be employed in the study process. As each project is drawn in a variety of ways and different aspects are studied, each new drawing reveals a new set of problems to be addressed in the process of design.*

*In my conceptual drawings, I concentrate on the plan and the quick elevation which usually and quite suddenly get transmogrified into a perspective sketch, the former two testing an organisational structure against measurable standards, the latter confirming or not the capacity of that idea to establish an appropriate character. These drawings are very personal things to me; not the stuff of art which always has an implication of public communication. Though they play a vital part in my design process, like the many study models we make in the office, they are essentially ephemeral in nature (though I confess that they are saved just as the models are photographed). In any case what you see of ours in this book is intended to make a point about the work after the direction of work has been established; it is intended to crystallise the character of an architectural idea, to keep a kind of vigil for architect and client alike during the arduous and frequently confusing process of making working drawings, letting contracts and building buildings. It is the icon that keeps the faith; we hope our building will be better than our drawings for them, but at the very least the drawings provide a record of our intentions, a standard for measure.*

## Robert A. M. Stern

# Selected Projects

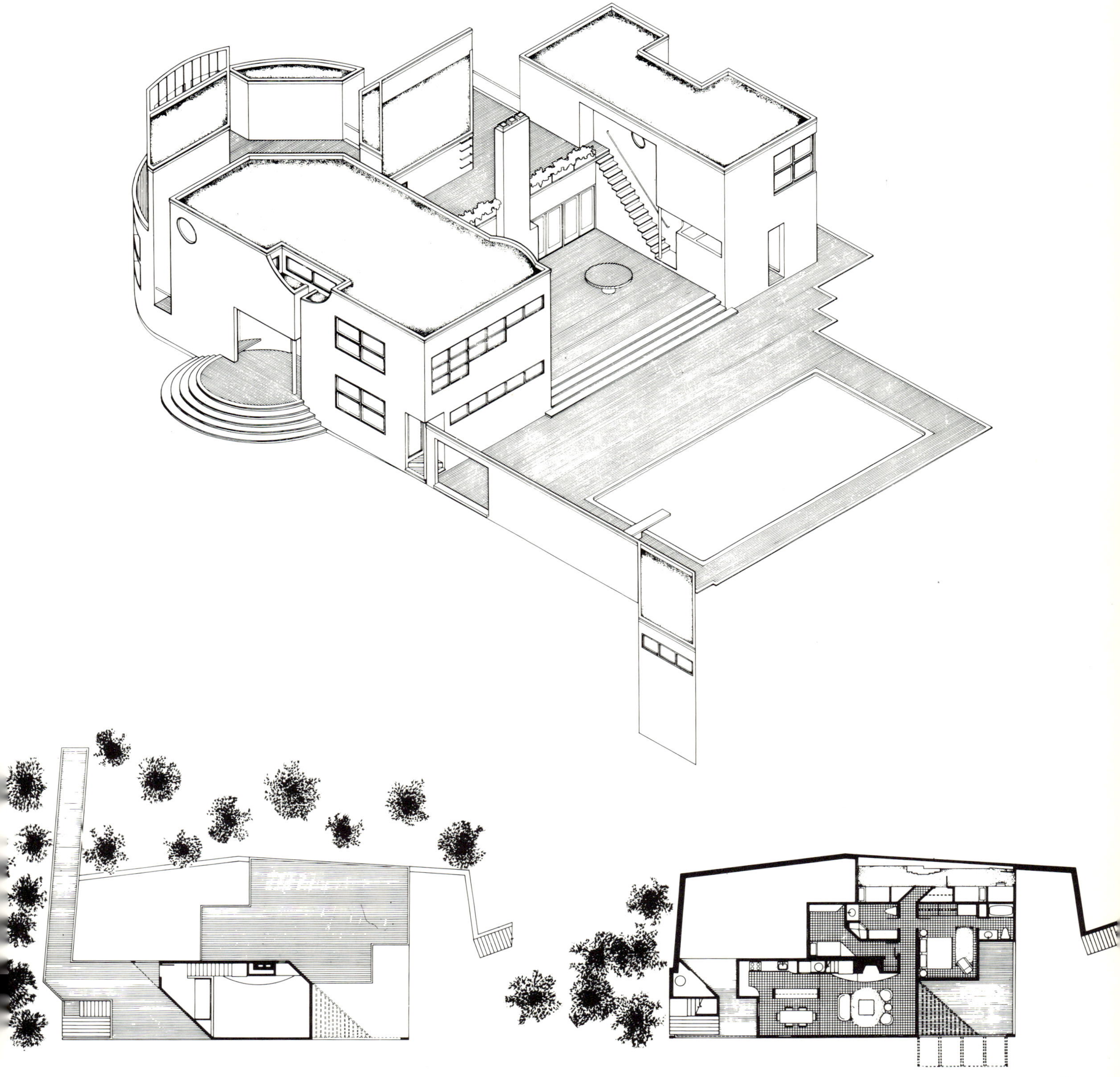

023 Guest house, house and cabana, Montauk, New York, 1972

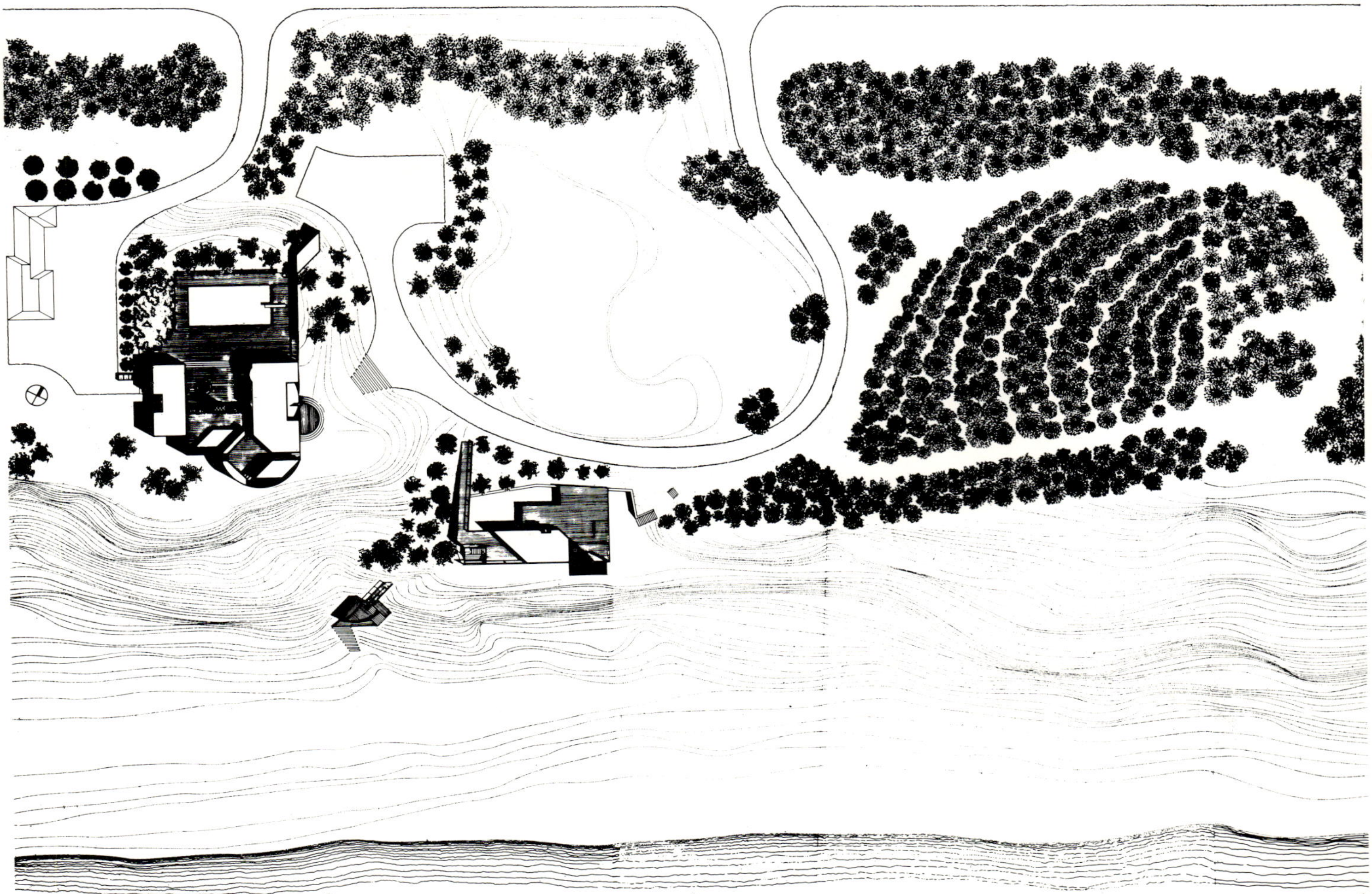

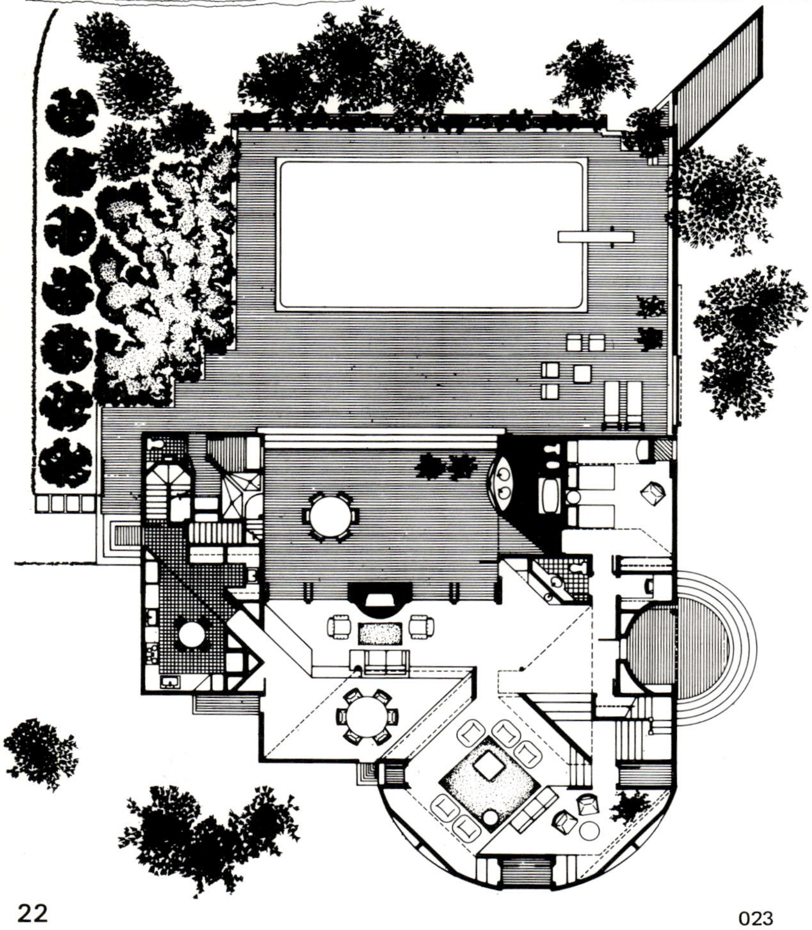

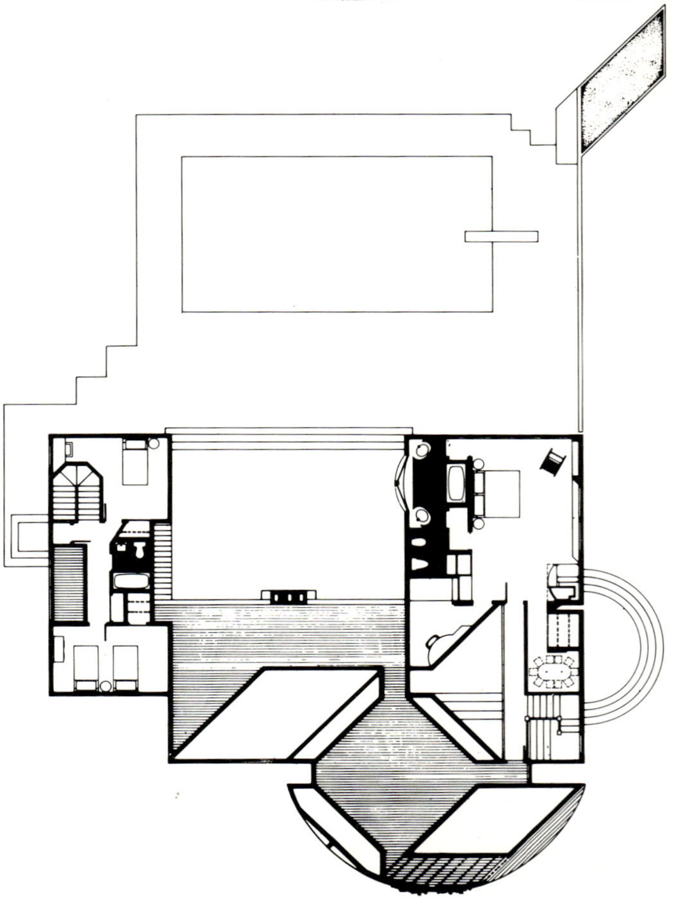

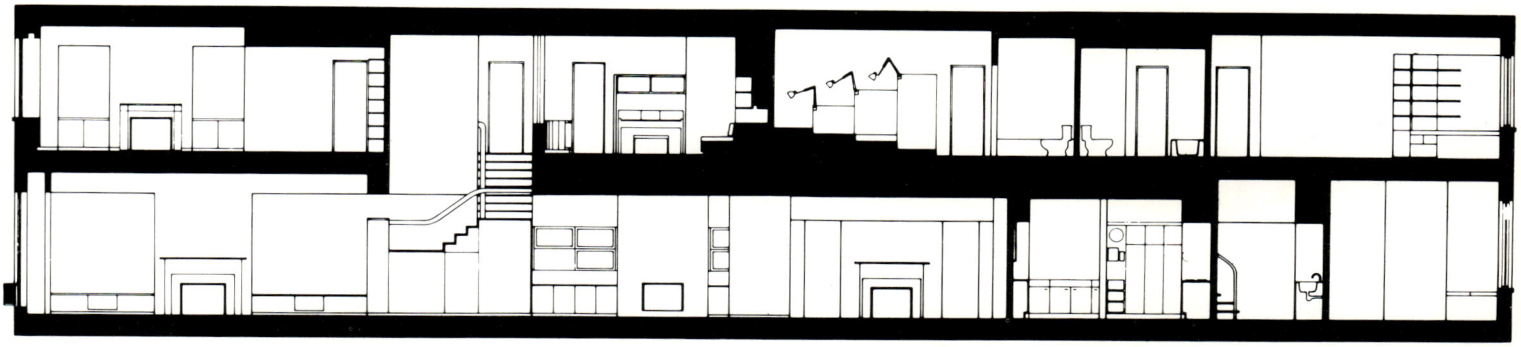

**Duplex Apartment**

**Sections**

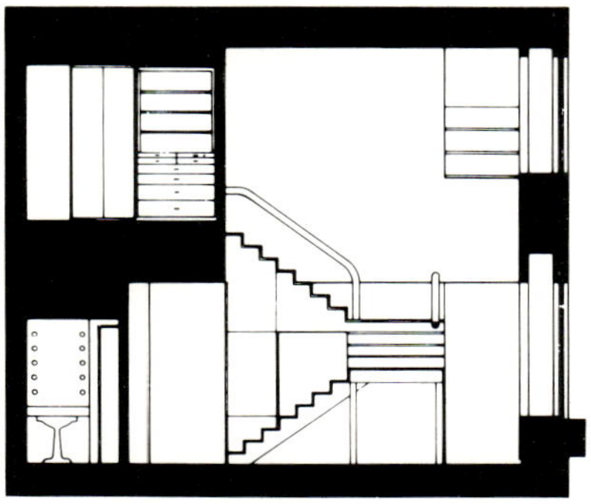

029 Duplex apartment, New York City, 1973

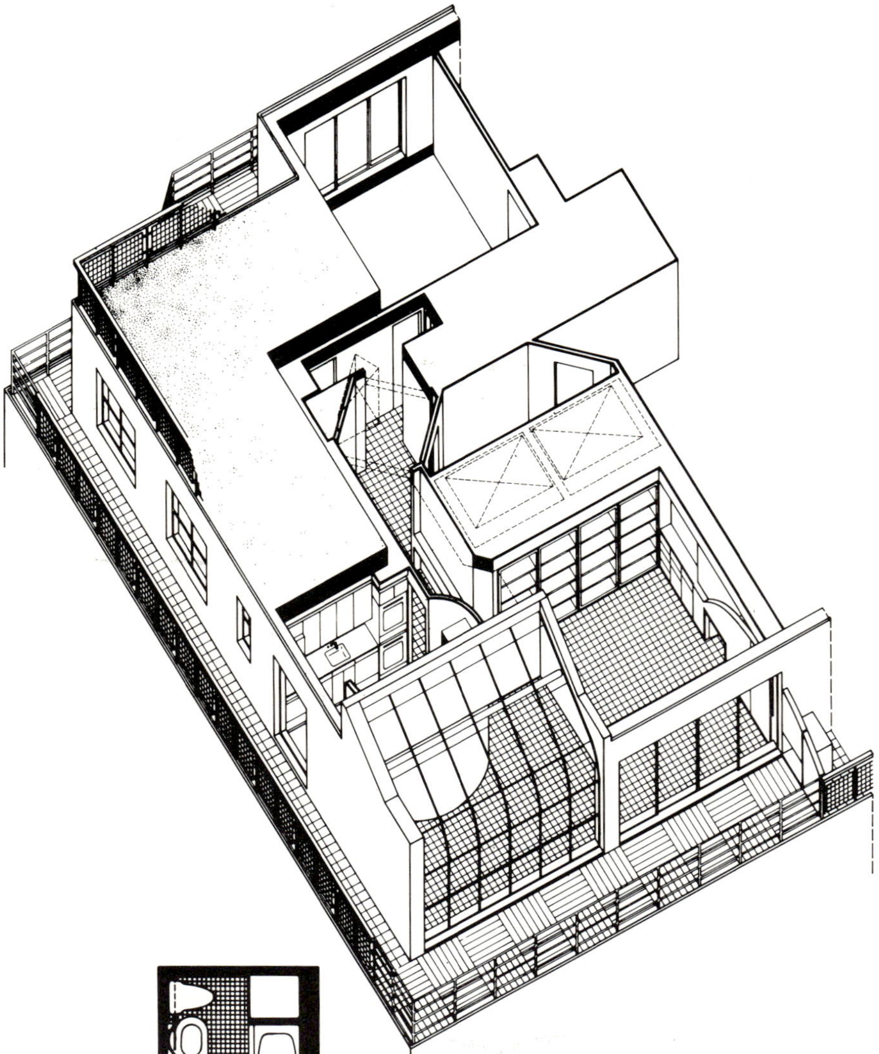

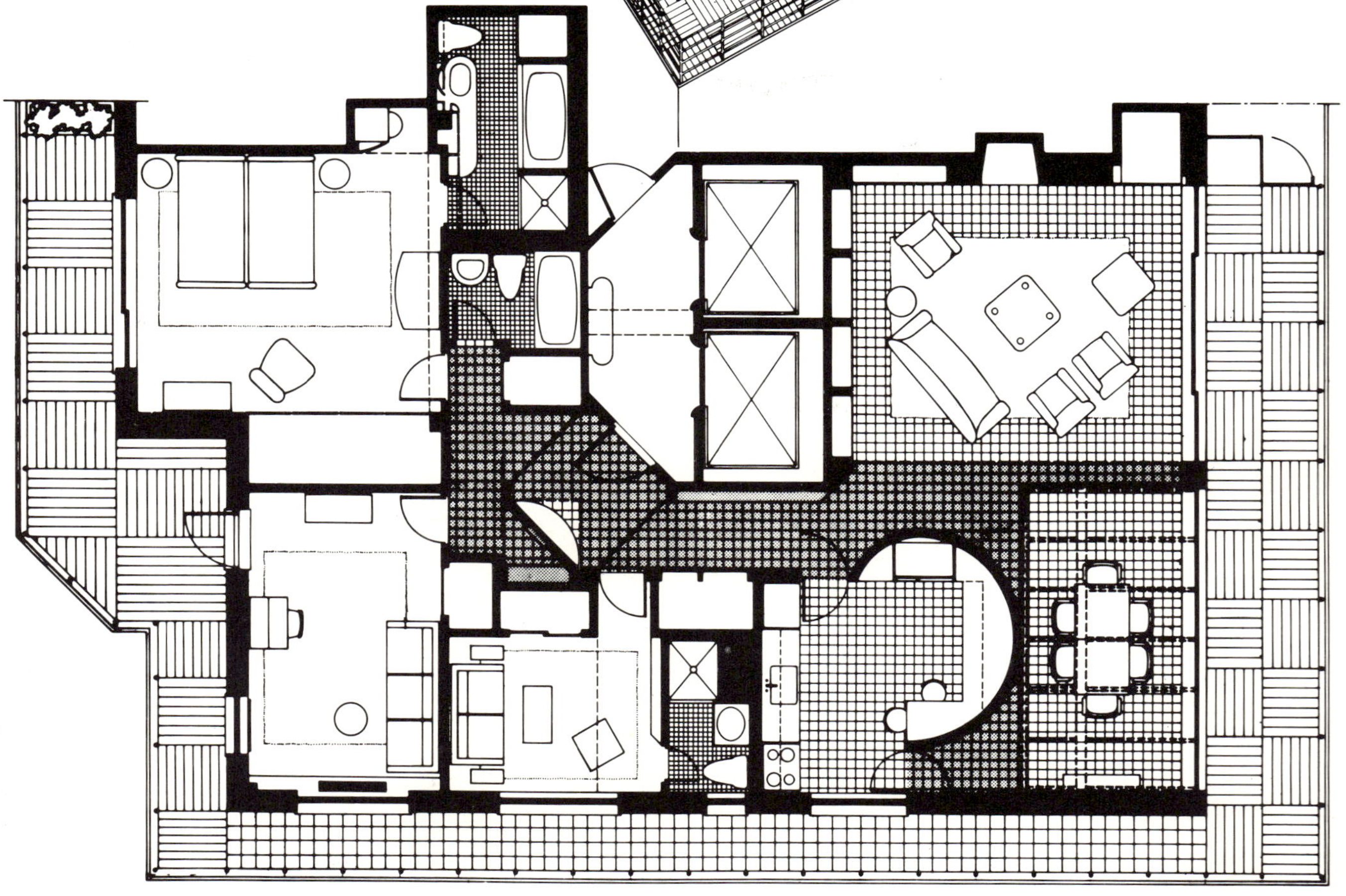



033 Rooftop apartment, New York City, 1973

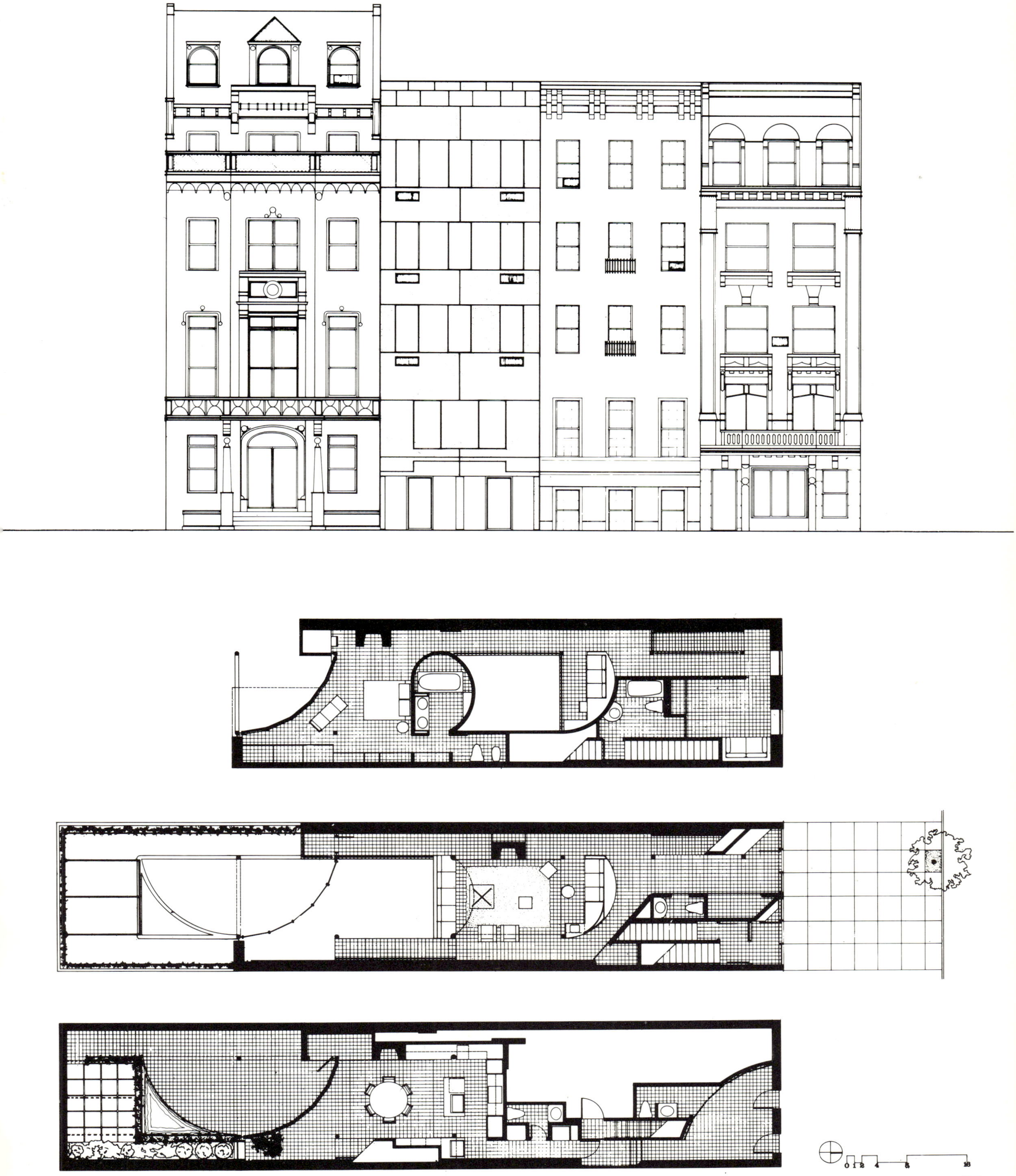

038 New York Greystone, New York, New York, renovation, 1972-79

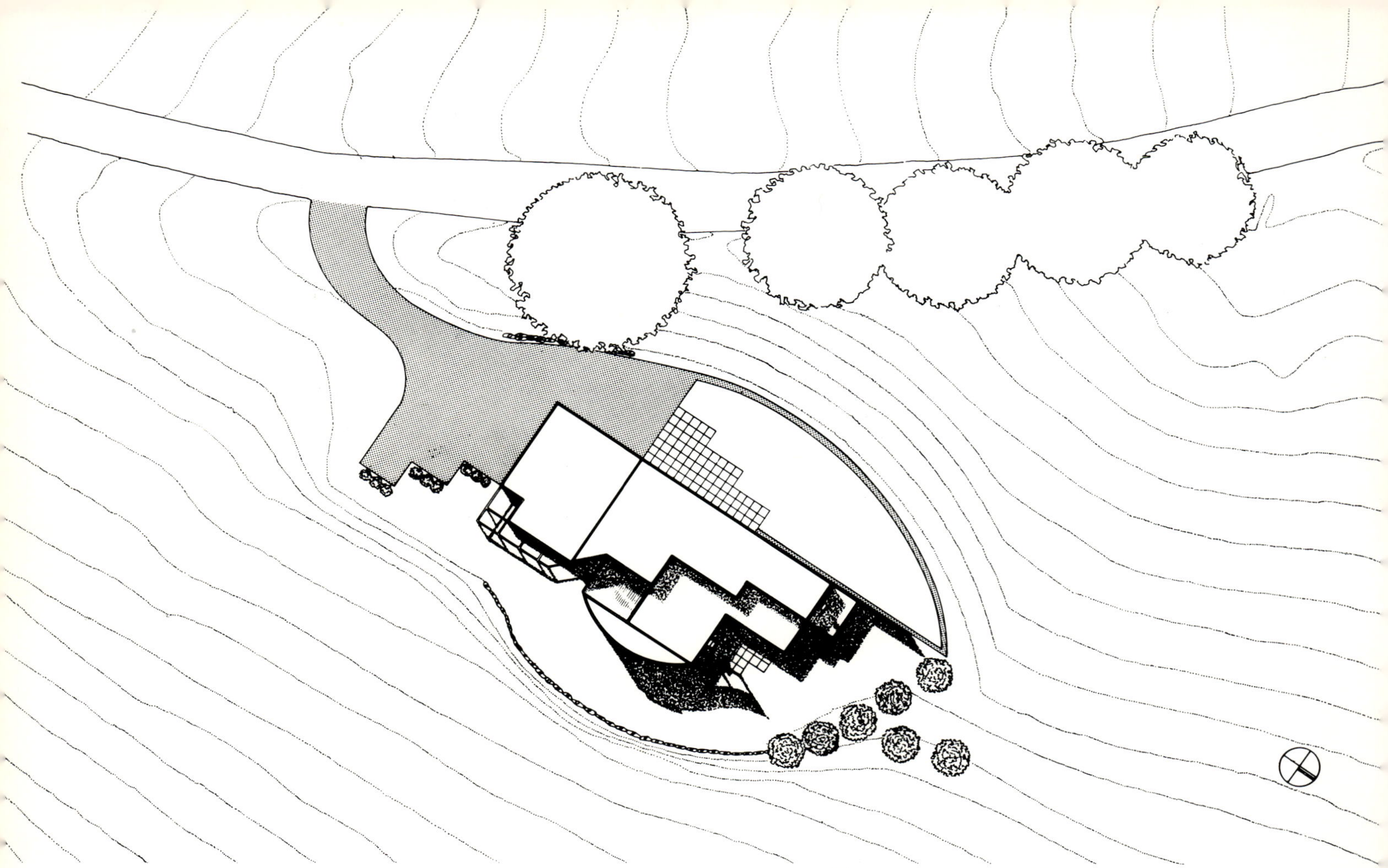

East Elevation

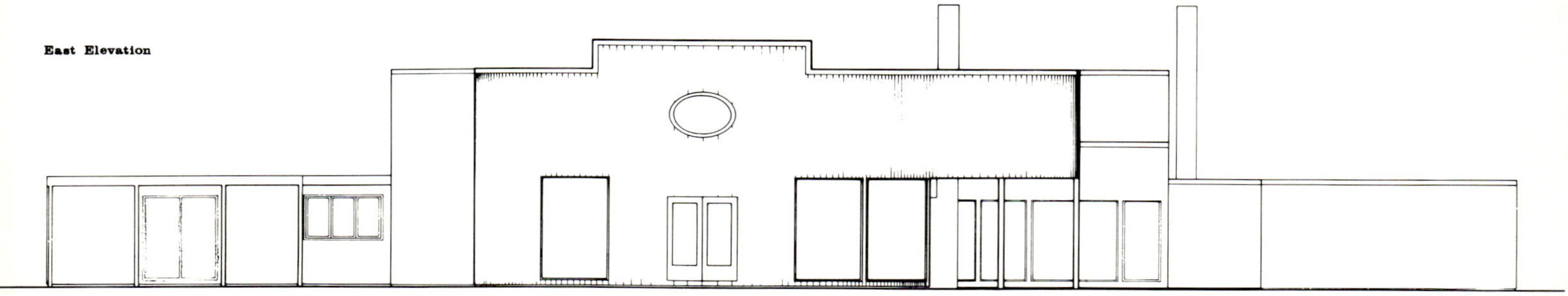

West Elevation

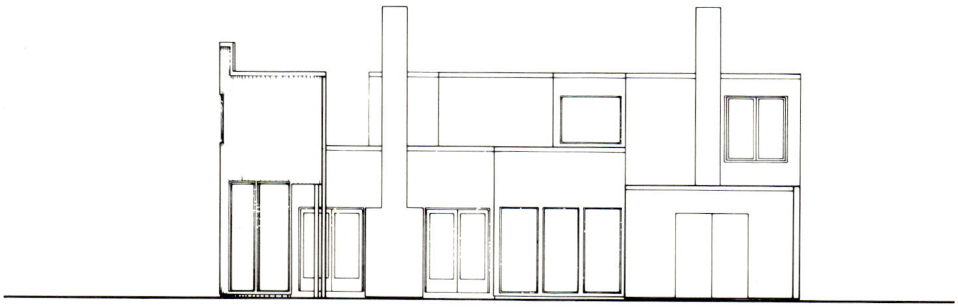

North Elevation

047 Lang House, Washington, Connecticut, 1972-79

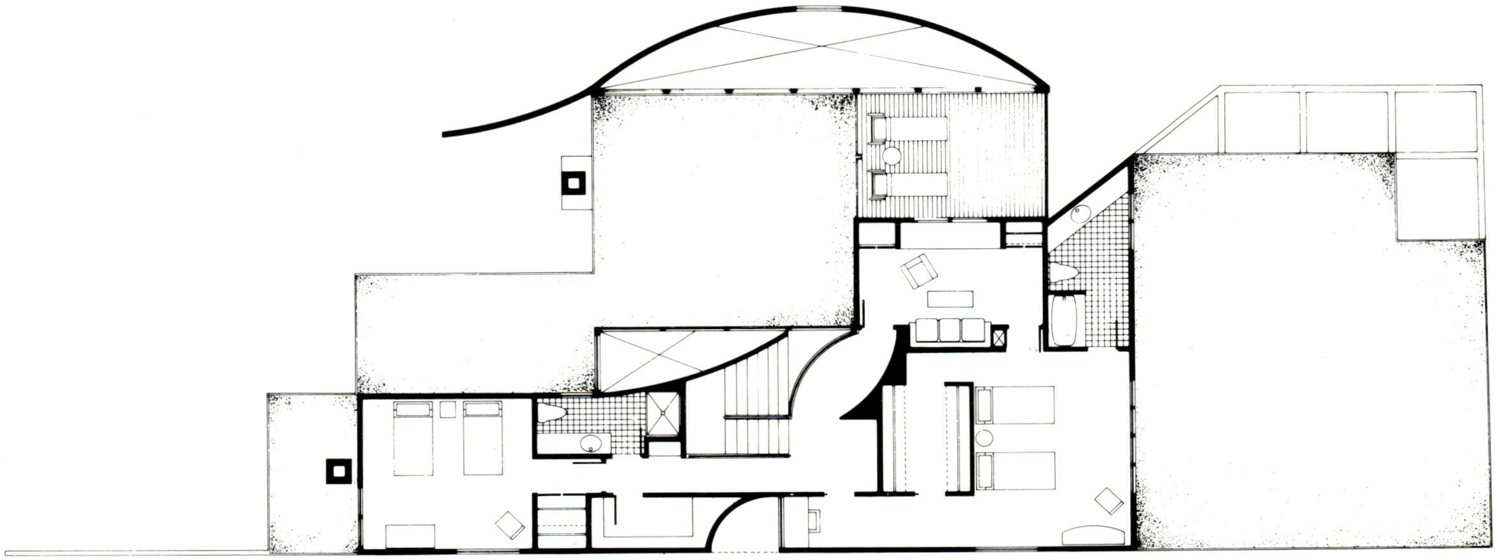

SECOND FLOOR PLAN

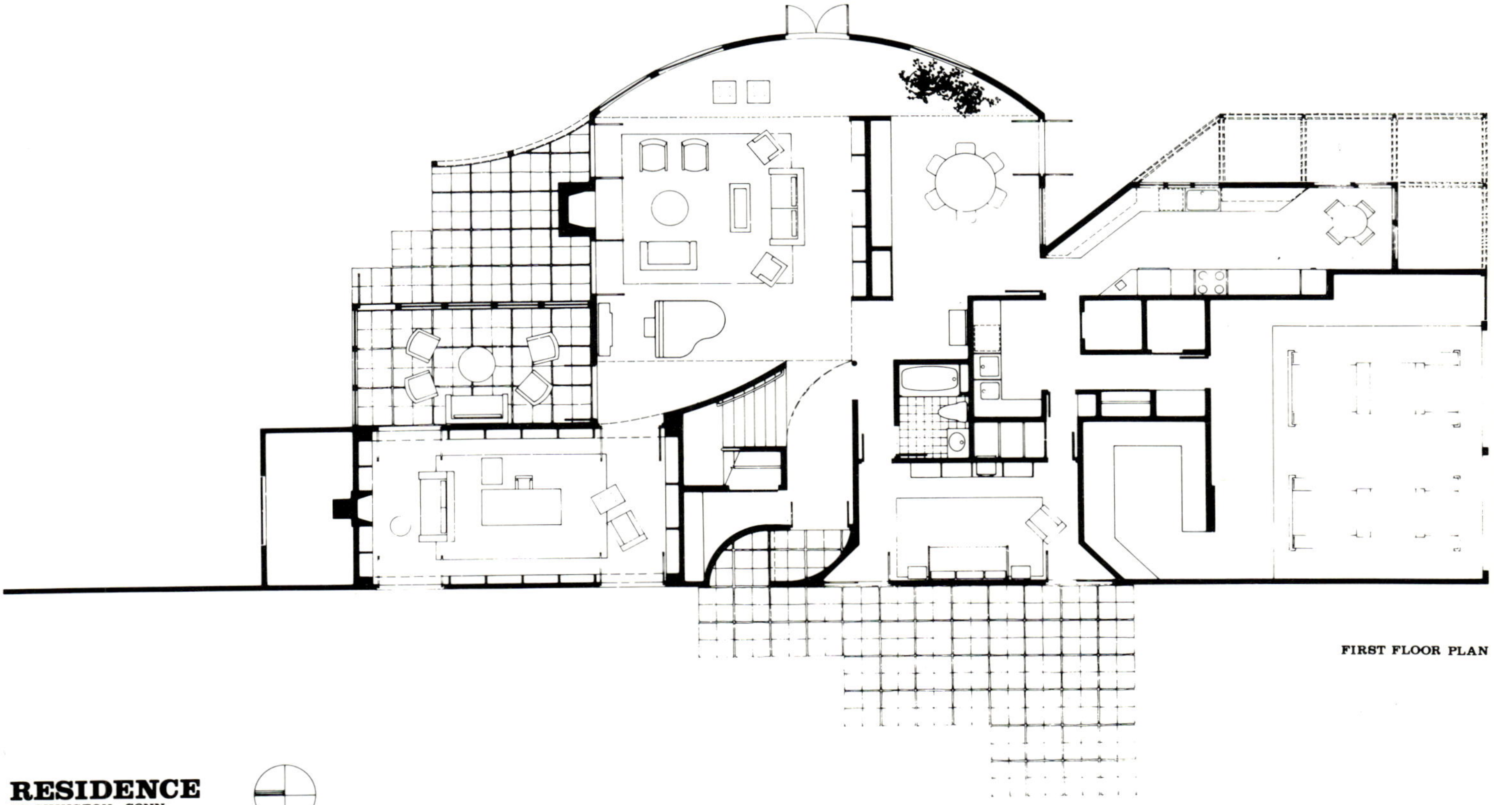

FIRST FLOOR PLAN

**RESIDENCE**
WASHINGTON, CONN.

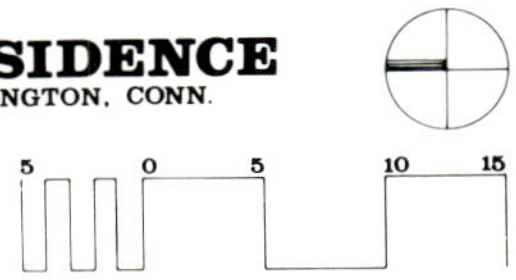

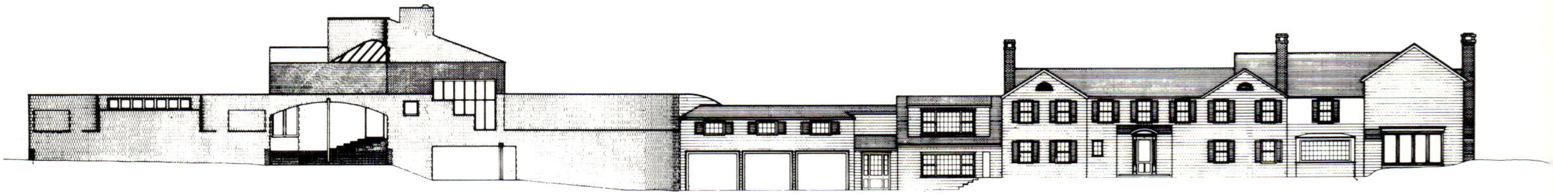

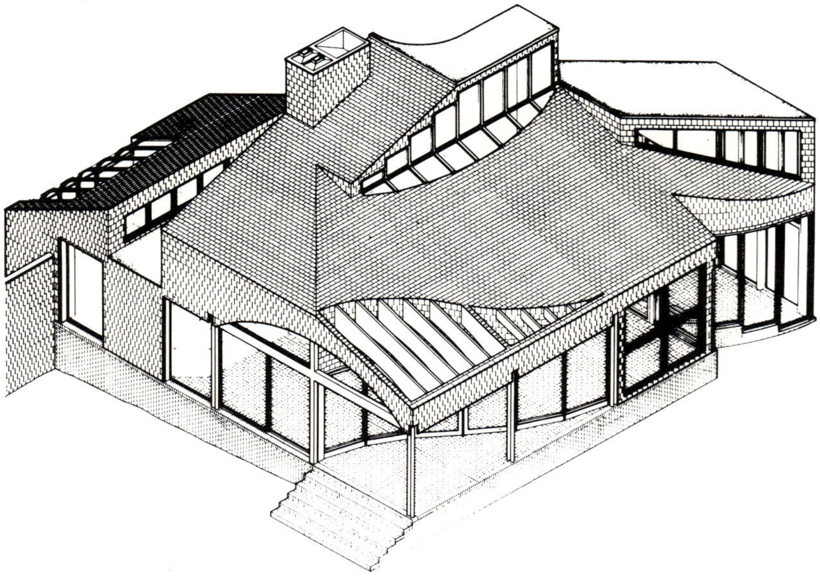

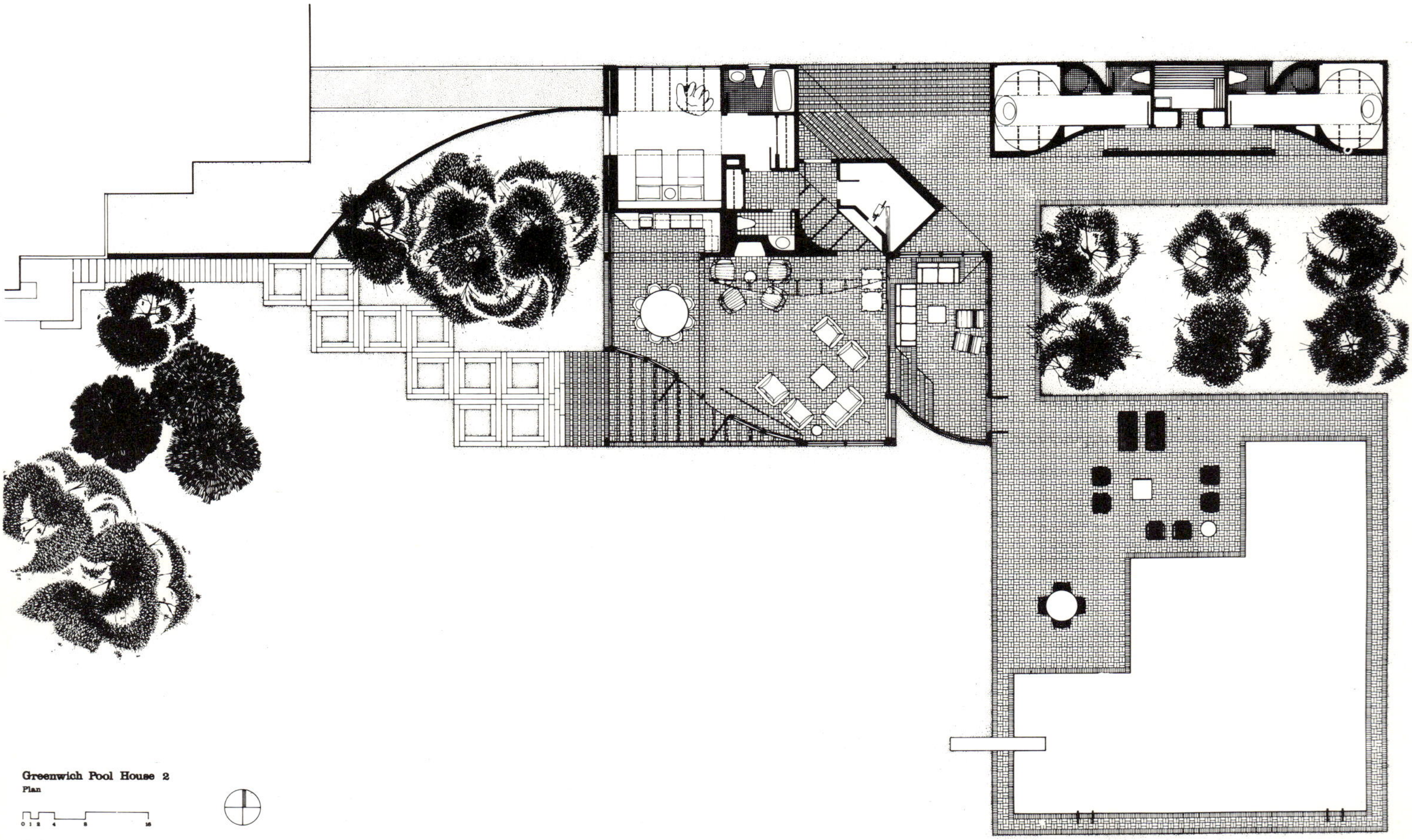

Greenwich Pool House 2
Plan



048 Poolhouse, Greenwich, Connecticut, 1973-75

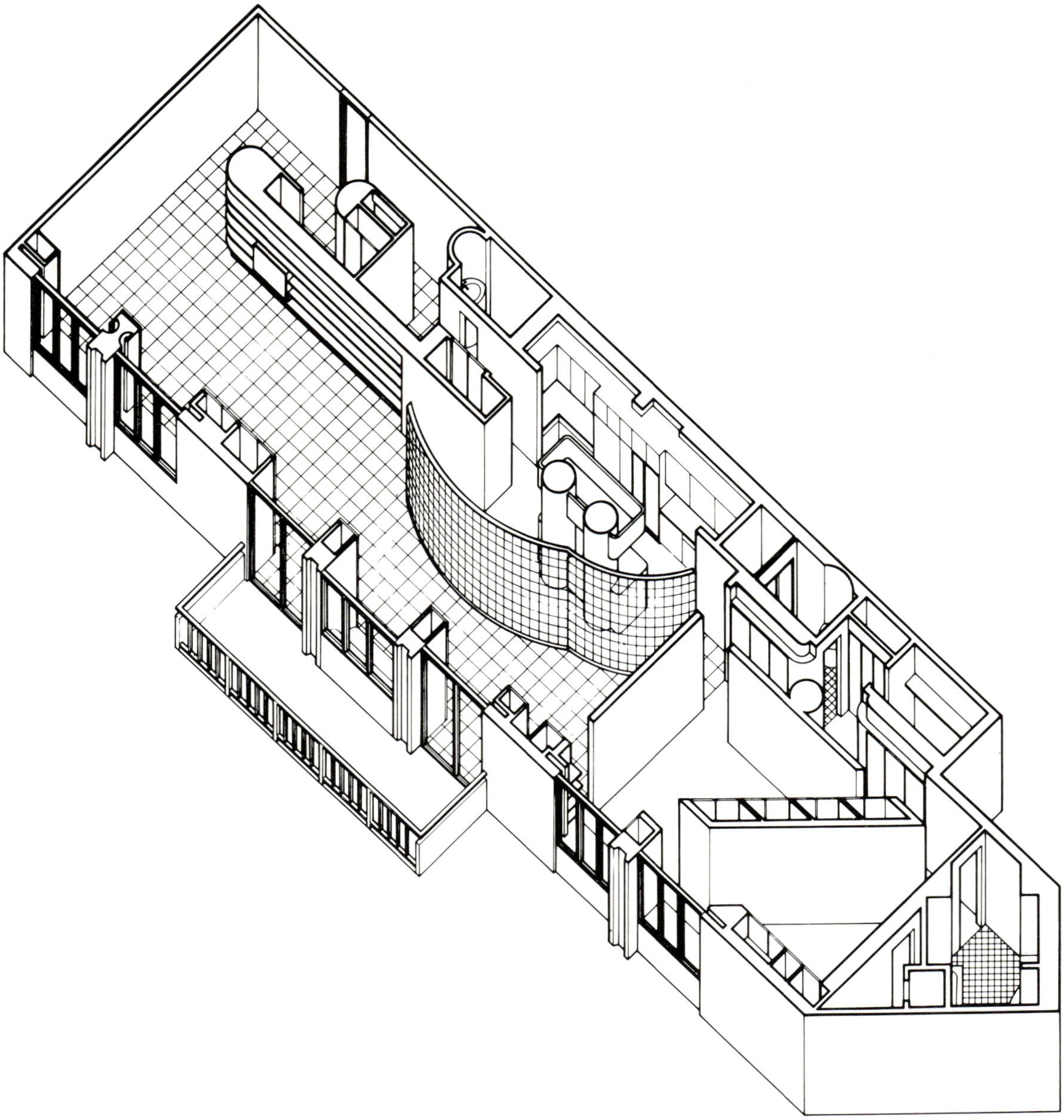

**Apartment**

Plan

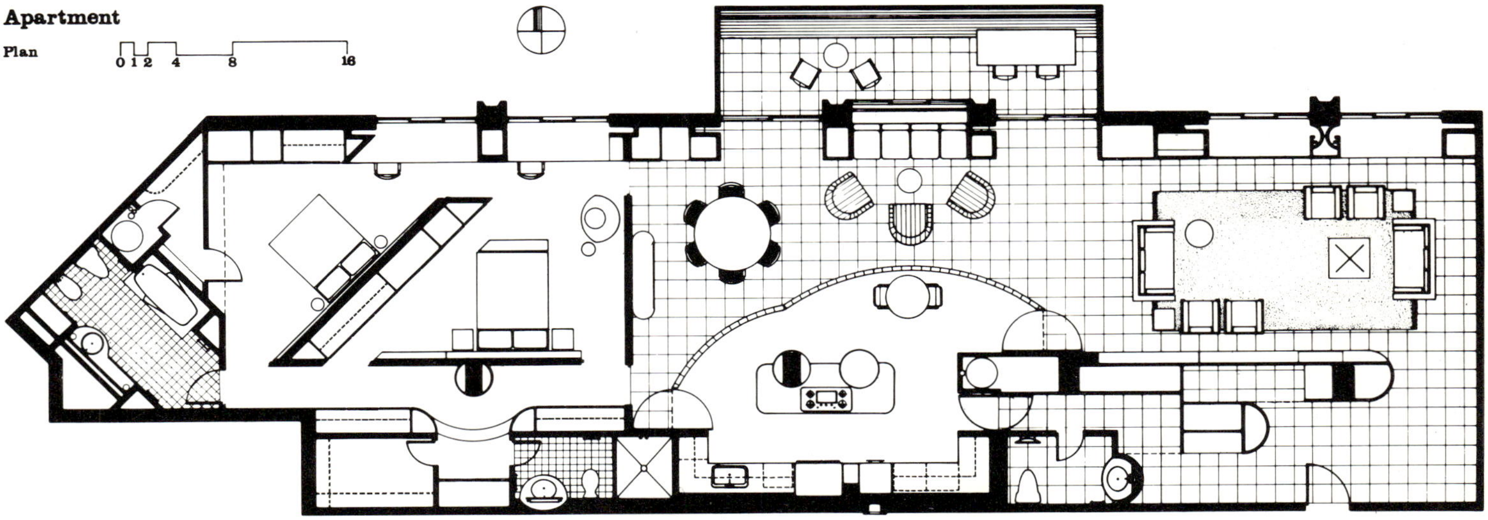


051 Apartment renovation, Elkins Park, Pennsylvania, 1975

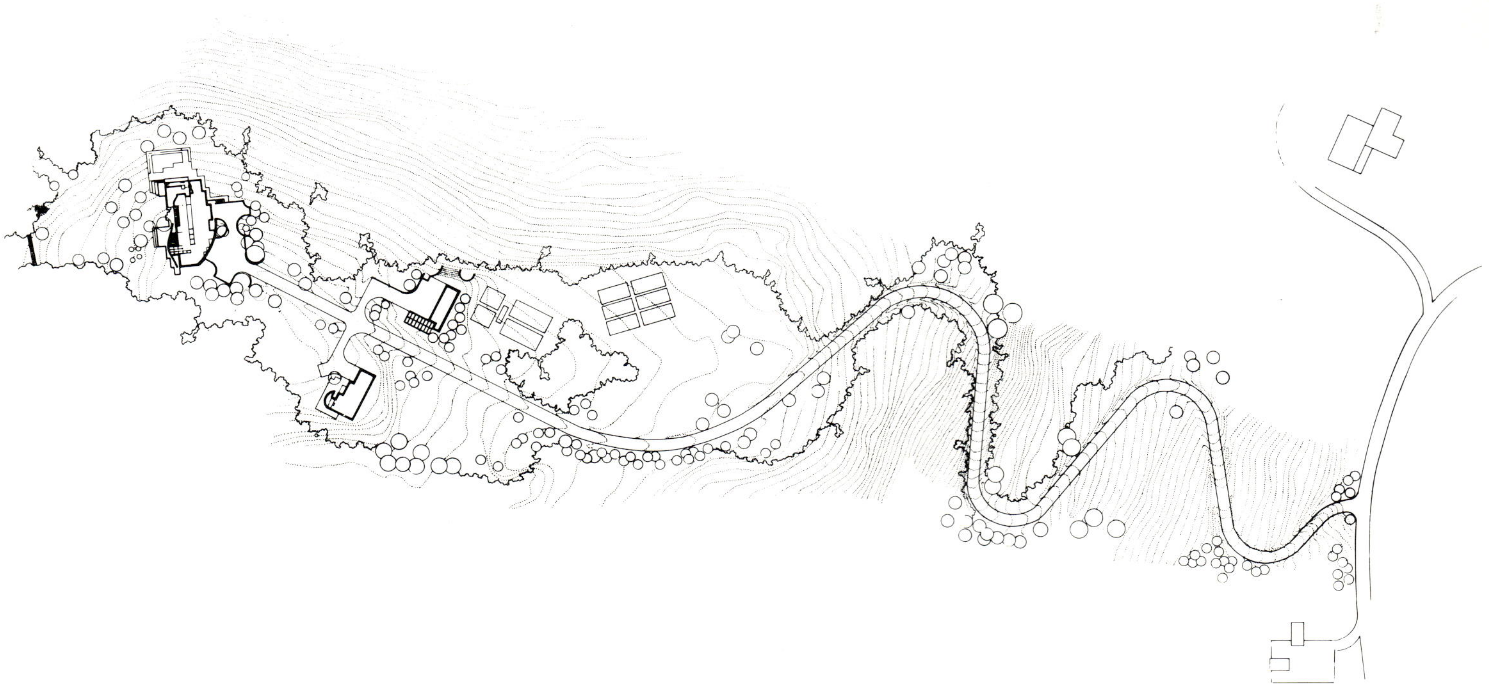

**Residence and Outbuildings**
Westchester County, New York

Site Plan



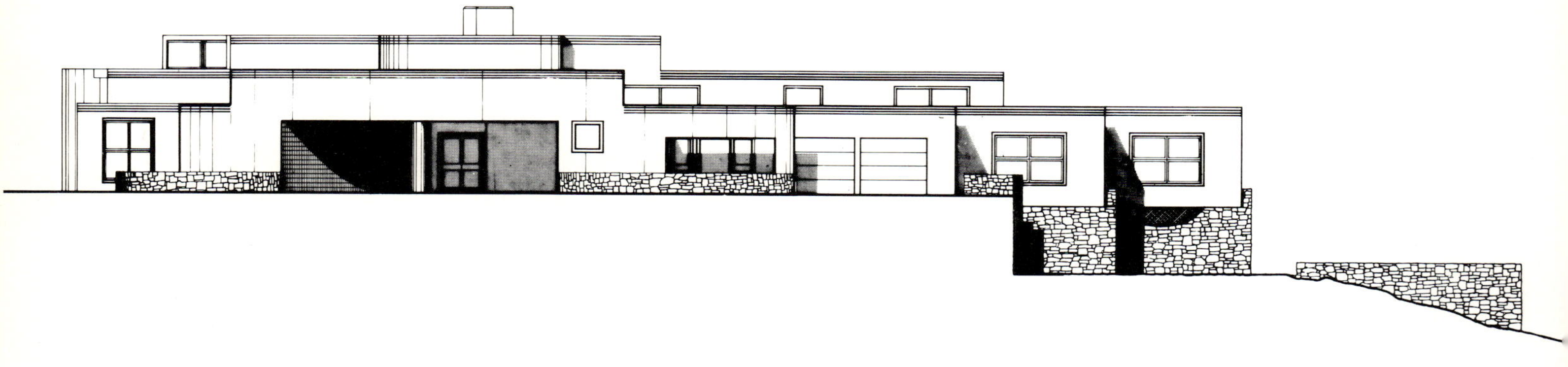

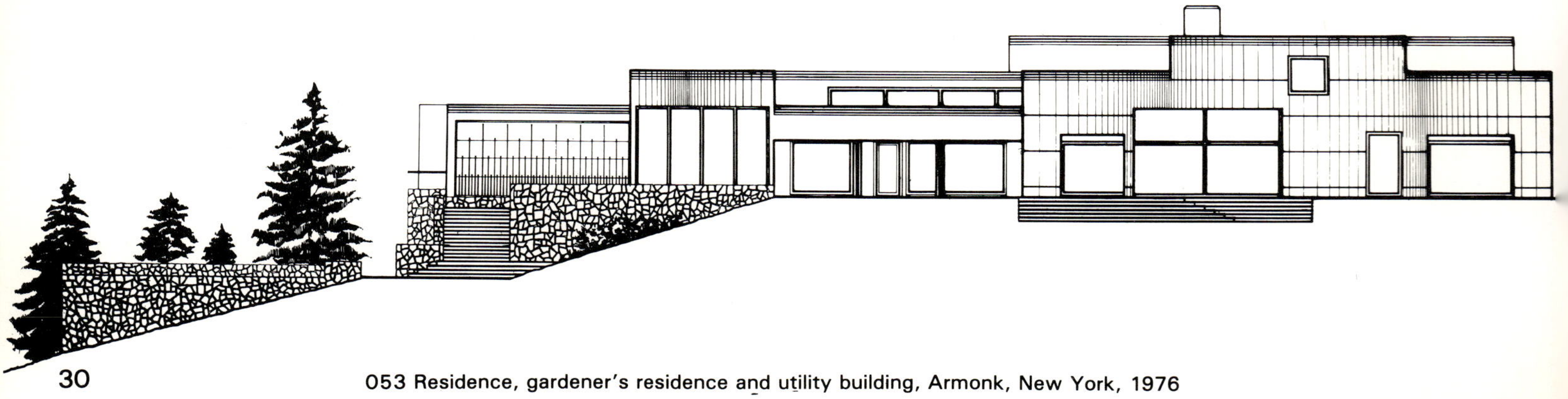



053 Residence, gardener's residence and utility building, Armonk, New York, 1976

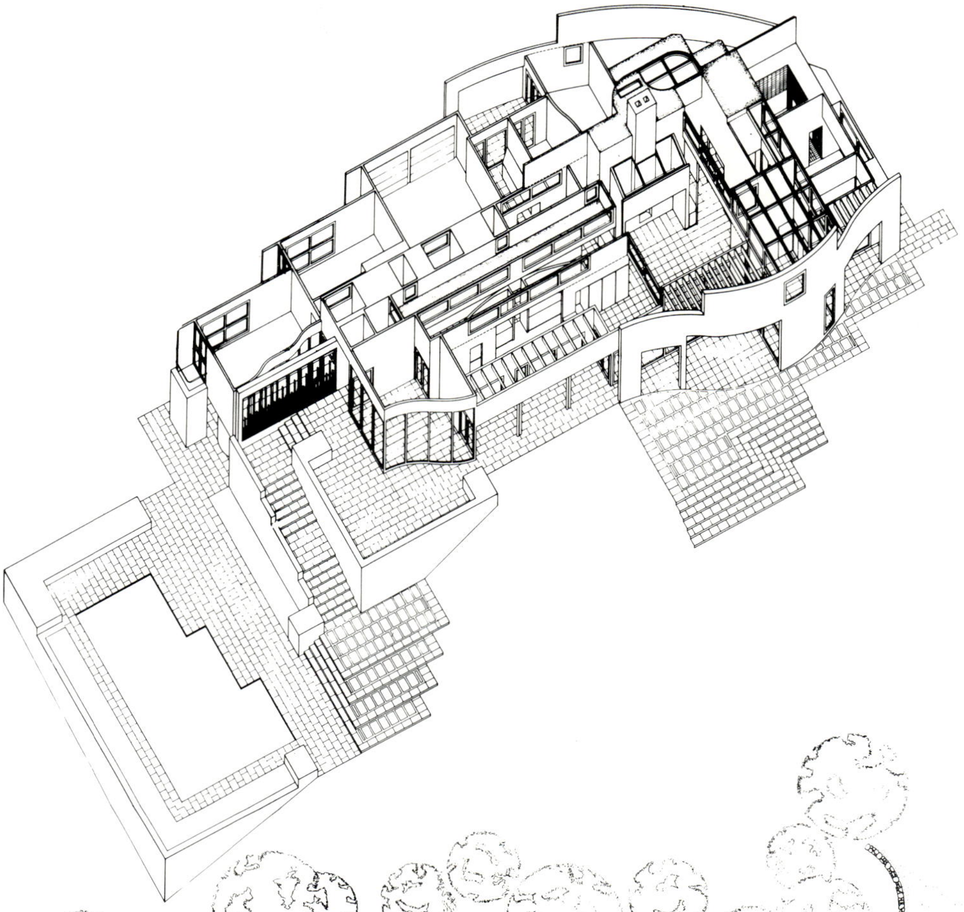

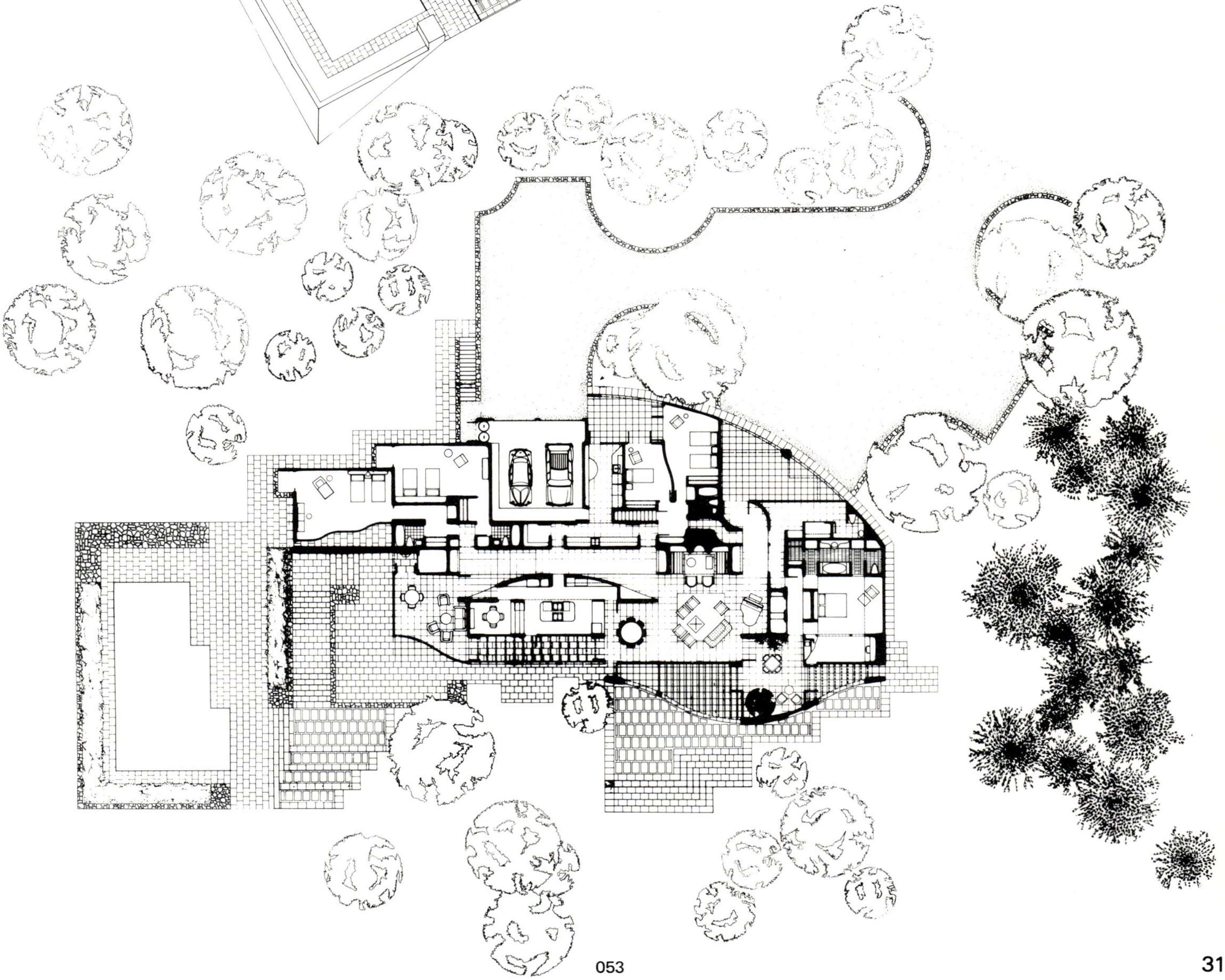

**New York Townhouse**

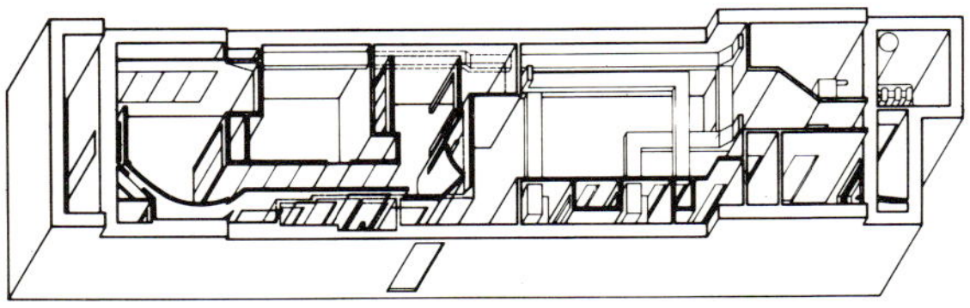
1

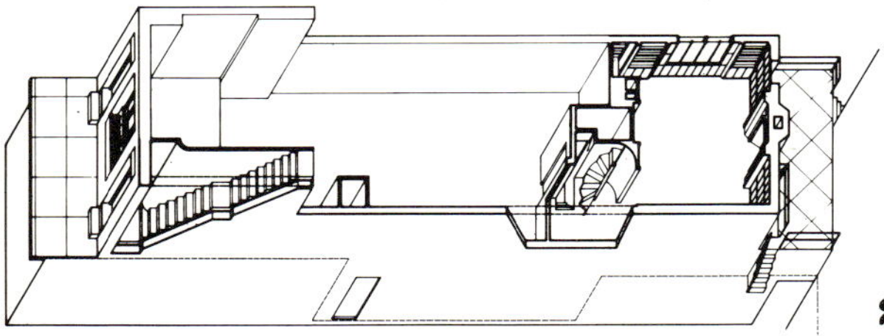
2

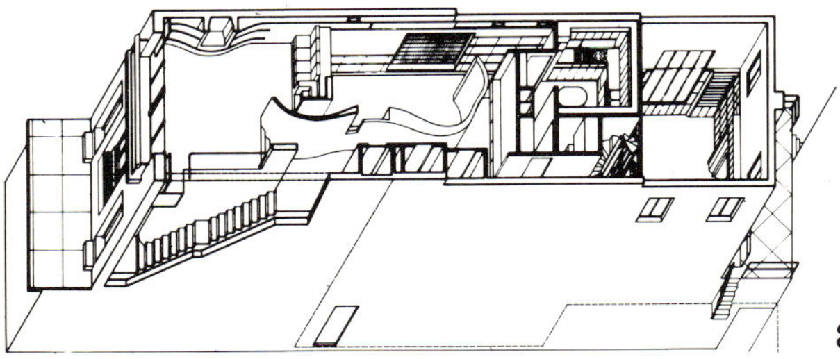
3

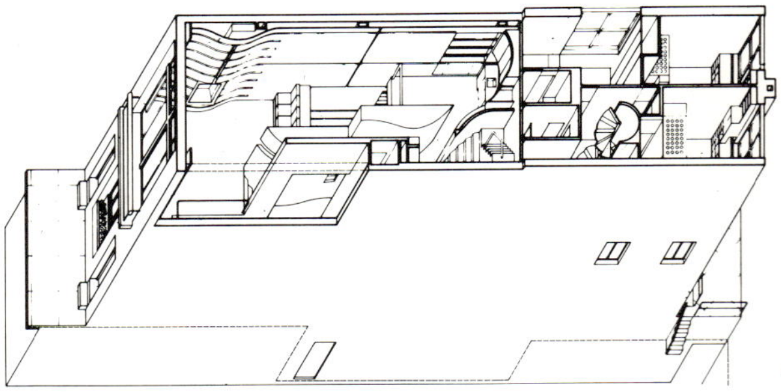
4

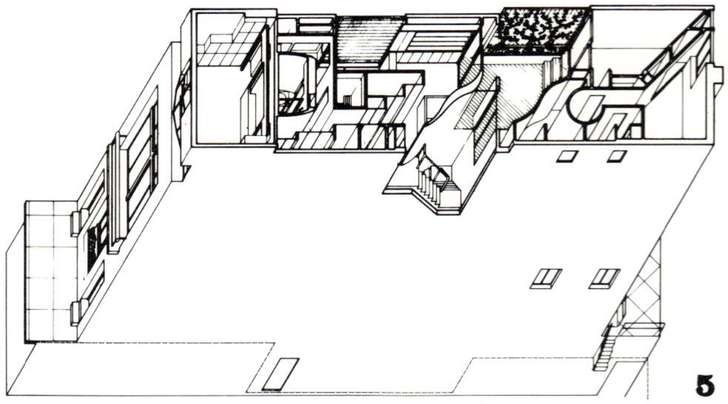
5

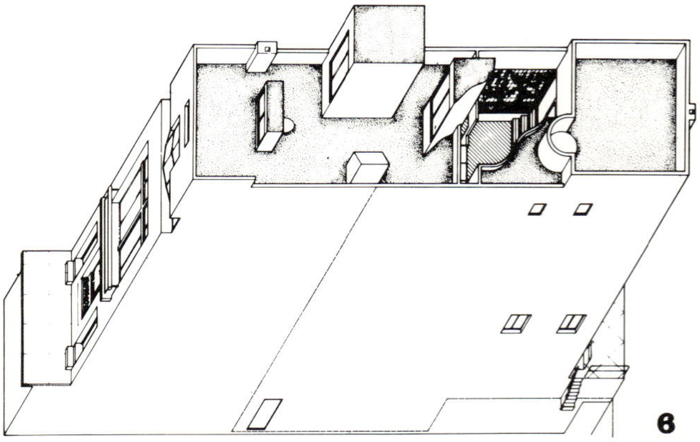
6



055 Townhouse, New York, 1975

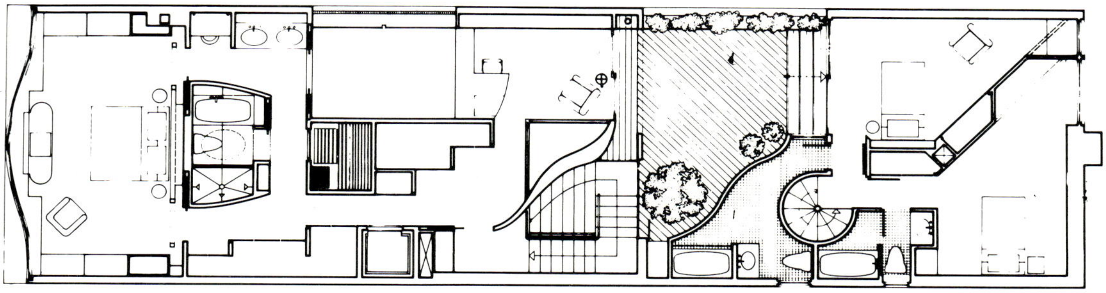

4

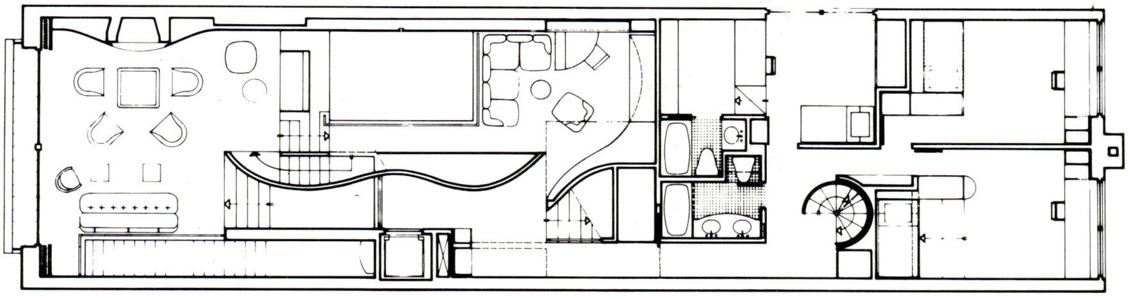

3

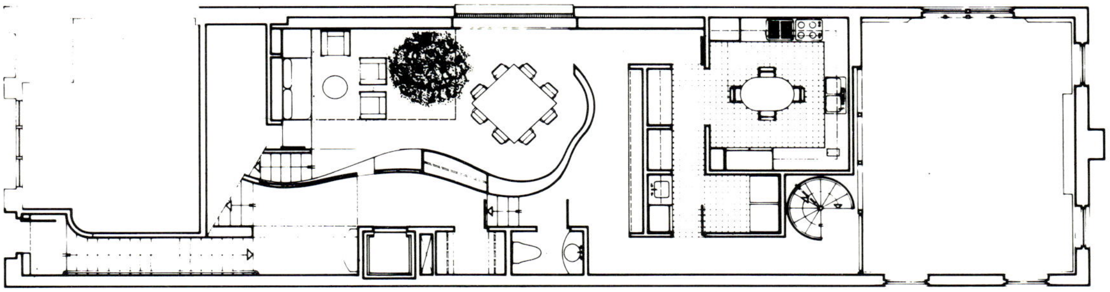

2

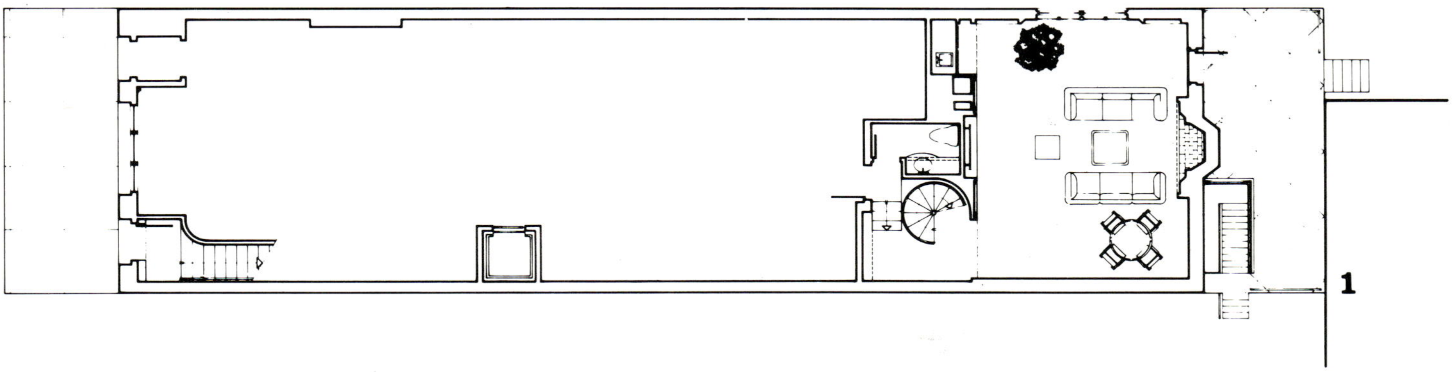

1

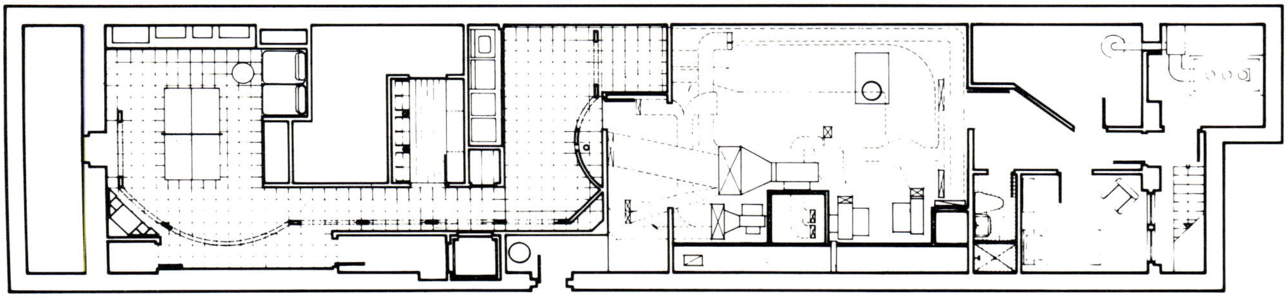

B

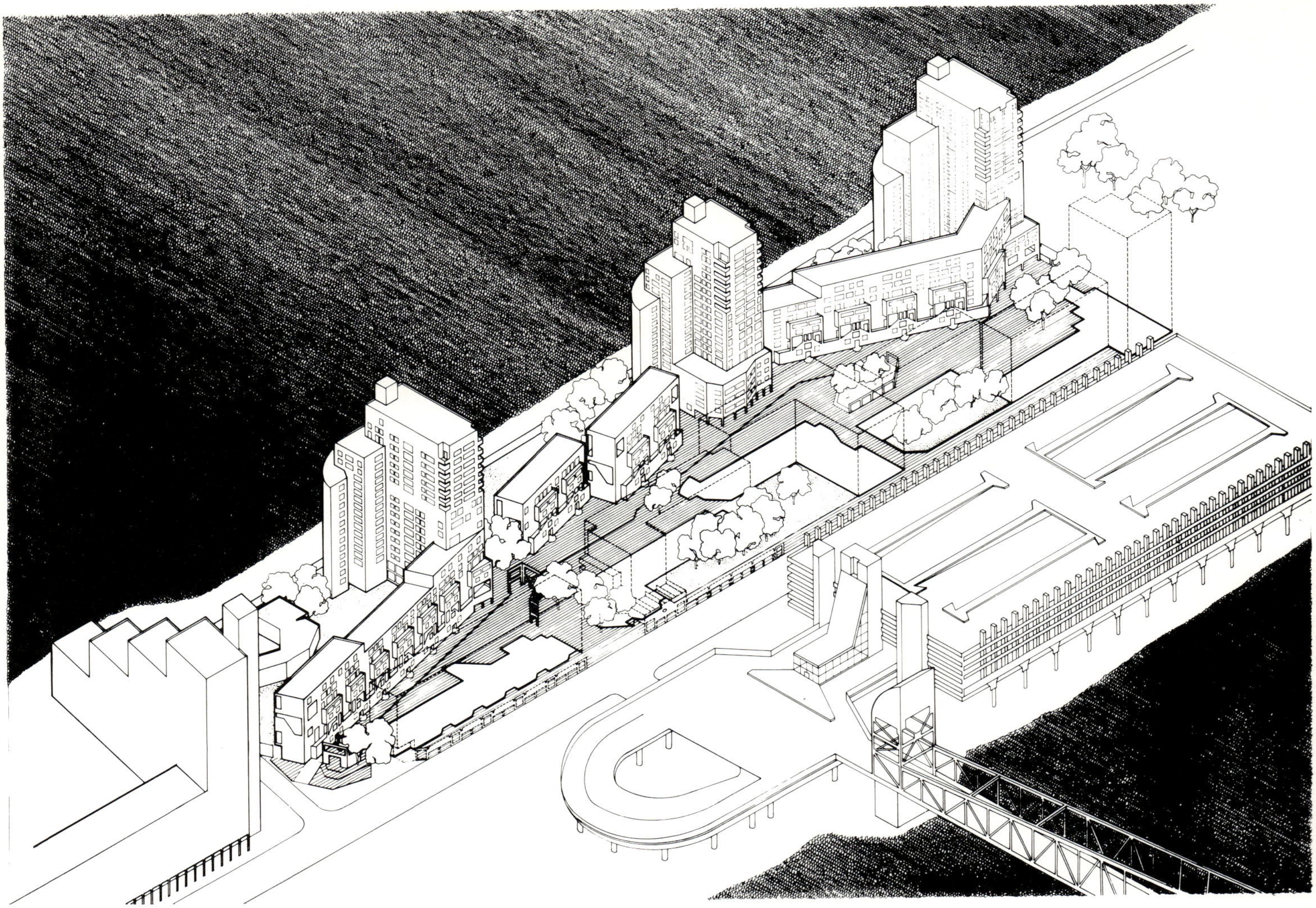

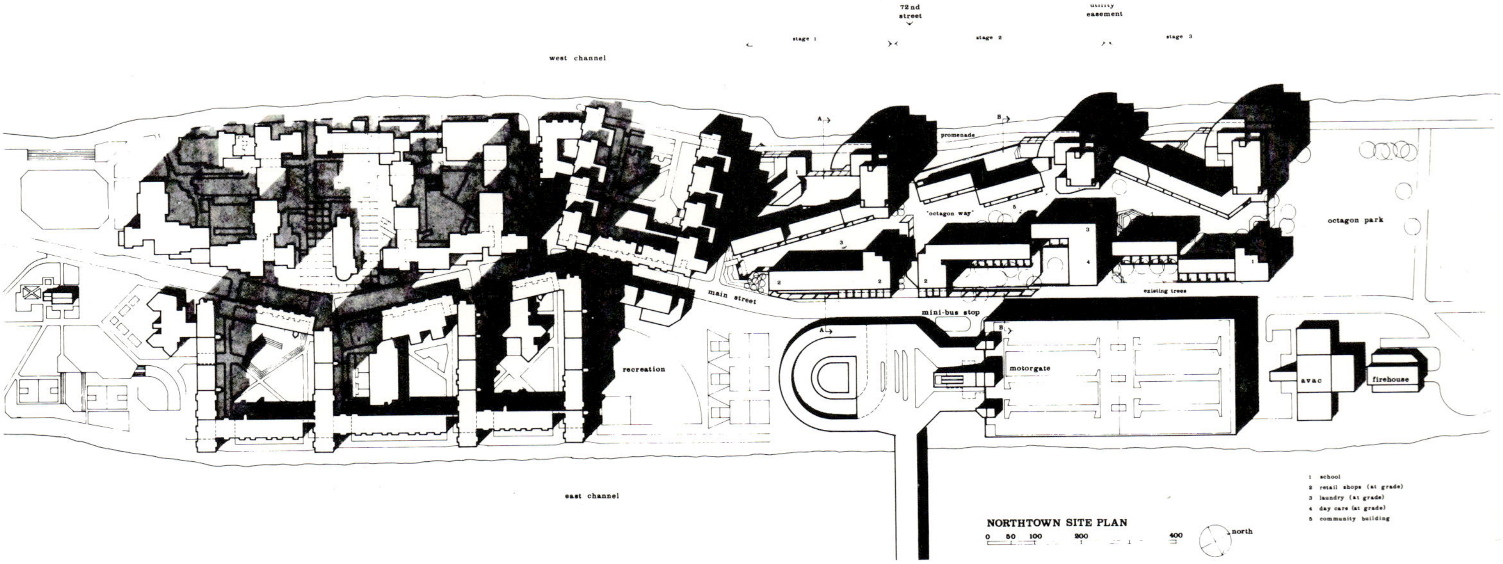




059 Roosevelt Island housing competition, project, 1975

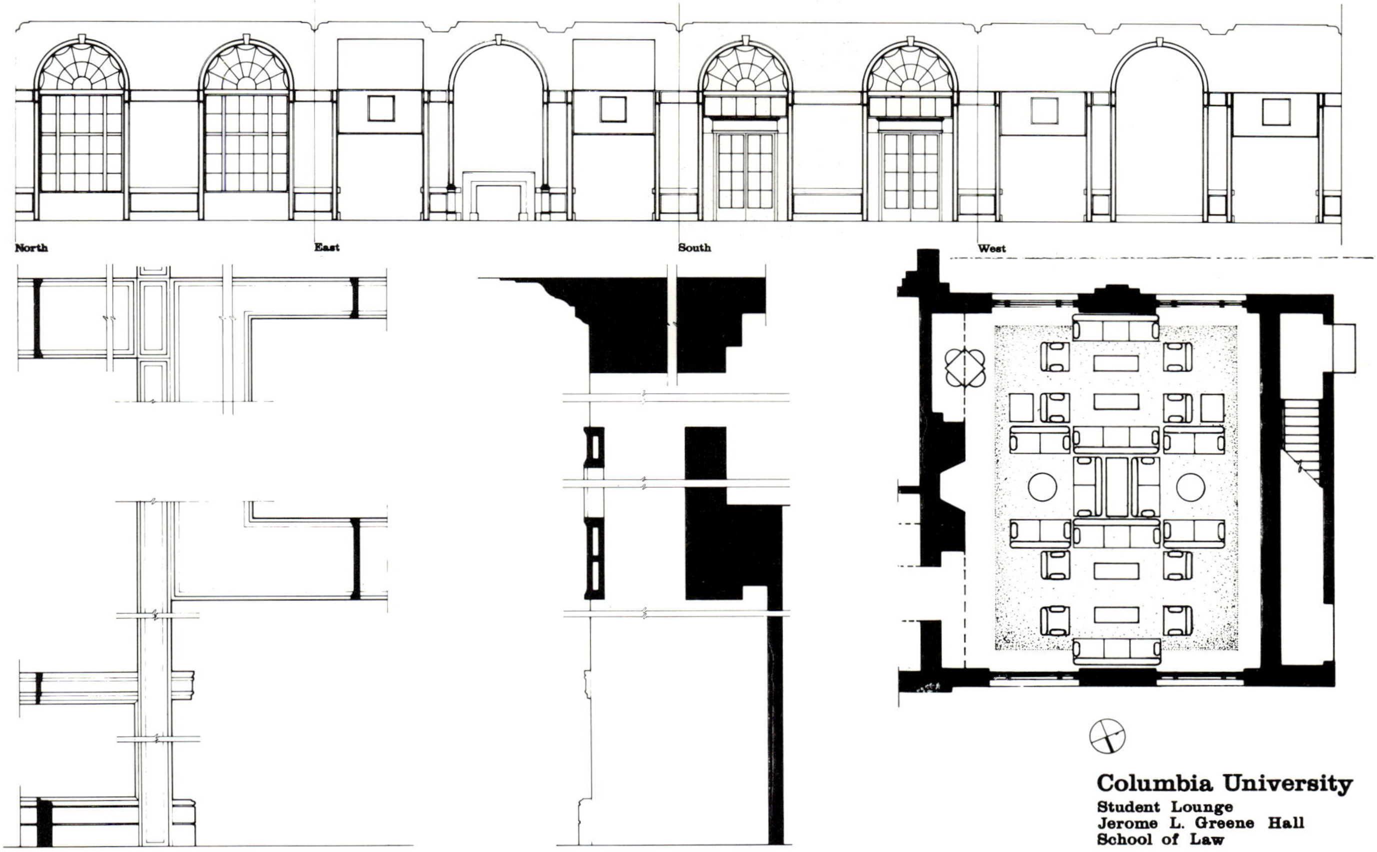


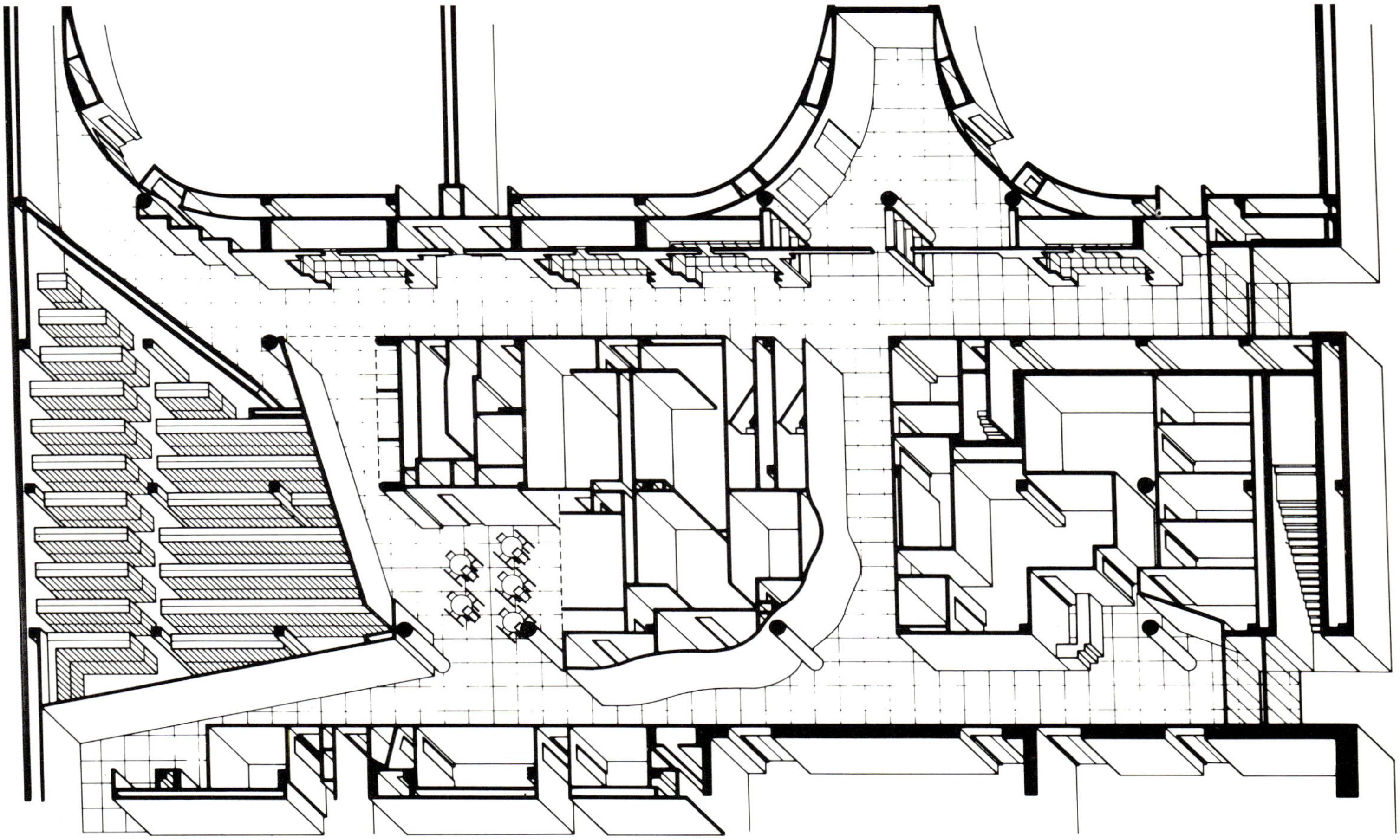

060 School of Law, Columbia University, New York City, 1975

View down Scarth Way from Dewdney Avenue 1

View down Mews from Scarth Square 2

Scarth Neighbourhood - Courtyard View 3

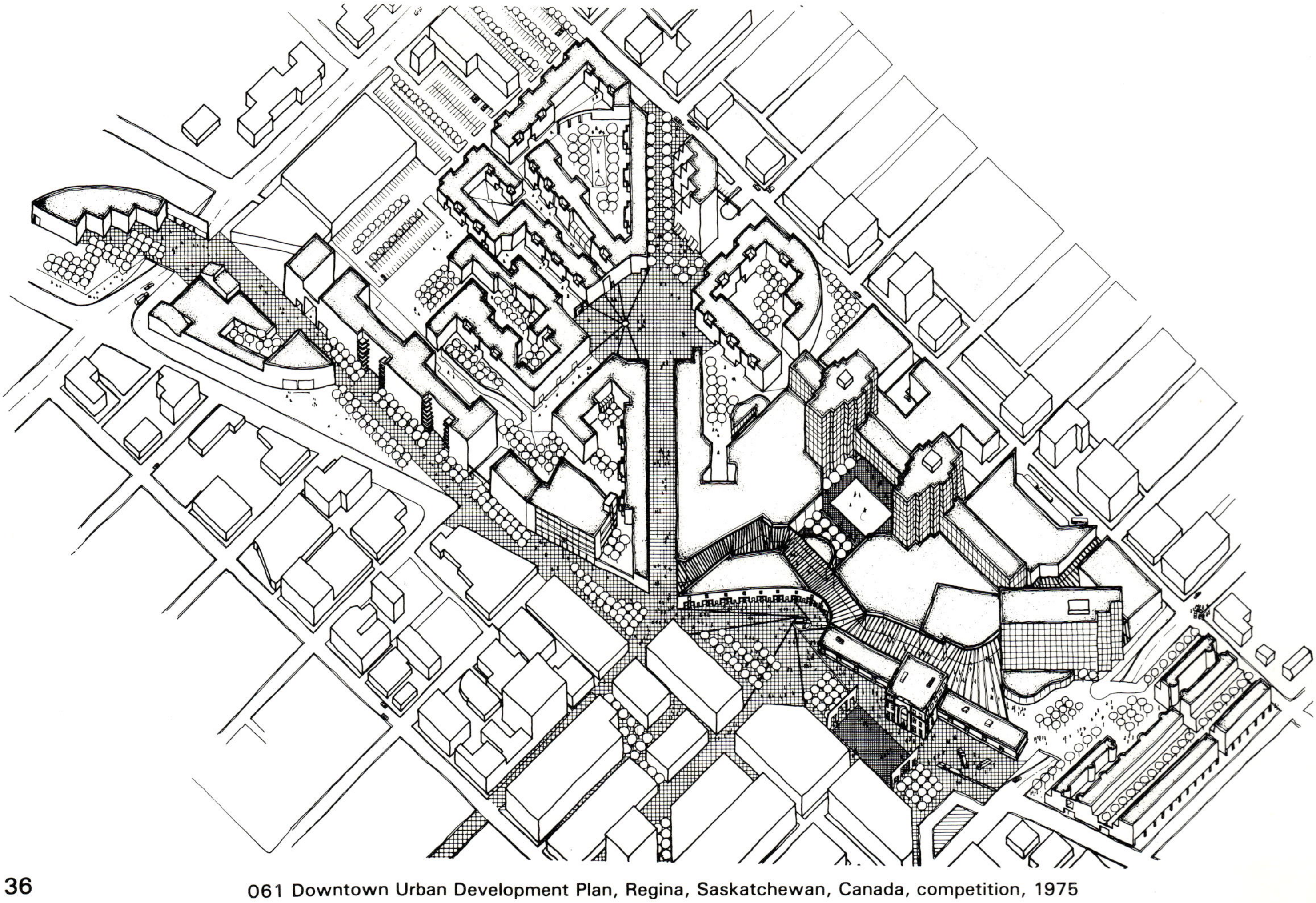



061 Downtown Urban Development Plan, Regina, Saskatchewan, Canada, competition, 1975

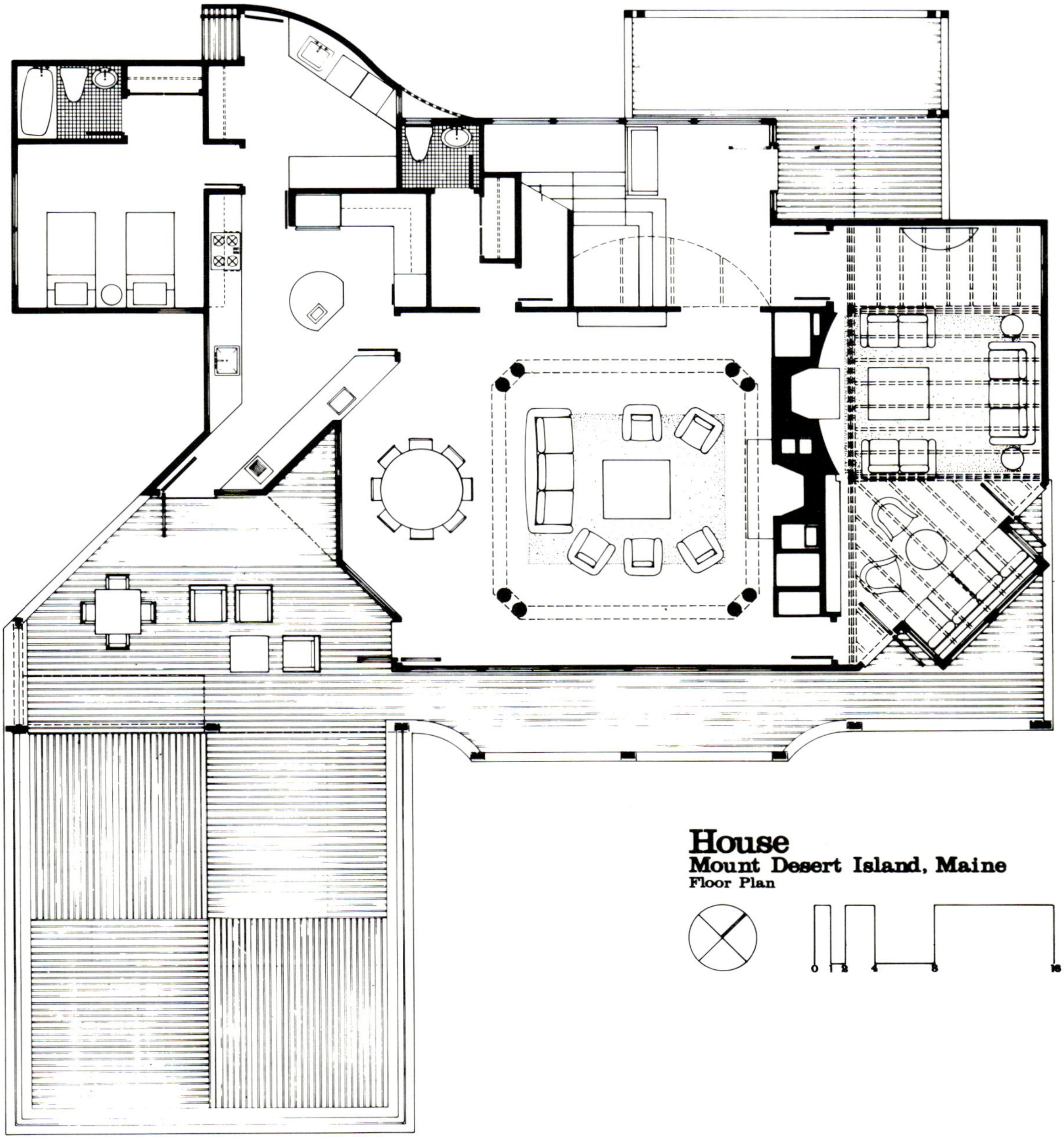

# House

**Mount Desert Island, Maine**

**Floor Plan**

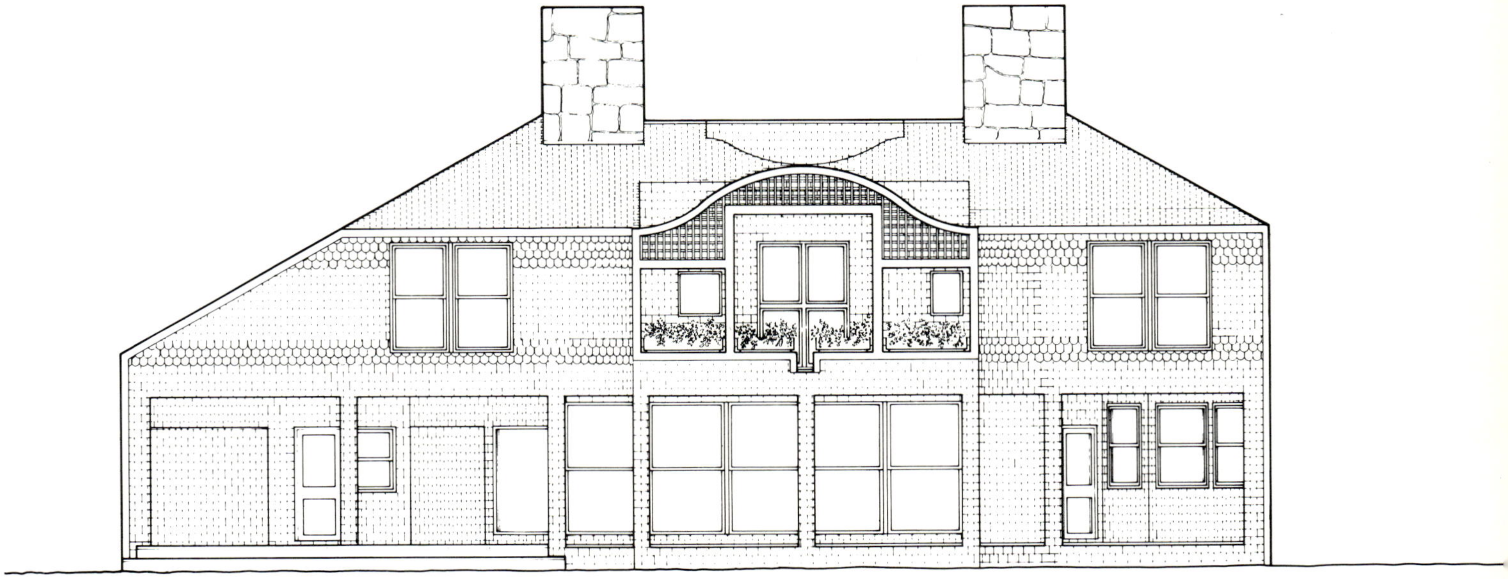

062 Points of View, Mount Desert Island, Maine, 1975-76

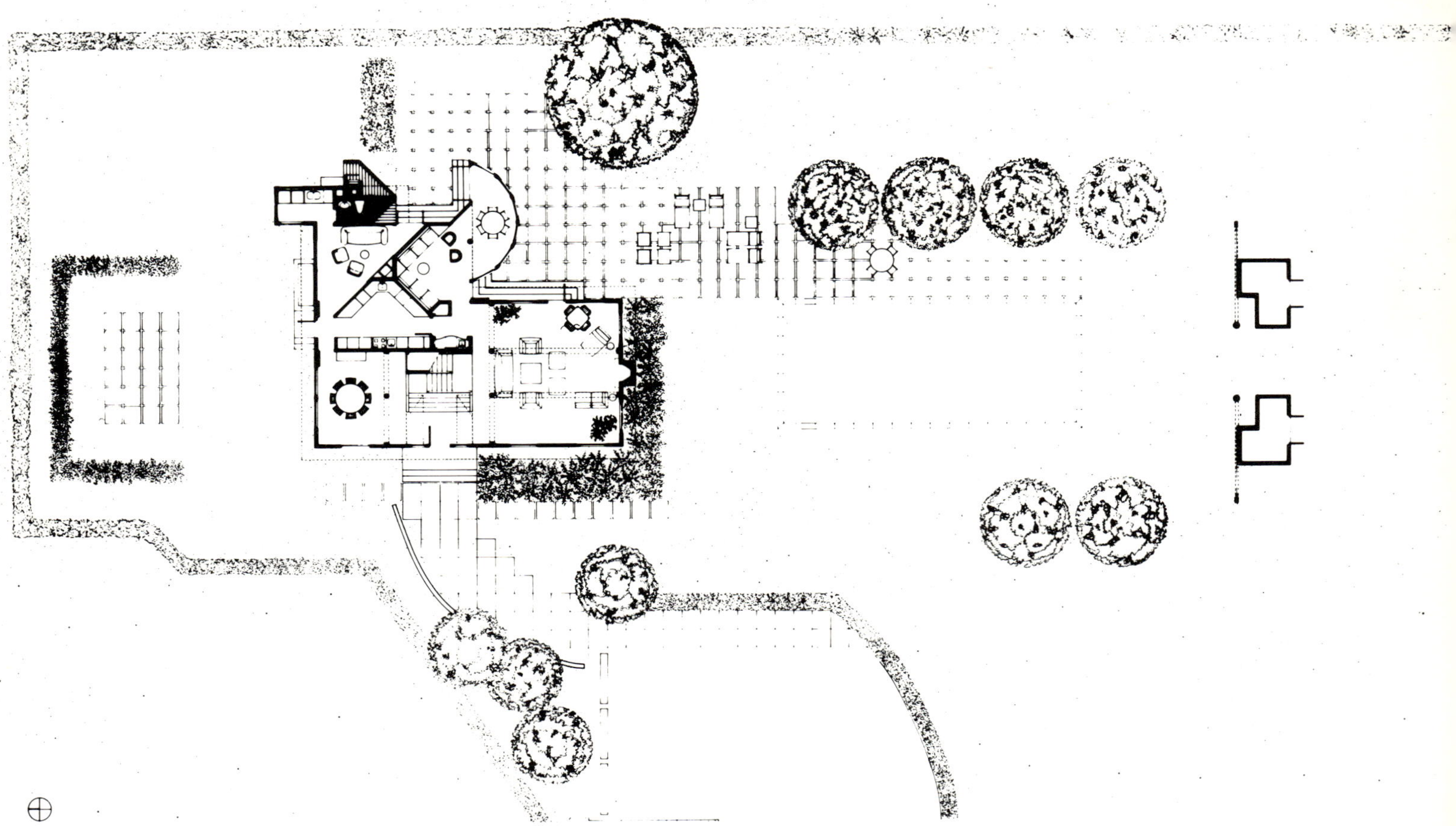

**Residence**
**Eastern Long Island**
**Entry Hall Elevation**



064 Residence, Eastern Long Island, 1975-77

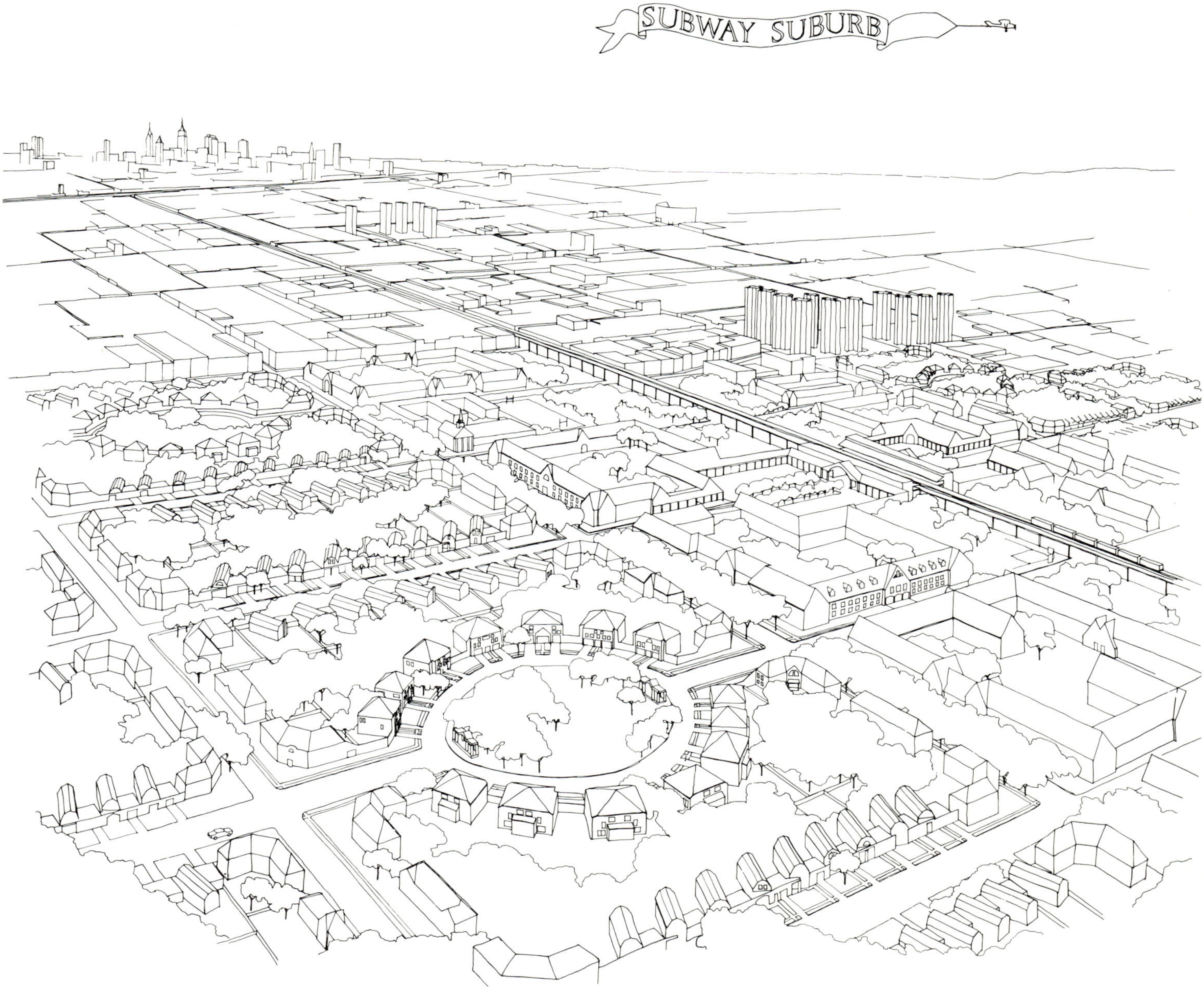


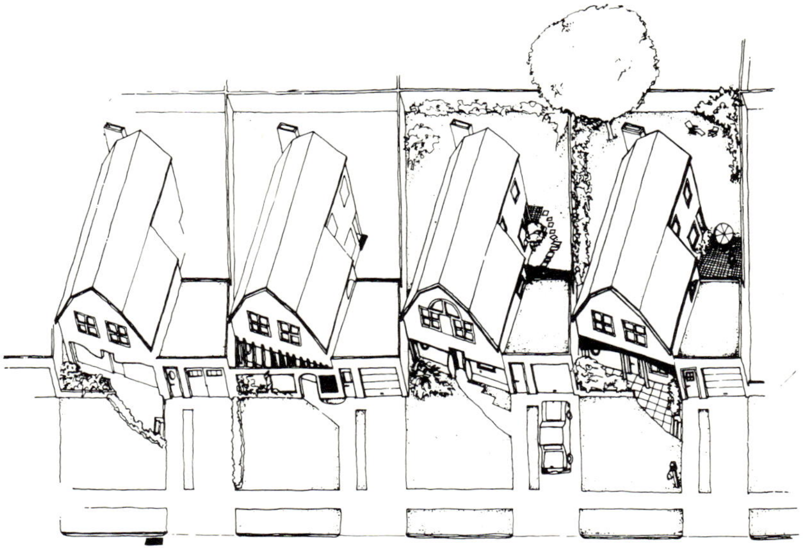

069 Subway Suburb, project for the Venice Biennale, 1976

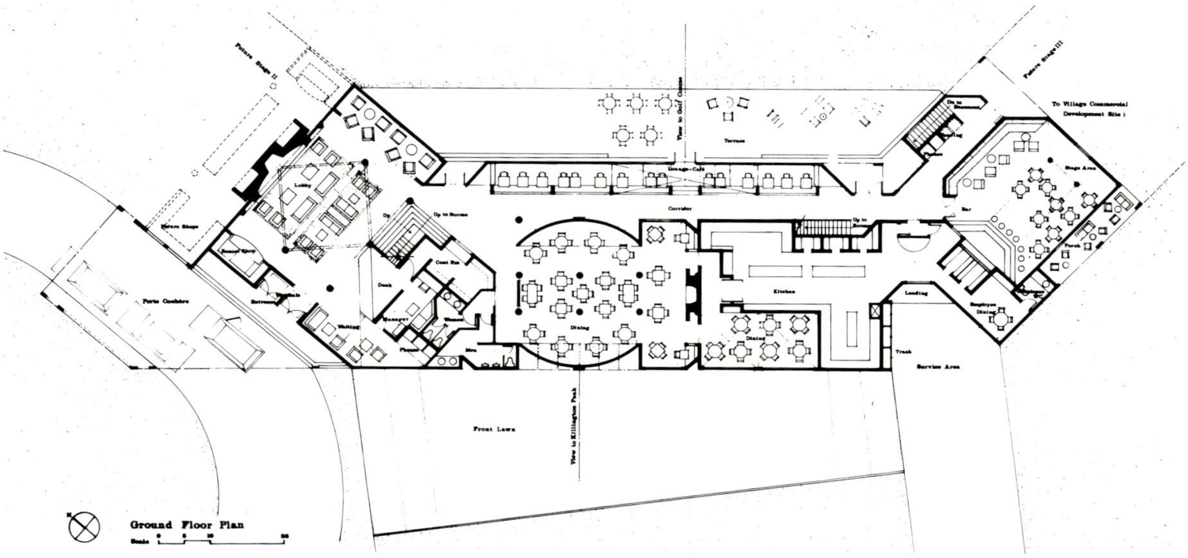




070 Killington ski lodge, Vermont, national competition, project, 1976

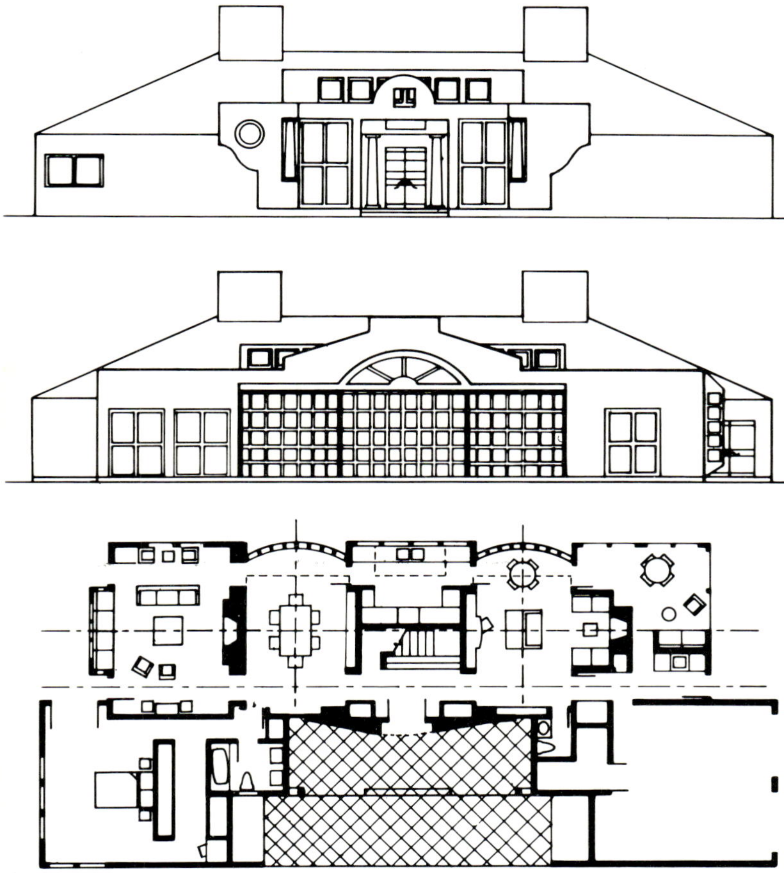

**1**

**2**

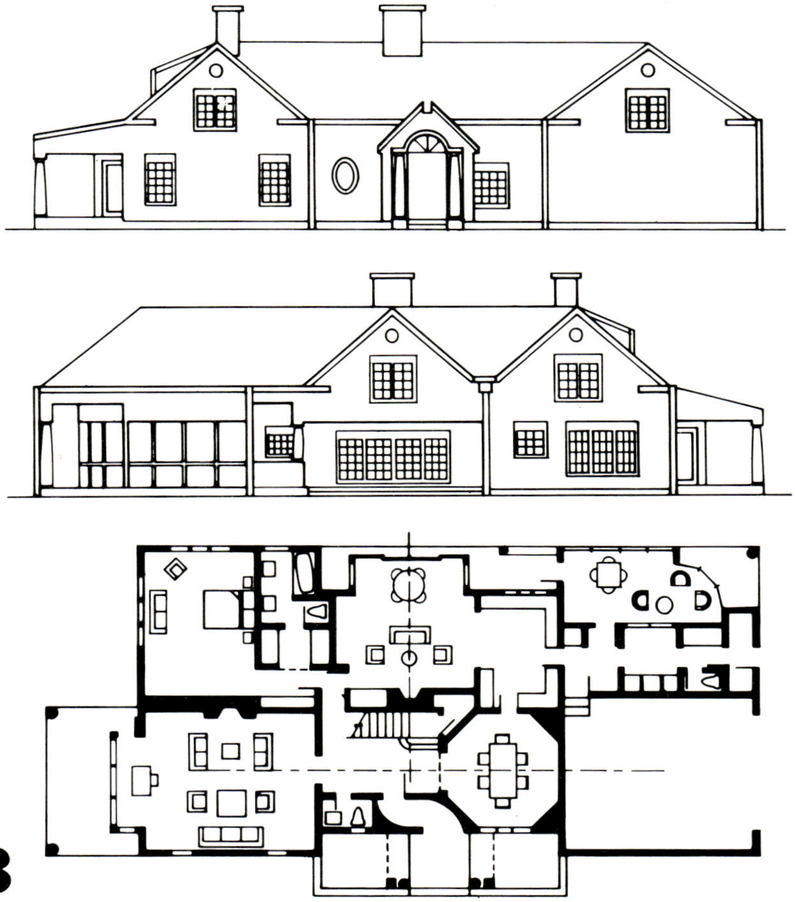

**3**

077 Residence, Fairfield County, project, 1977-78

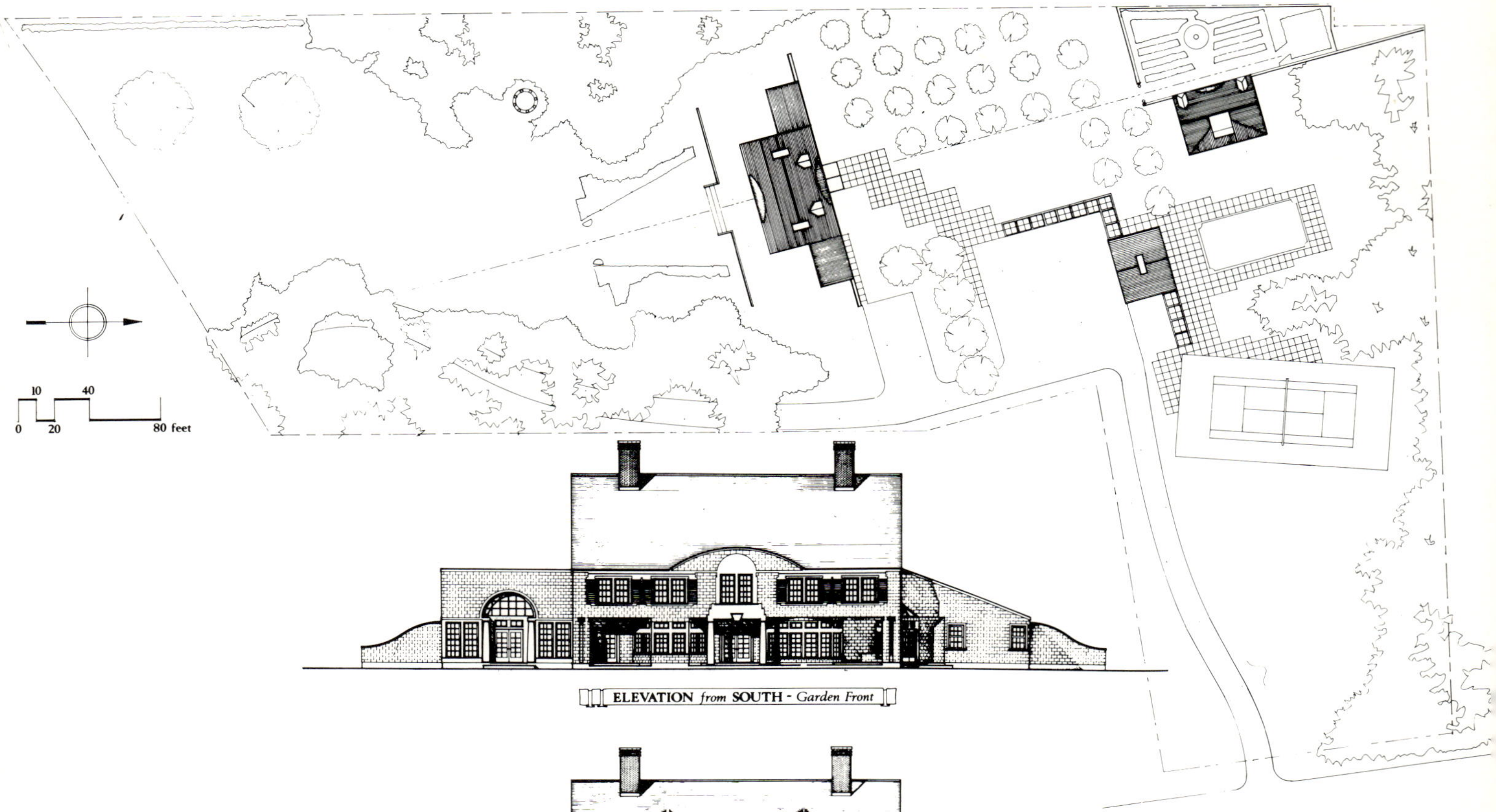


ELEVATION *from* SOUTH - *Garden Front*

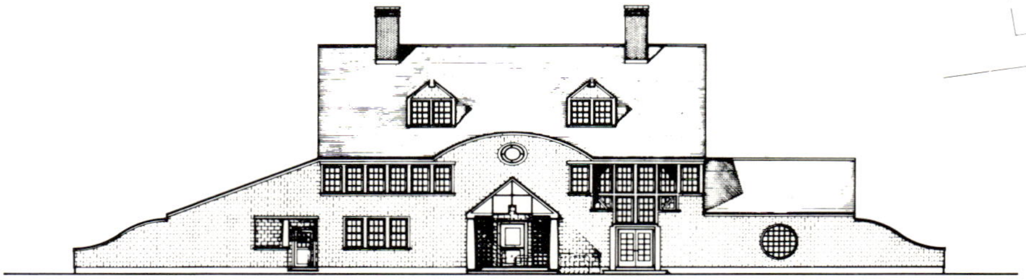

ELEVATION *from* NORTH - *Entrance Front*

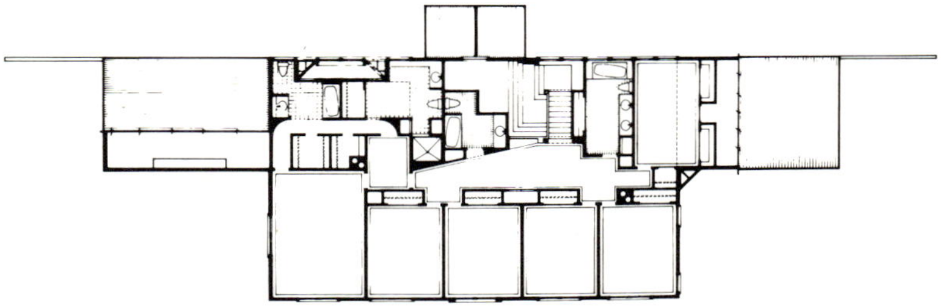

PLAN *of the* FIRST FLOOR

PLAN *of the* GROUND FLOOR

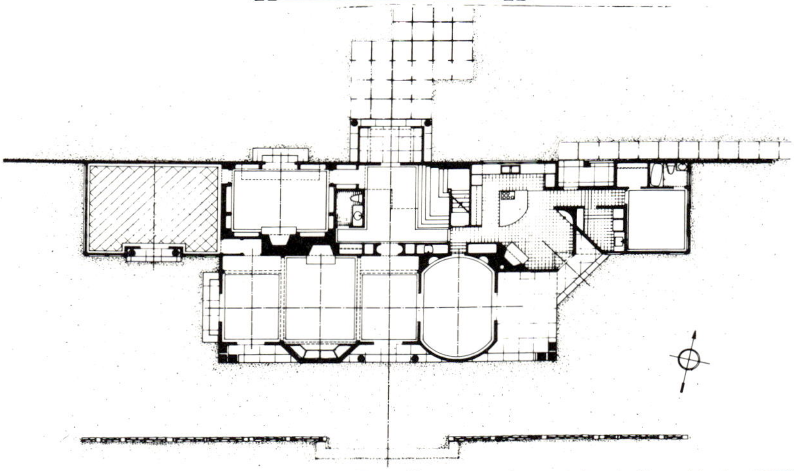



087 Residence, studio and outbuilding, East Hampton, Long Island, New York, 1978-79

# POOLHOUSE - GARAGE

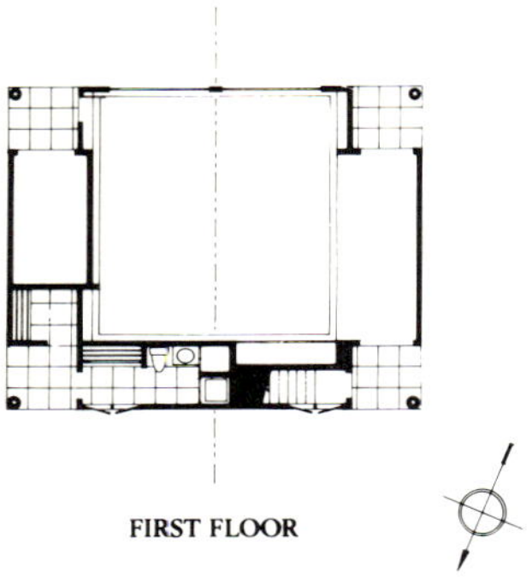
FIRST FLOOR

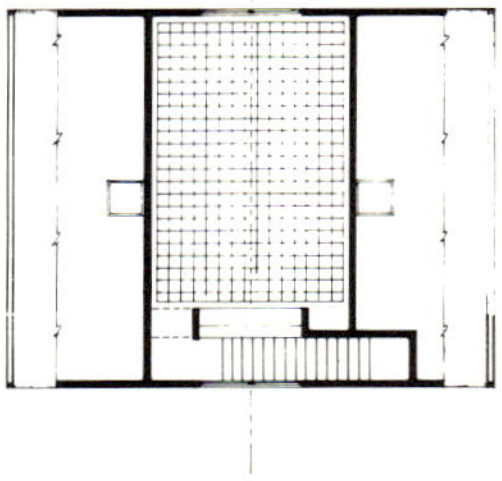
SECOND FLOOR

PLANS

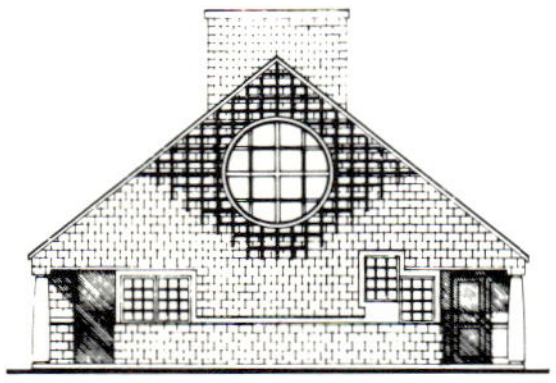
NORTH

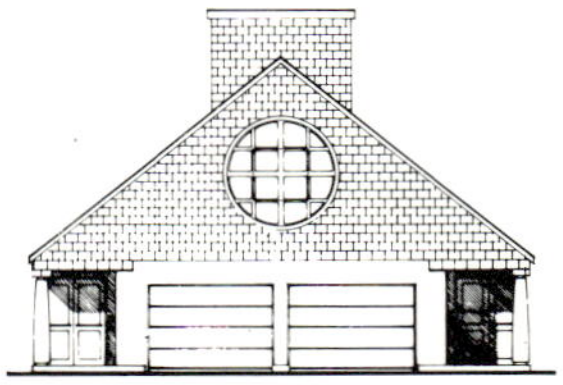
SOUTH

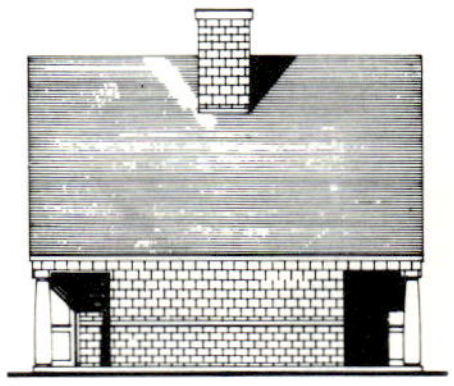
EAST

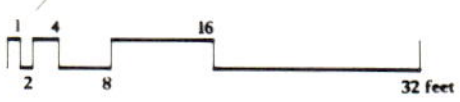


ELEVATIONS

# STUDIO

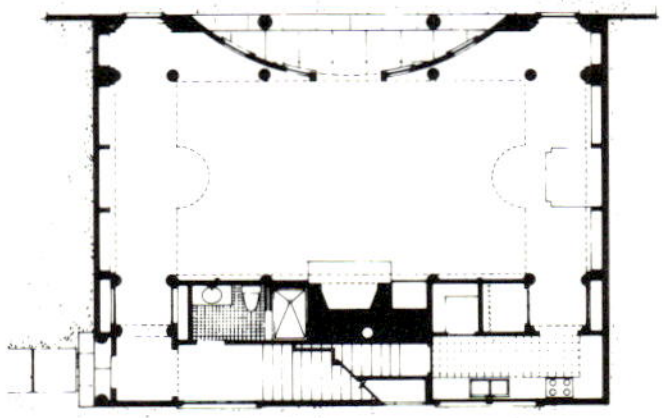
GROUND FLOOR

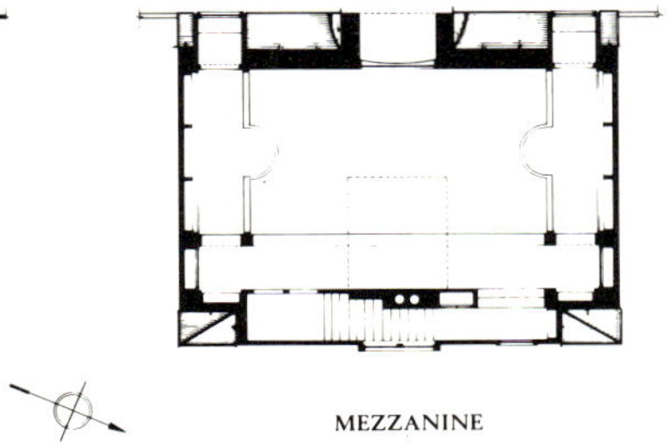
MEZZANINE

PLANS

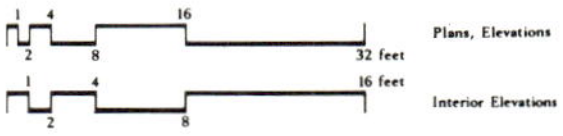


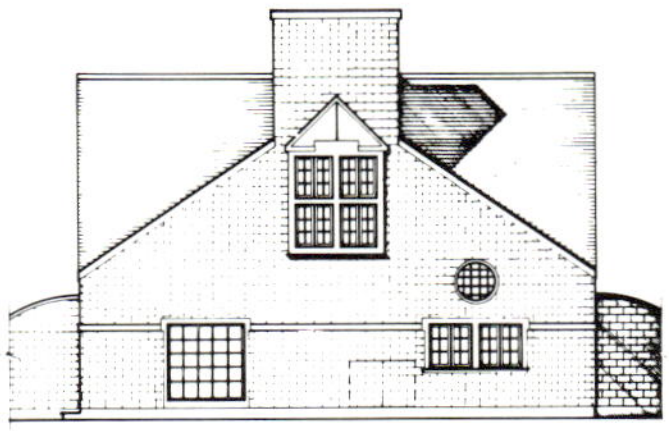
EAST

WEST

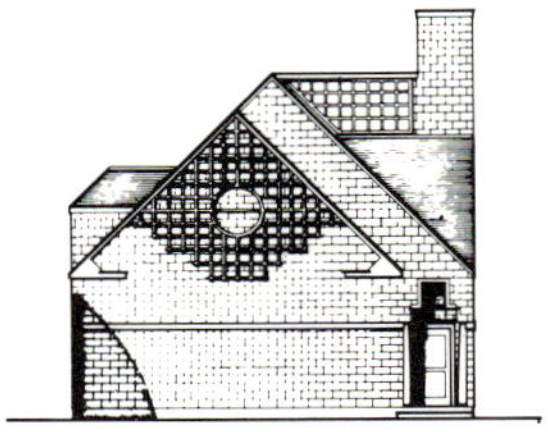
SOUTH

ELEVATIONS

TOWARDS EAST

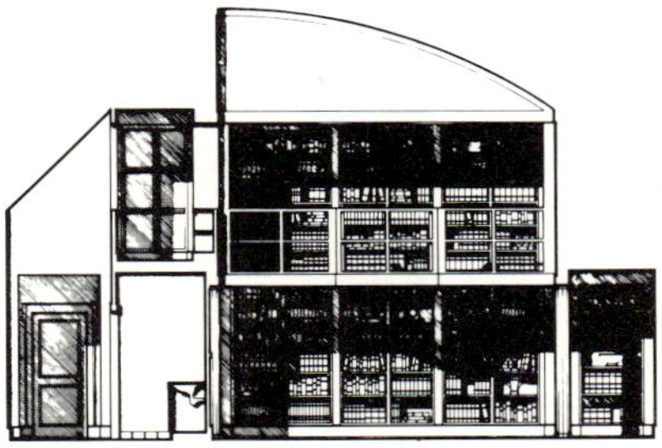
TOWARDS SOUTH

TOWARDS WEST

INTERIOR ELEVATIONS

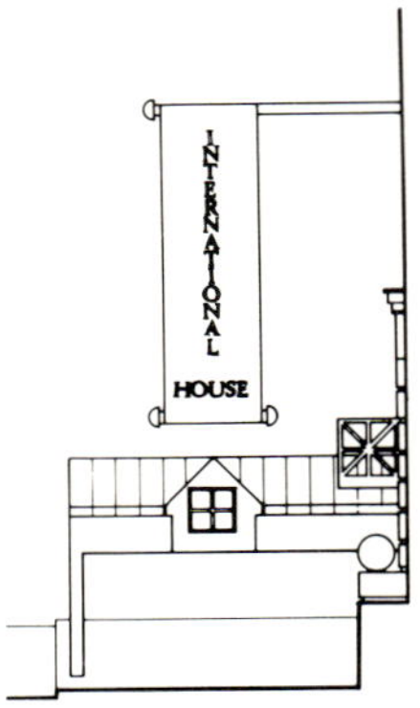


SECTION · ELEVATION A·A

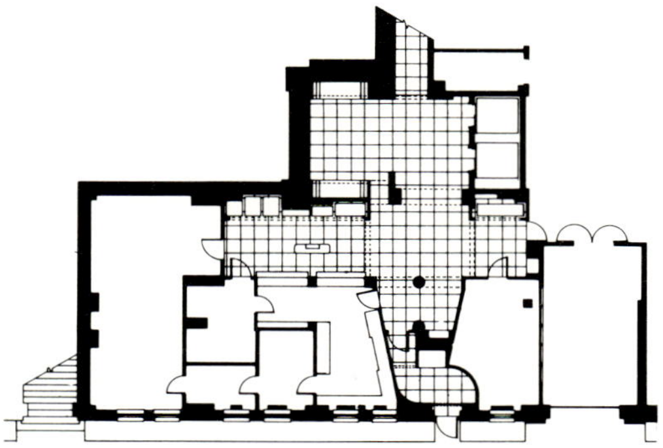

PLAN

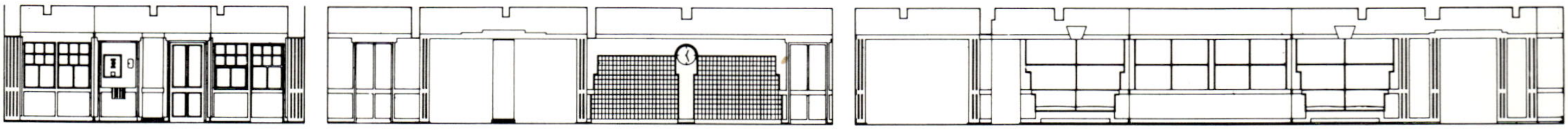

INTERIOR ELEVATIONS

# INTERNATIONAL HOUSE

## CLAREMONT AVENUE LOBBY



089 Renovations to International House, New York, New York, 1979

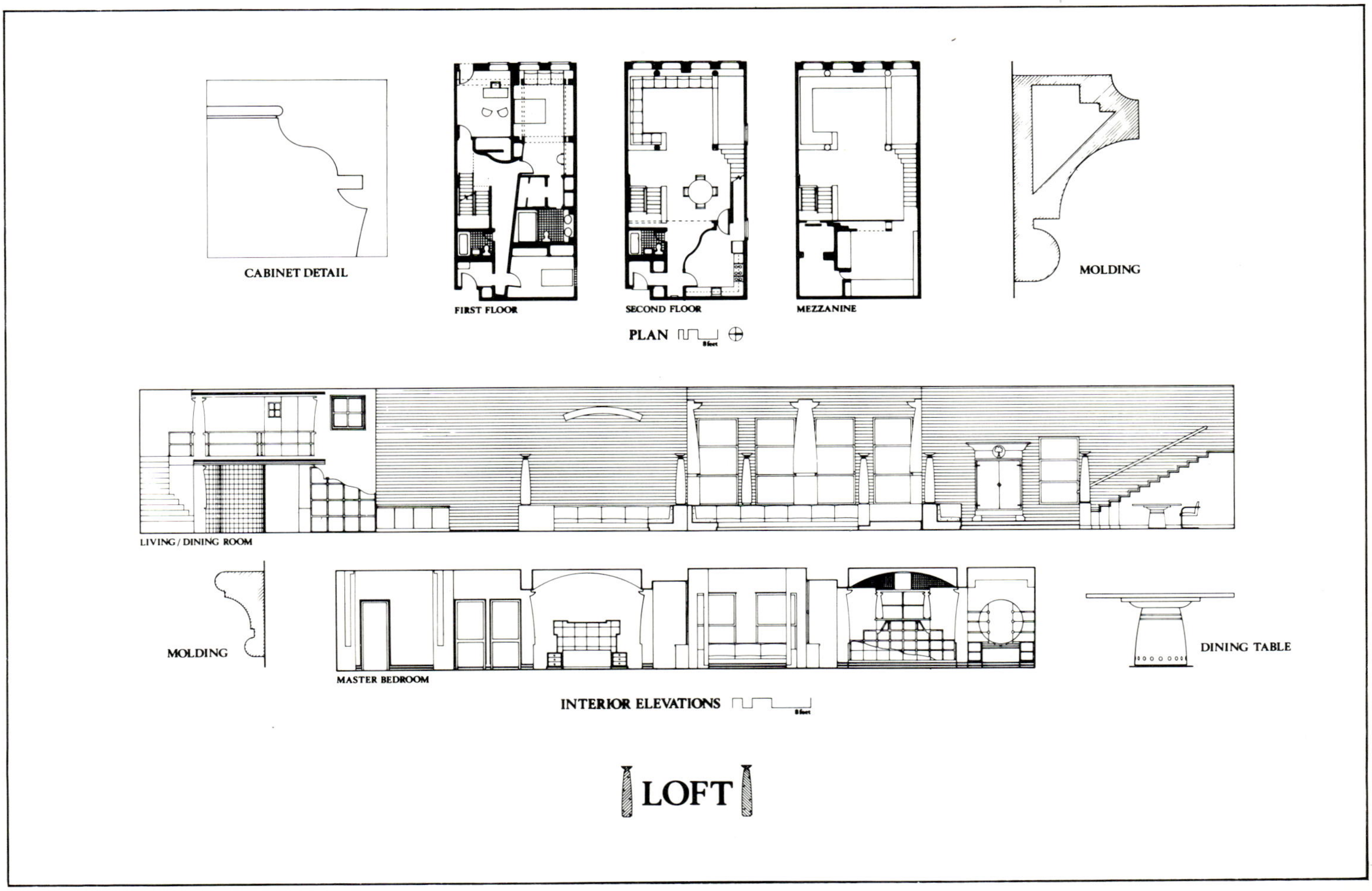


090 Smetana Loft, New York, under construction

SOUTH ELEVATION

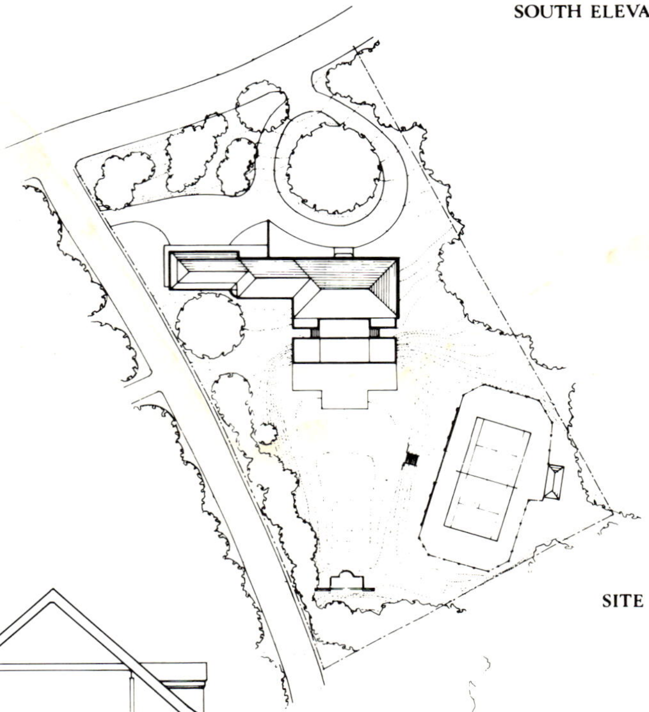

SITE PLAN

SECTION

# RESIDENCE · LLEWELLYN PARK · NEW JERSEY

0 2 4 8 16 32 FEET·SECTION·ELEVATION

0 10 20 40 80 160 FEET·SITE PLAN



094 Residence, Llewellyn Park, New Jersey, under construction

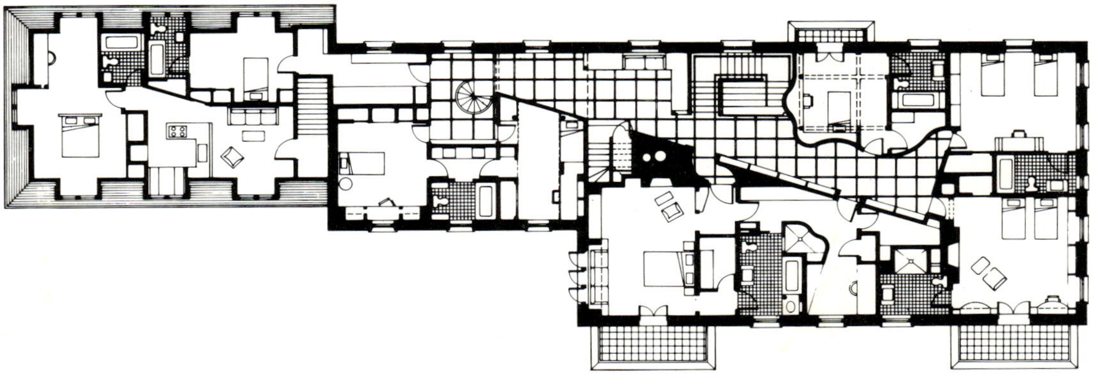

SECOND FLOOR

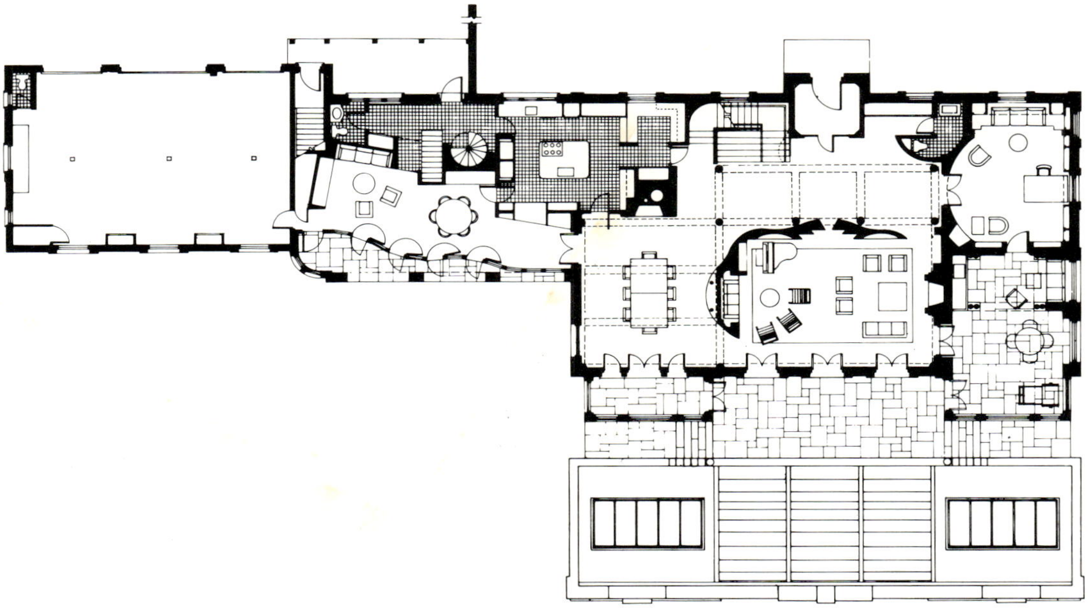

FIRST FLOOR

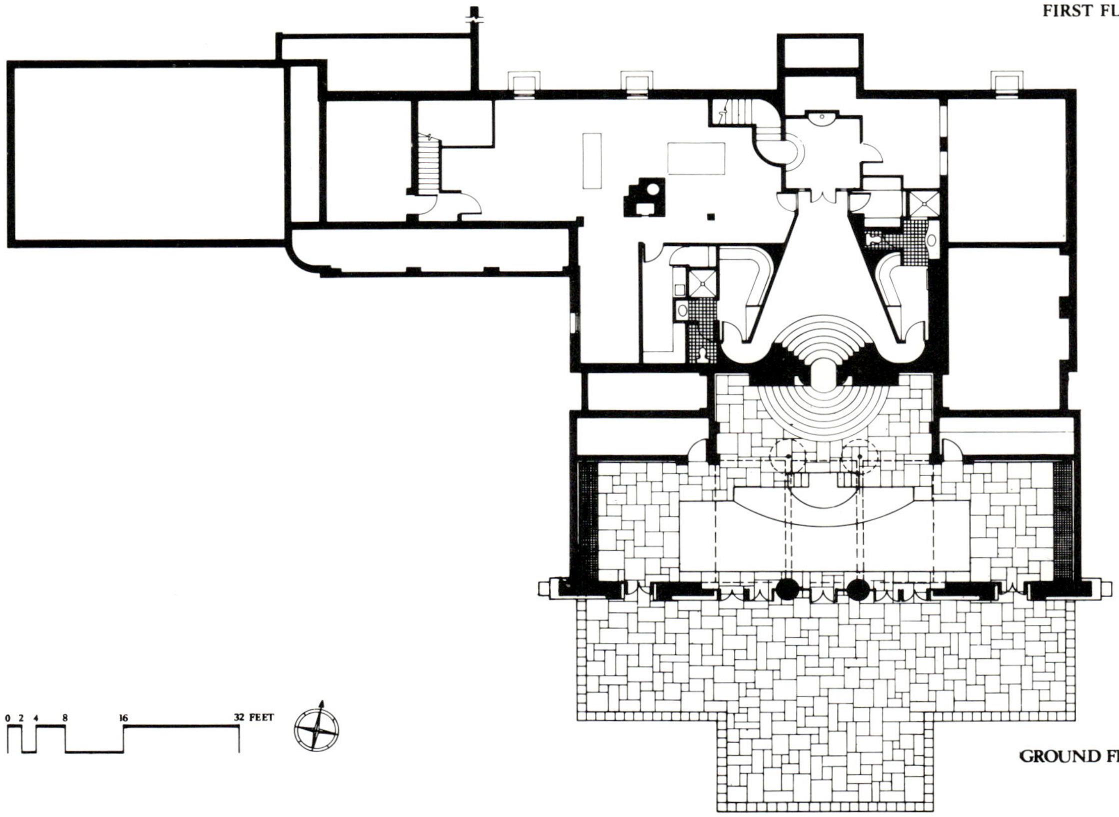


GROUND FLOOR

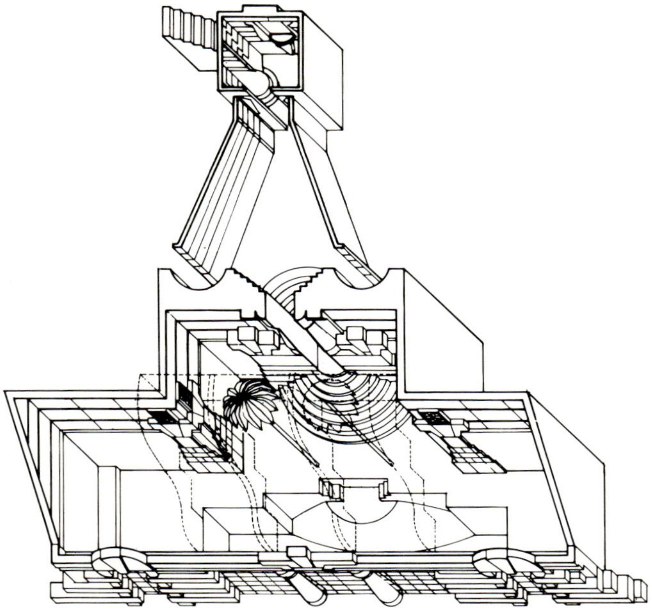

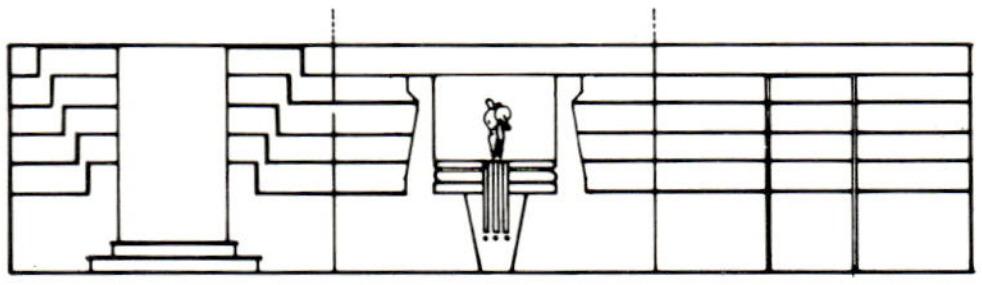

VESTIBULE

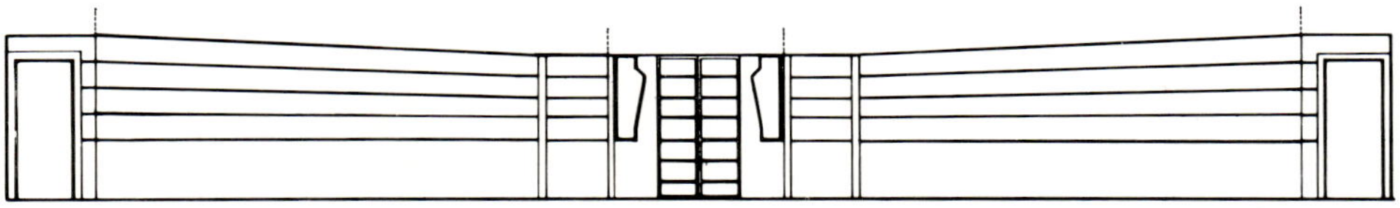

HALL

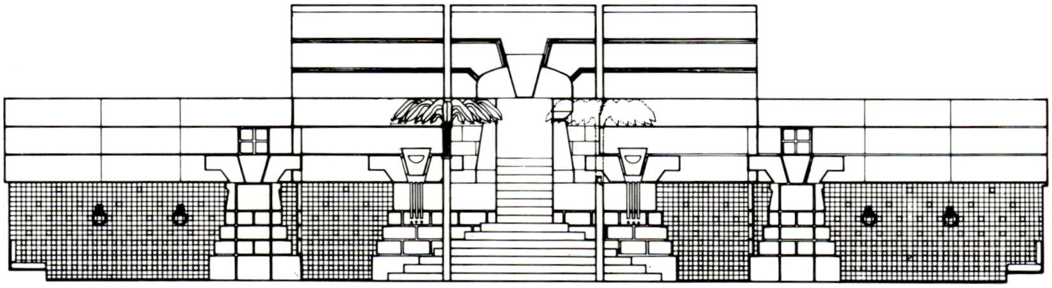

INTERIOR ELEVATION

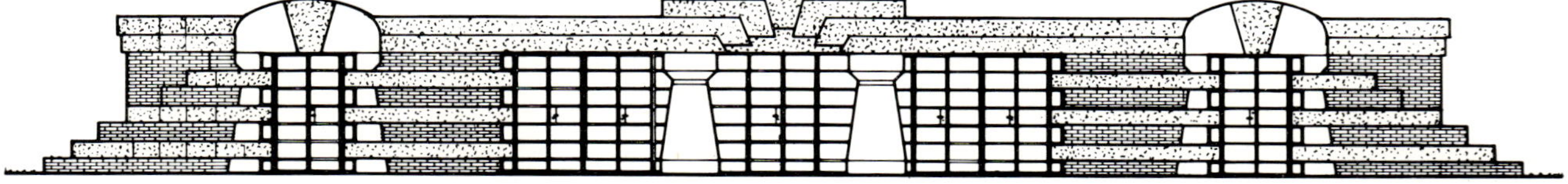

EXTERIOR ELEVATION

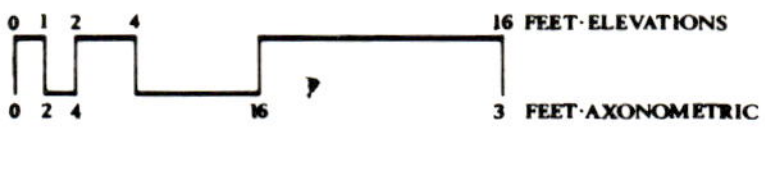


POOLHOUSE

West

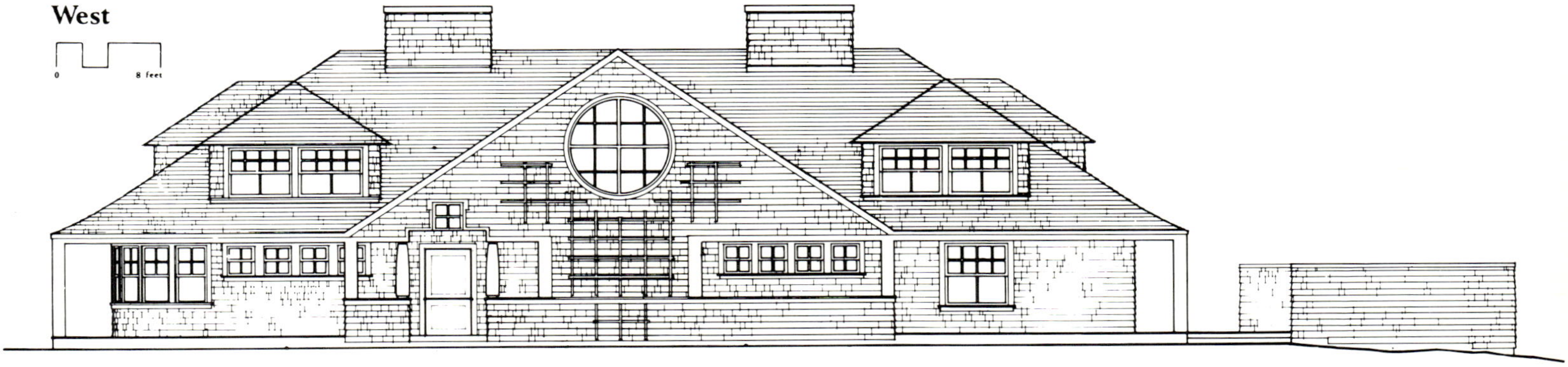

East

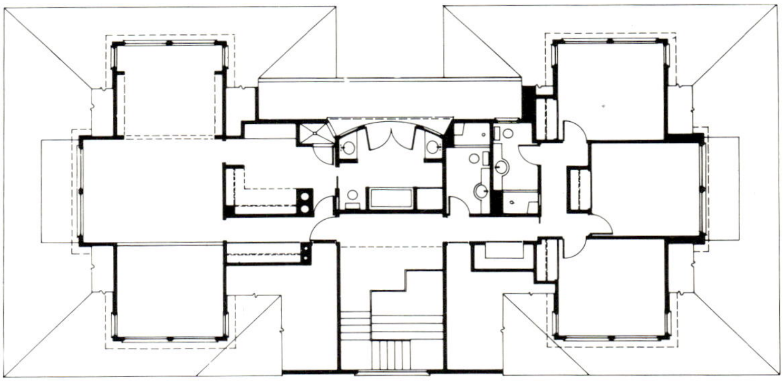

Second Floor

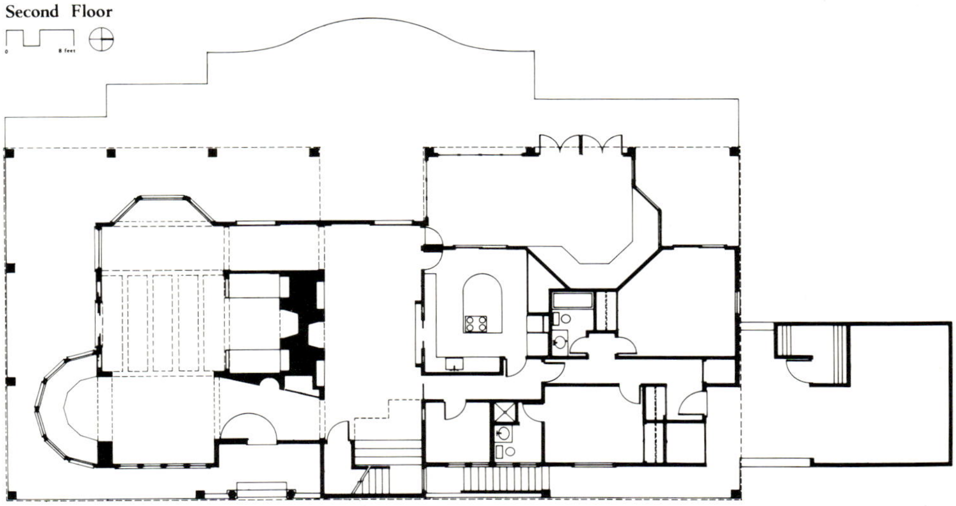

First Floor

095 Residence, Chilmark, Martha's Vineyard, Massachusetts, under construction 49

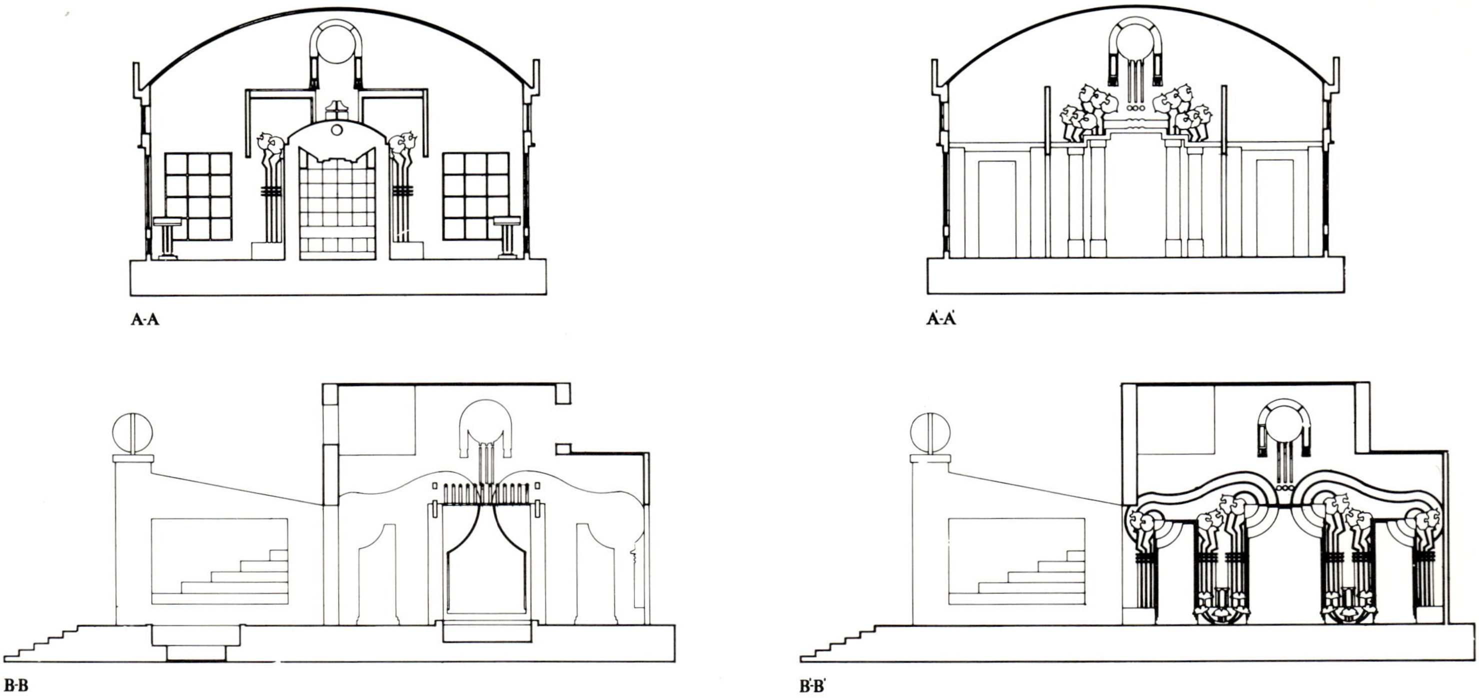


SECTIONS



# SUPER SPA

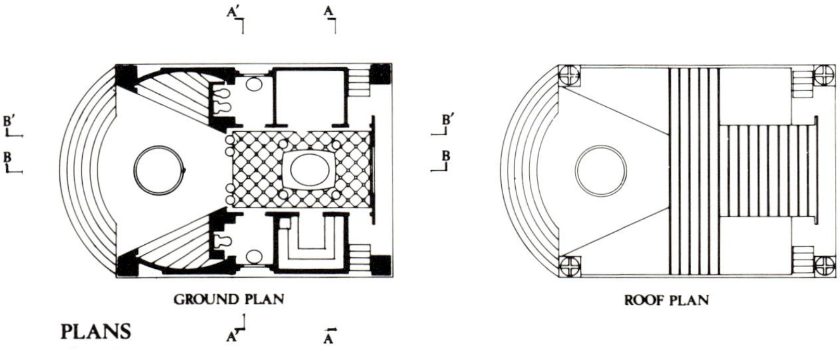


PLANS



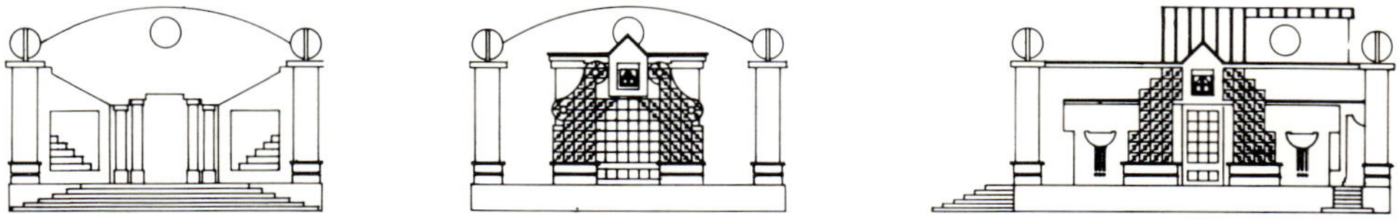

ELEVATIONS





097 Super Spa, for House Beautiful and the Kohler Company, project, 1979

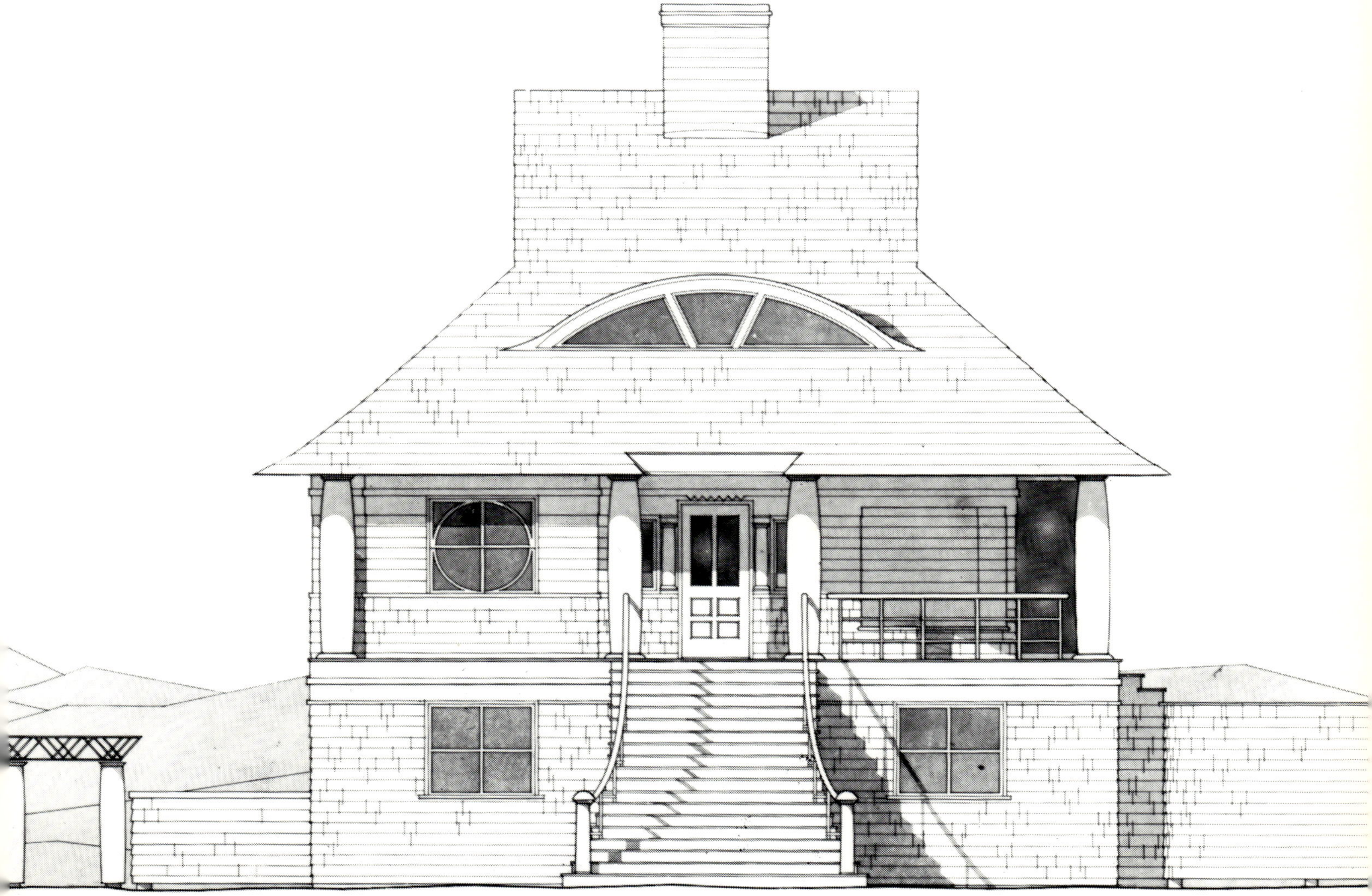

098 Lawson House, Quogue, New York, under construction, 1979-80

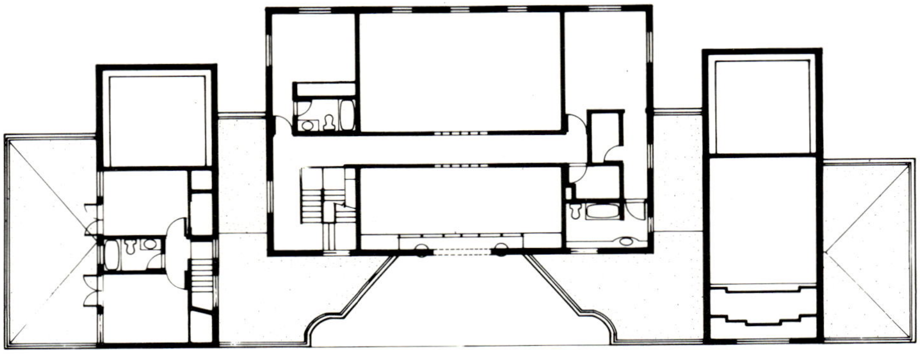

SECOND FLOOR

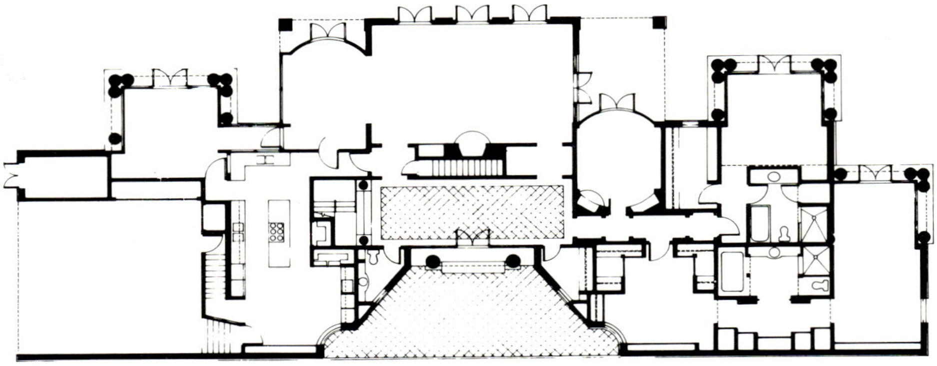

FIRST FLOOR

## PLANS

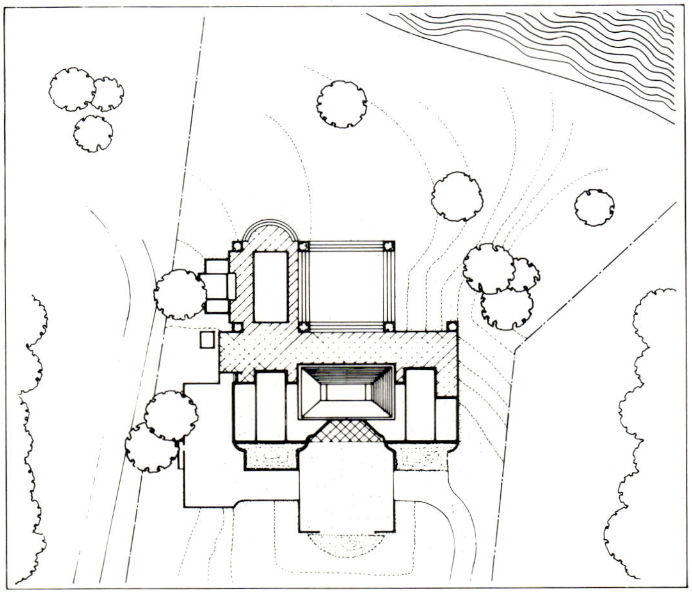

## SITE PLAN

104 Residence, King's Point, New York, 1979-80

EAST

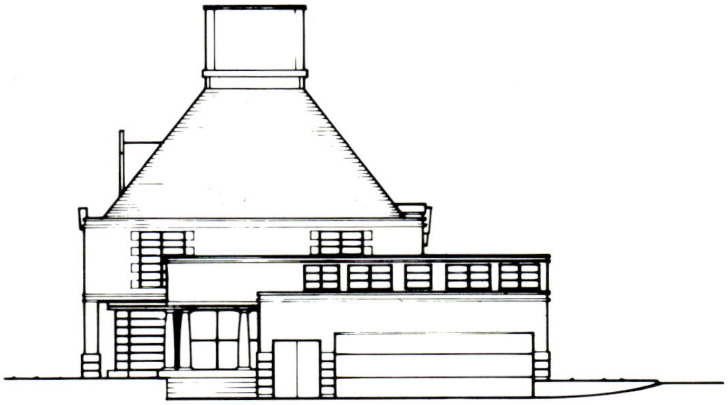

NORTH

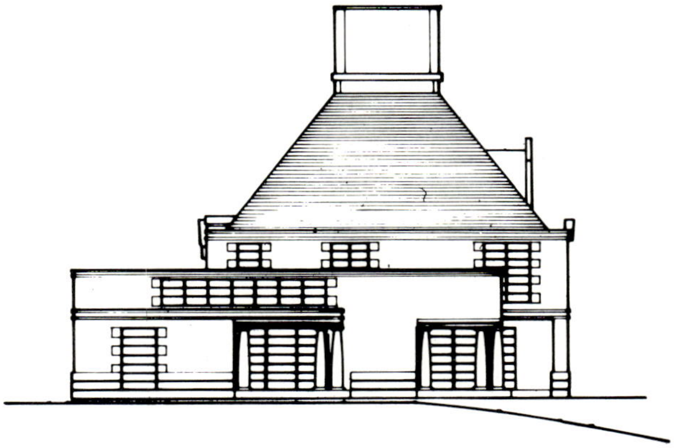

SOUTH

WEST

## ELEVATIONS

# RESIDENCE · KING'S POINT · NEW YORK

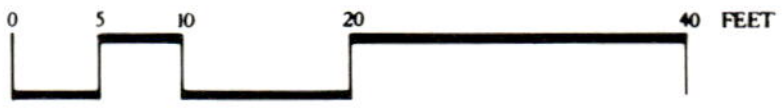

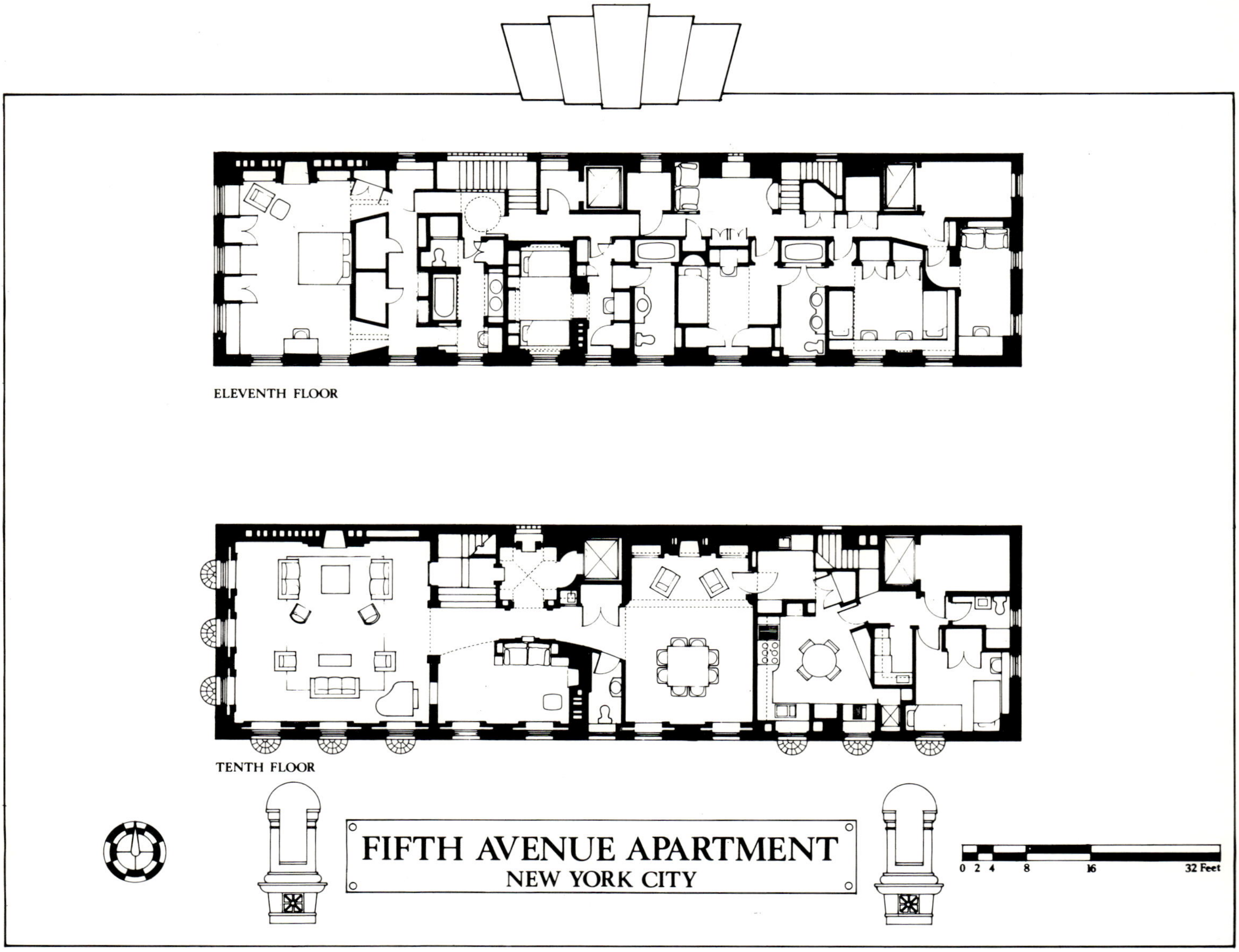


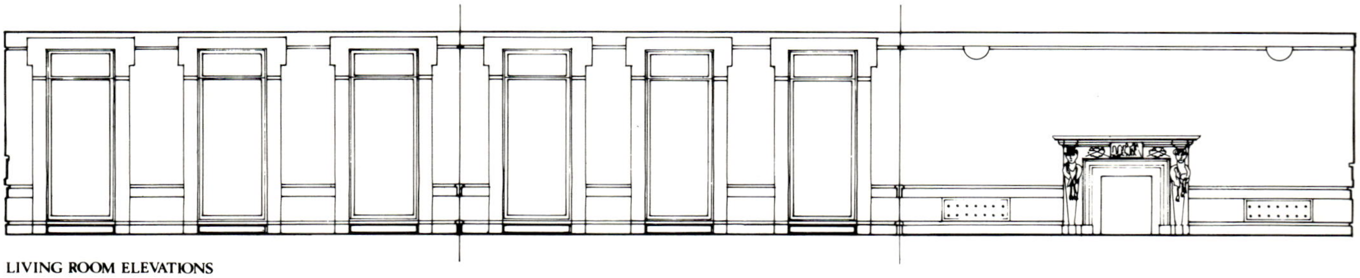

LIVING ROOM ELEVATIONS

DINING ROOM ELEVATIONS

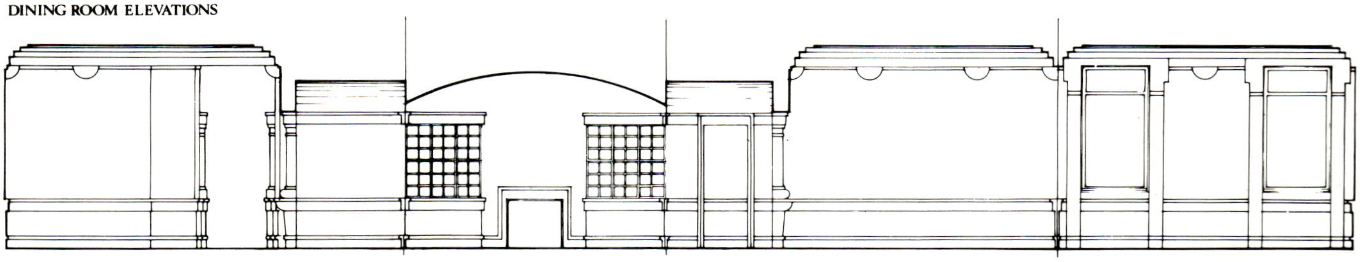

113 Capasso residence, New York City, 1980

# CINCINNATI CITY HALL ANNEX

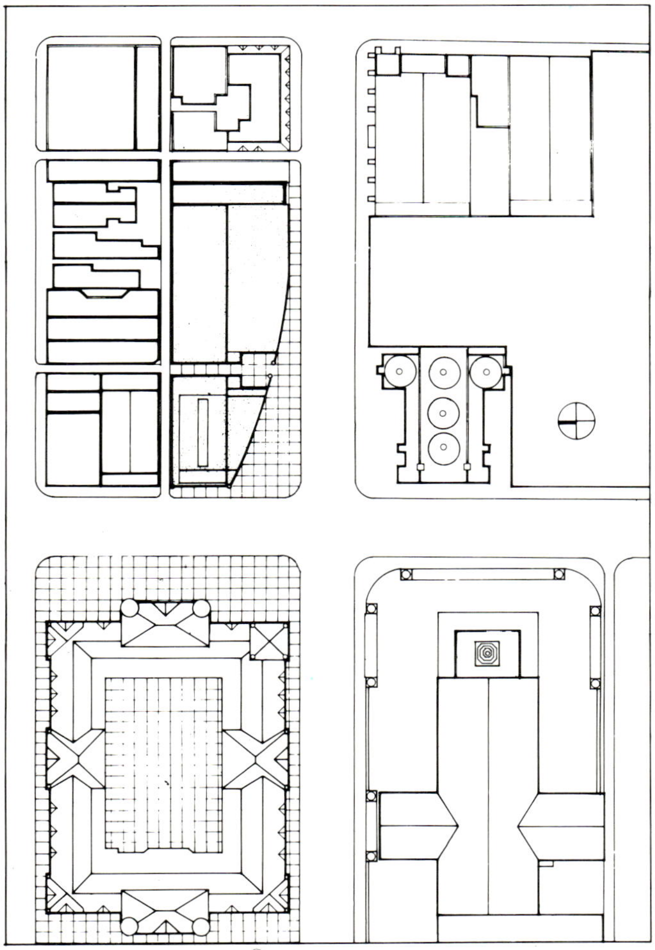

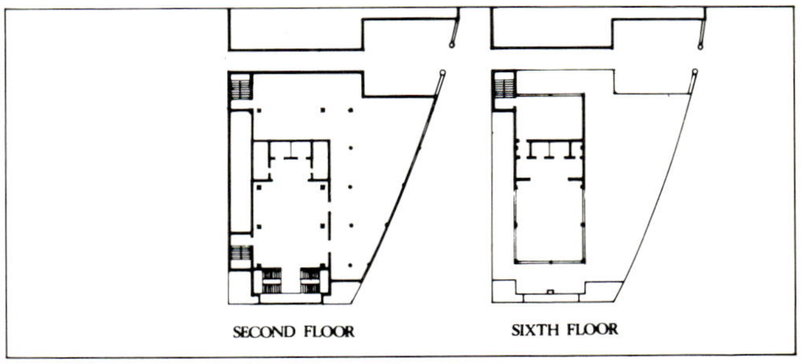


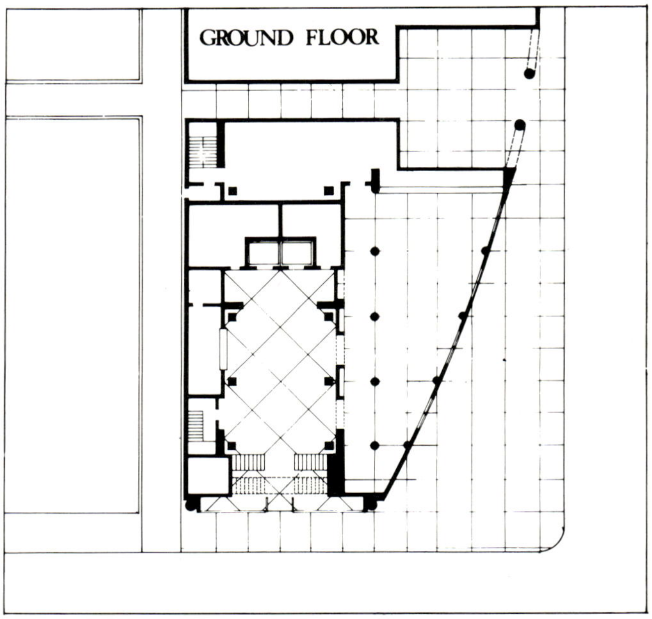


120 Cincinnati City Hall Annex, competition project, 1980

SOUTH ELEVATION

NORTH ELEVATION

LIVING ROOM

FAMILY ROOM

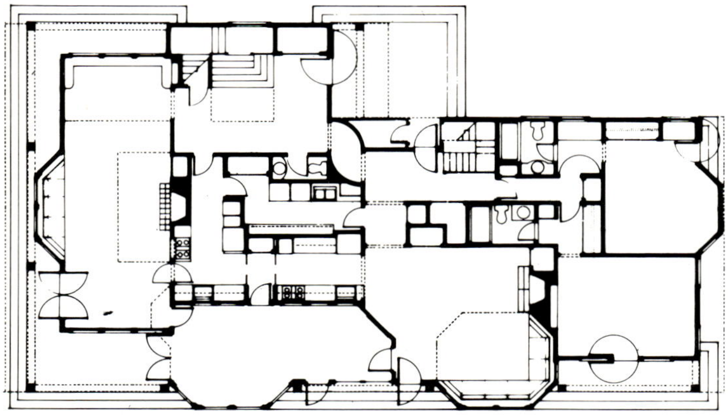

FIRST FLOOR

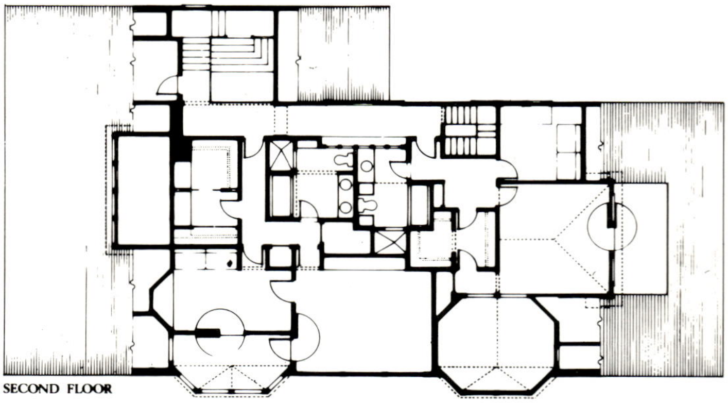

SECOND FLOOR

## RESIDENCE AT FARM NECK
### OAK BLUFFS, MASSACHUSSETTS

0 2 4 8 16 32 Feet



121 Residence at Farm Neck, Oak Bluffs, Massachusetts, 1980

DOM HEADQUARTERS
Bruhl, Germany

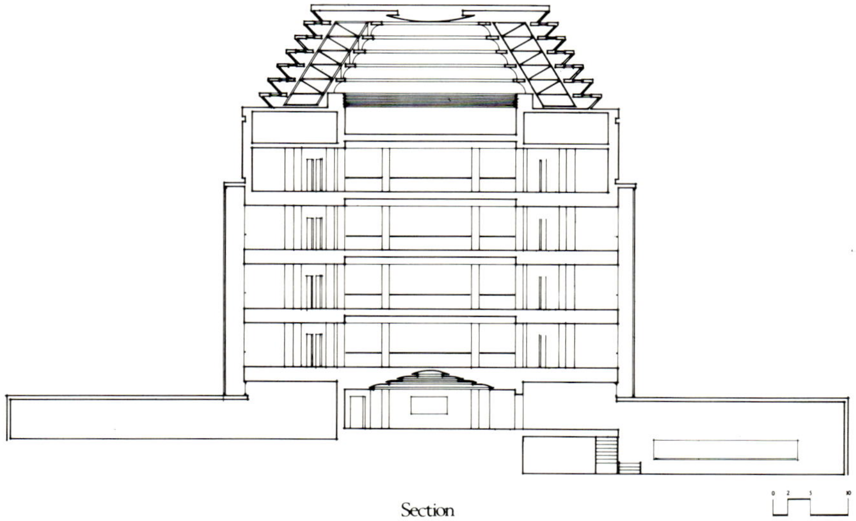

Section

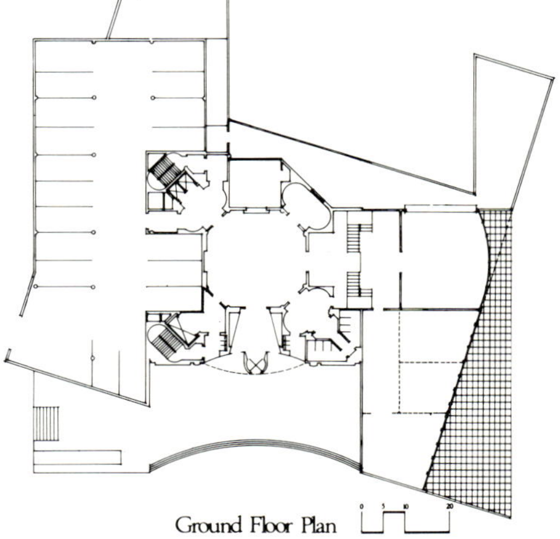

Ground Floor Plan

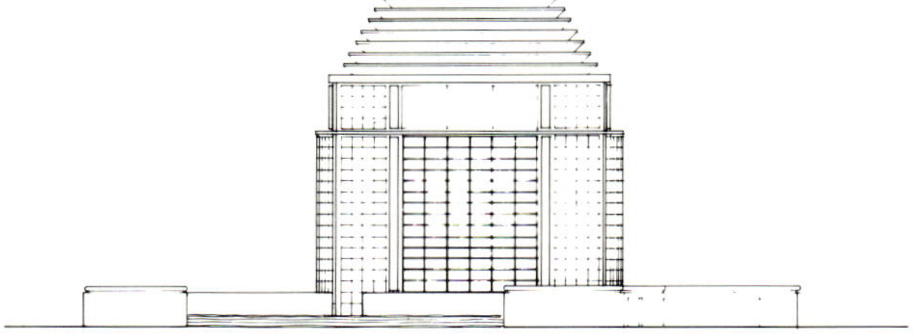

East Elevation

124 DOM Headquarters, competition project, Bruhl, Germany 1980

HALL OF FAME

# GARIBALDI-MEUCCI MEMORIAL MUSEUM
## STATEN ISLAND, NEW YORK

ENTRY

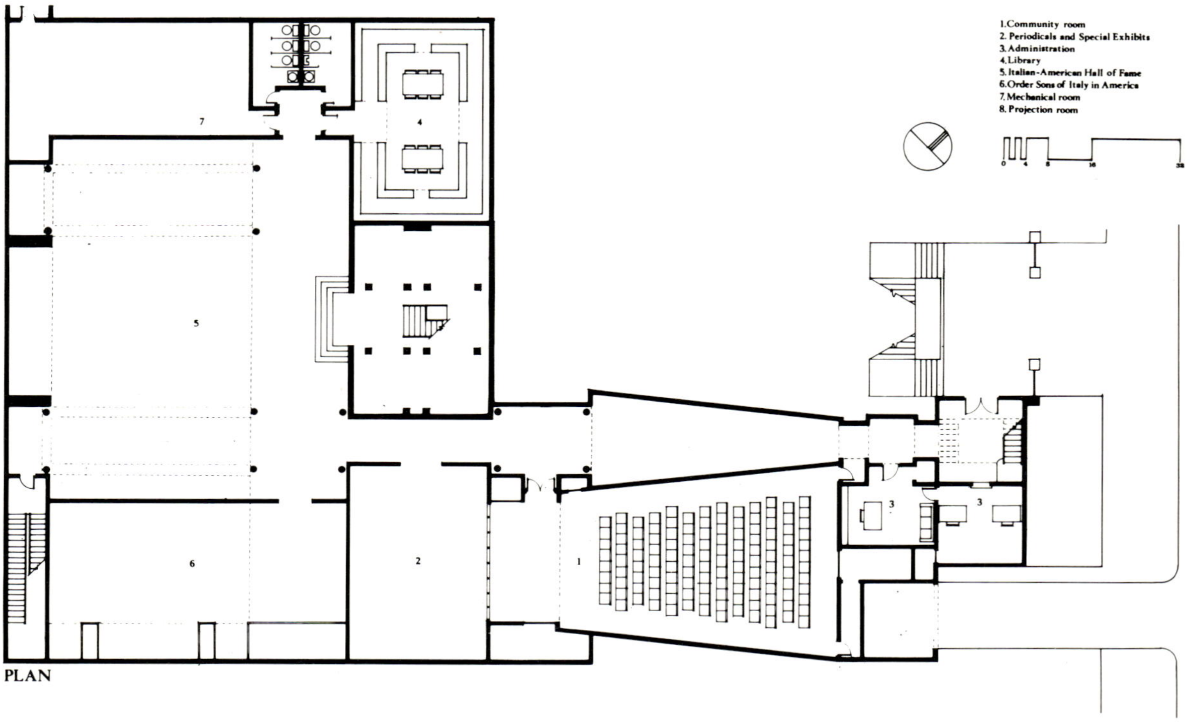


PLAN



125 Garibaldi Meucci Museum, Staten Island, New York, 1980

LIVING ROOM

DINING ROOM

ENTRY HALL

BACK PORCH

128 Residence at East Hampton, Long Island, New York, 1980

EAST ELEVATION

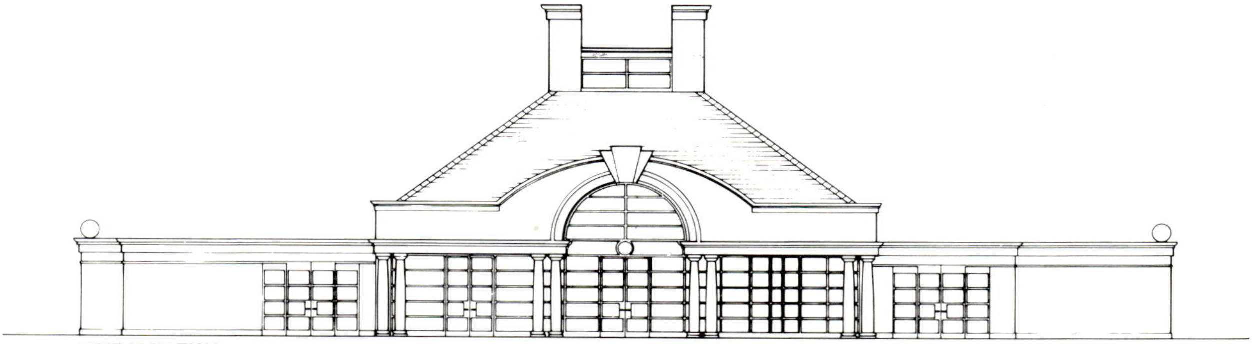

WEST ELEVATION

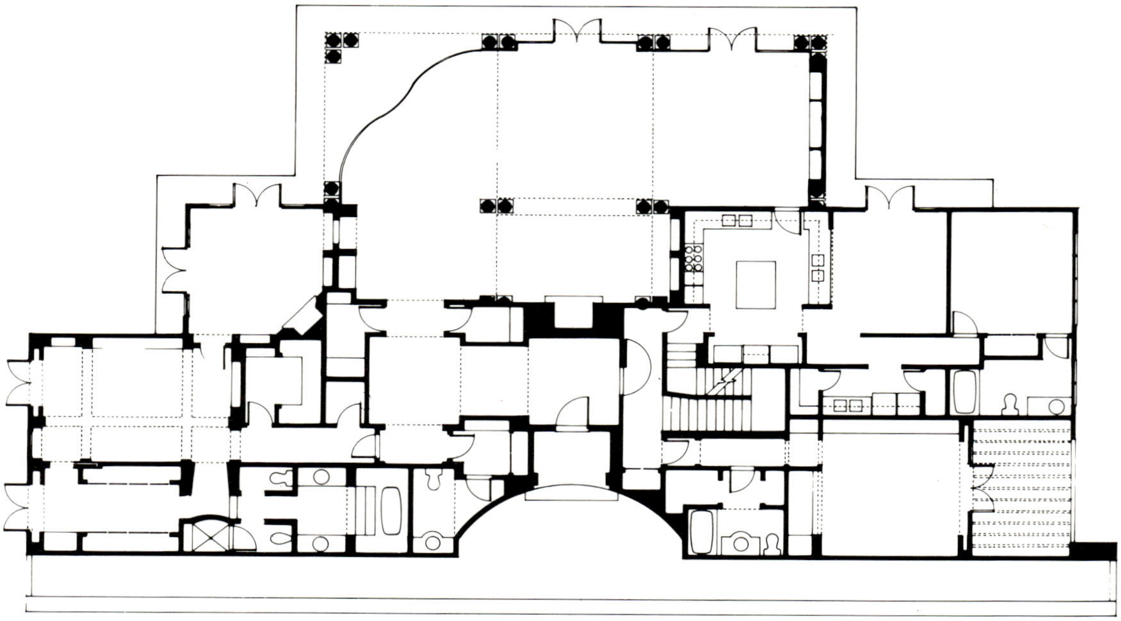

# RESIDENCE IN GLEN COVE
## LONG ISLAND, NEW YORK

129 Residence in Glen Cove, Long Island, New York, 1980

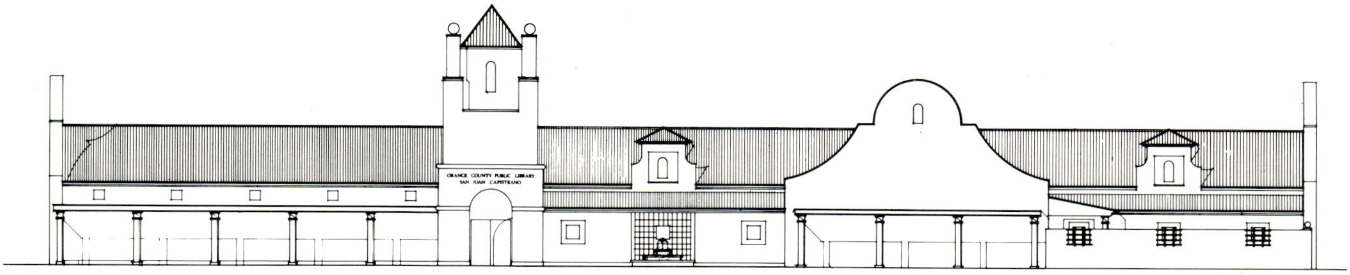

WEST ELEVATION

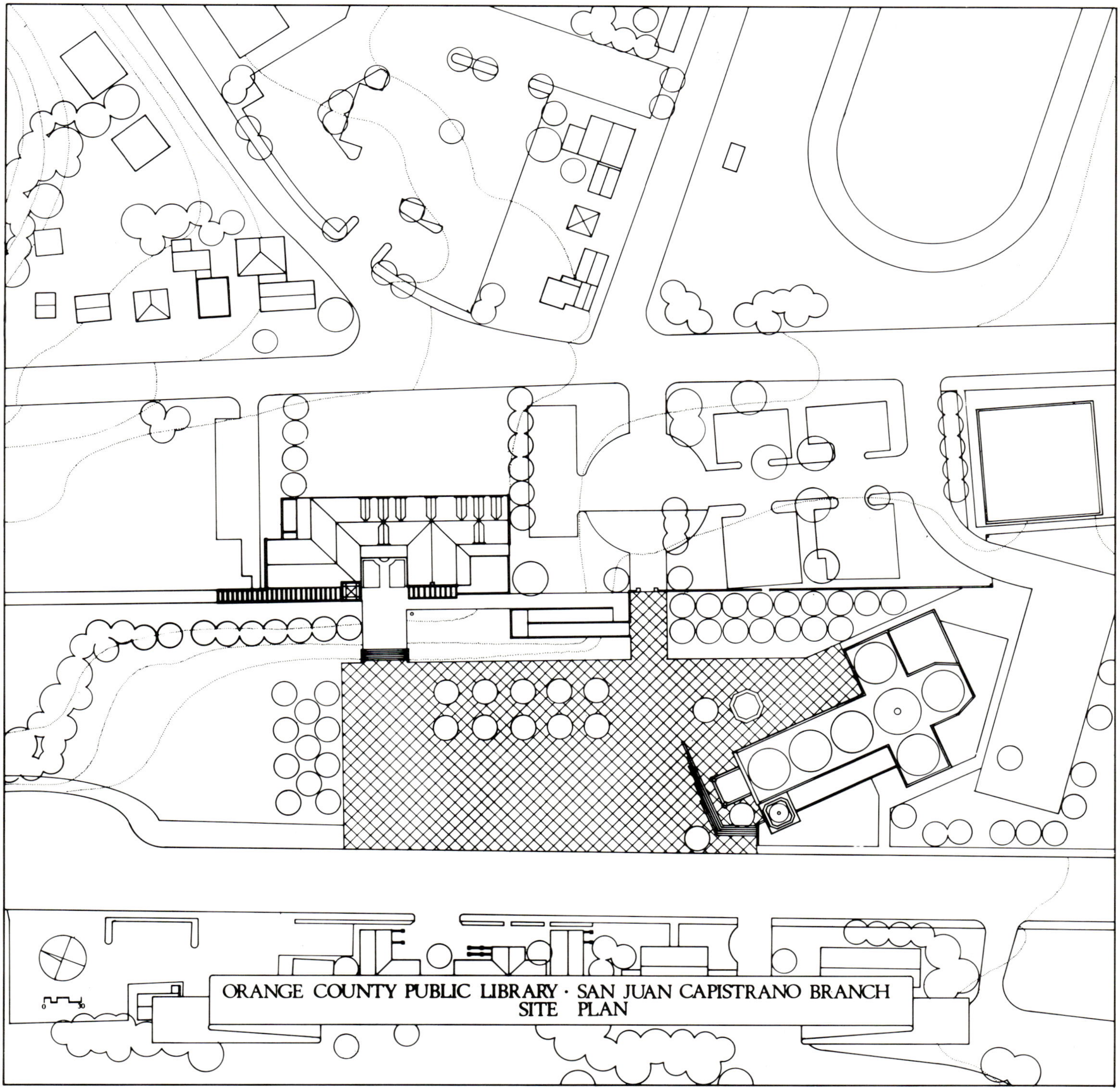


133 San Juan Capistrano library, competition project, California, 1980

YOUNG ADULT AREA

BROWSING LOUNGE

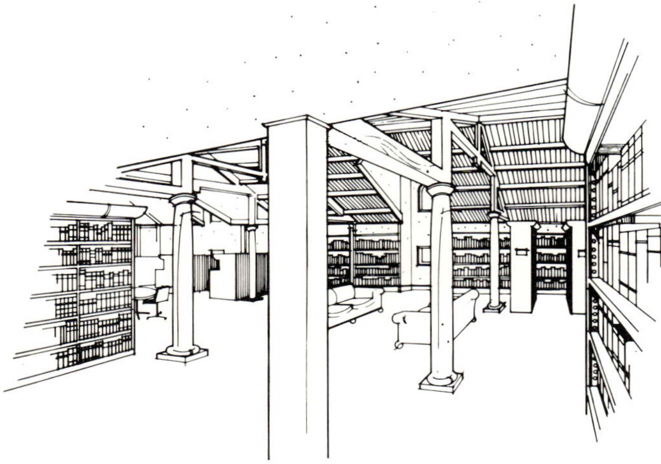

MAIN READING ROOM

INFORMATION AREA

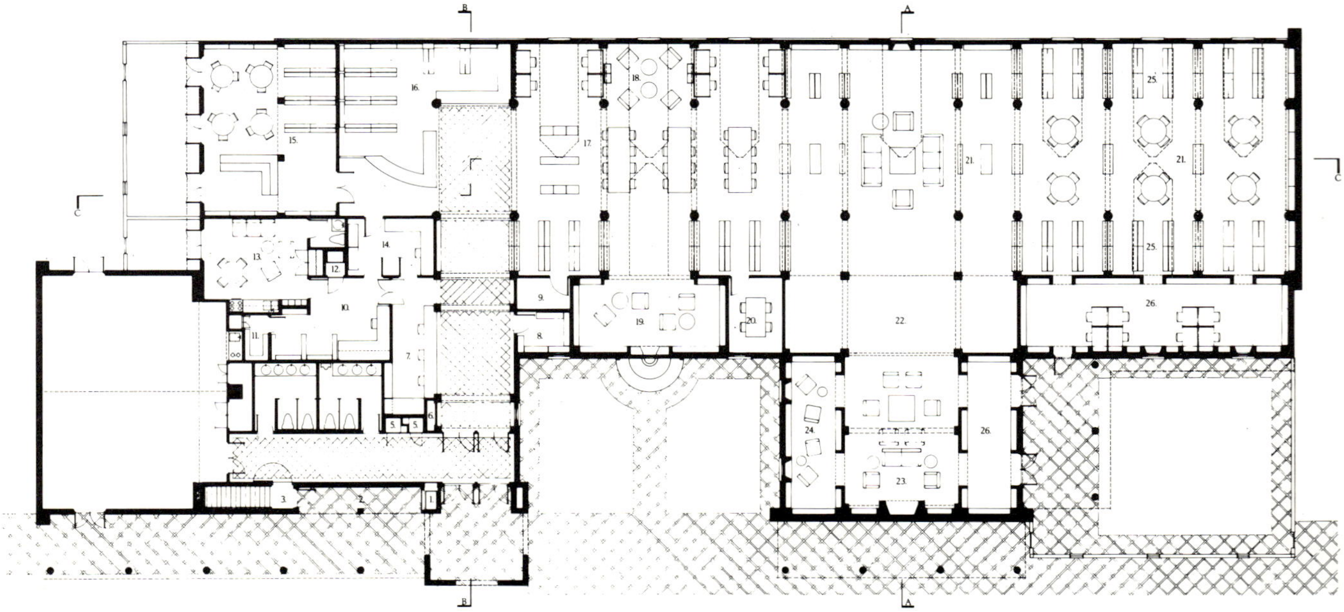

KEY TO FLOOR PLAN

1. BOOK DROP
2. COVERED BICYCLE RACKS
3. STAIR DOWN TO MECHANICAL ROOM
4. MEETING ROOM
5. PUBLIC TELEPHONES
6. DISPLAY CASE
7. CHARGE DESK
8. FRIENDS' GIFT BOOKS
9. XEROX ROOM
10. WORK ROOM
11. SUPPLY ROOM & DIAL-A-STORY EQUIPMENT
12. JANITOR'S CLOSET
13. STAFF ROOM
14. LIBRARIAN'S OFFICE
15. CHILDREN'S AREA
16. INFORMATION AREA
17. REFERENCE AREA
18. AUDIO VISUAL AREA
19. YOUNG ADULTS' AREA
20. TYPING/CONFERENCE AREA
21. MAIN READING ROOM
22. EXHIBITION AREA
23. BROWSING/LOUNGE AREA
24. SPANISH LANGUAGE CORE COLLECTION
25. COMMON STACKS
26. ADULT FICTION

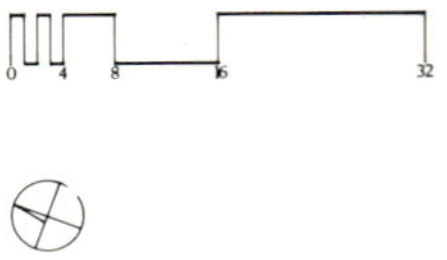

Robert A. M. Stern

# The Doubles of Post-Modern

*'...cubism and superrealism (surrealism), far from being the dawn of a style, are the end of a period of self-consciousness, inbreeding and exhaustion. One thing seems clear to me: that no new style will grow out of a preoccupation with art for its own sake. It can only arise from a new interest in subject matter. We need a new myth in which the symbols are inherently pictorial'.*[1]

What has been called Modern architecture for the past fifty years is in disarray: though such leading architects as Paul Rudolph, I.M.Pei, and Kevin Roche continue to produce major new work, the forms as well as the theories on which that work is based are systematically being questioned by a growing number of younger architects who perceive the waning of modernism and who are questioning the prevailing philosophic basis for architecture and its form language. The questioning sensibility has come to be described, alternately and rather imprecisely, as 'Post-Modern' or 'Post-Modernist'.[2]

Charles Jencks' book, *The Language of Post-Modern Architecture*, is the first to explore the new mood and to begin to erect a scaffolding of theory for post-modernism.[3] Jencks suggests that the term 'Post-Modern' is at best *'negative and evasive'*. Nonetheless it does enjoy some precedent in architecture.[4]

The terms 'modernism' and 'post-modernism' have been used in other disciplines besides architecture, including political history, and literary and art criticism. In each of these disciplines, they suggest two different conditions resulting in related sets of what I would describe as 'doubles' — the doubles of modernism and of post-modernism. Both grow out of the same two distinct but interrelated sensibilities or conditions, and both fall within the Modern — that is Western Humanist/Post-Renaissance — period.

These conditions affect both modernism and post-modernism. Borrowing the term from Frank Kermode, I would label the first of these conditions 'schismatic'. The schismatic condition argues for a clean break with Western Humanism. I would label the second condition 'traditional', borrowing the term from Stephen Spender. It argues for a recognition of the continuity of the Western Humanist tradition. Traditional modernism can be *'conceived of as a return, at once spontaneous, willed to eternal values long forgotten or buried but which a reborn or renewed historical memory makes once again present'*; schismatic modernism can be seen as a sensibility in which *'the new and the modern (are) seen in terms of a birth rather than a rebirth, not a restoration but ... a construction of the present and future not on the foundations of the past but on the ruins of time'*.[5]

The two modernisms can be distinguished by their attitudes toward the past: 'traditional' modernism, typified by the writings of Proust or Eliot or the paintings of Picasso, views the past as a source of order; 'schismatic' modernism, typified by the work of Duchamp or Mondrian, views the past as a burden. Although the two kinds of modernism are distinct, they are linked by an apocalyptic view of the future and by a recognition of Western Humanism as an on-going condition.

It is important to reiterate that the Modern period as a whole encompasses a continuing tradition of humanistic thought and action though some of its stylistic movements — for example Dada and Surrealism — regard humanism as a yoke.

Like the two modernisms, the two post-modernisms can be distinguished by their attitudes toward the past. While the schismatic Post-Modern condition posits a break with both modernism and the Modern period itself, the traditional Post-Modern condition proposes to free new production from the rigid constraints of modernism, especially from its most radical and nihilistic aspects (as exemplified by Dada and Surrealism) while simultaneously reintegrating itself with other strains of Western Humanism, especially those which characterise its last pre-modernist phase, that of the Romanticism which flourished between 1750 and 1850.[6] Thus, schismatic post-modernism is a sensibility that considers itself not only beyond modernism but also outside the Modern period, one which seeks to establish the mode of thought and artistic production that is as free from the 500-year old tradition of Western Humanism as that mode was, in its turn, free from the previous Gothic era of religious scholasticism. Traditional post-modernism, on the other hand, is one that seeks to reintegrate or subsume modernism within the broad category of the Modern period as a whole.

In post-modernism, the distinctions between traditional and schismatic conditions are useful in illuminating the distinctions between the work of John Gardner and William Gass in literature or of Peter Eisenman and Michael Graves in architecture. Though the term 'Post-Modern' appears to be used to describe sensibilities and theories that share as common ground a reaction to the modernism which has dominated much of the cultural activity of the past 125 years, the traditional and schismatic conditions serve to distinguish between distinct sensibilities within the Post-Modern devolution; these distinctions have at their core the question of the relationship between new work and the tradition of humanism which characterised the Modern period itself.

Thus the doubles of the Post-Modern: two distinct but interrelated Post-Modern sensibilities: a schismatic condition that argues for a *clean break* with the tradition of Western Humanism and a 'traditional' condition that argues for a return to, or a recognition of, the *continuity* of the cultural tradition of Western Humanism of which it holds modernism to be a part.

*'Somebody should write the history of the word "modern". The OED isn't very helpful, though most of the senses the word now has have been in the air since the sixteenth century, and are actually older than Shakespeare's way of using it to mean "commonplace" ... The New is to be judged by the criterion of novelty, the Modern implies or at any rate permits a serious relationship with the past, a relationship that requires criticism and indeed radical reimagining.'*[7]

In order to clarify what is meant by the term 'Modern' in the phrase 'Post-Modern', it is necessary to establish clear definitions for the related terms 'Modern' and 'modernism'. Such a seemingly pedantic exercise is necessary because the distinctions between the older terms have become blurred by daily use, and they have become ineffective for discourse.

What can be called the 'Modern period' begins in the fifteenth century with the birth of Humanism. The renaissance of classicism in architecture is the first of the Modern stylistic phases: the Baroque and the Rococo are subsequent Modern styles. The International Style of *c.* 1920-60 is also a Modern style, often thought to be *the* Modern Style in which the meaning of the word 'Modern' is transformed and limited so as to represent only those values more properly described as 'modernist', a term which describes the urge to produce new artistic work that eschews all known form-language and, ideally, all grammar, in favour of a new self-referential (i.e. in architecture, functionally and technologically determined) language of form whose principal cultural responsibility is toward its moment in time. Modernism sees art as a manifestation of the *zeitgeist*; it strives to reflect the moment of its conception. Modernism, in the most oversimplified terms, represents a moralistic application of a superior value to that which is not only new but also independent of all previous production.

Modernism views the present as a state of continuing crisis; it sees history only as a record of experiences, a body of myth, but not as objective truth, and it is apocalyptic in its relationship to the future. A person who believes in the sensibility of 'modernism' is a 'modernist' as well as a 'Modern', the latter term being the more general one and simply referring to someone who has lived in the 'Modern' period and has contended with or at least recognised the issue of 'modernity' but who has not necessarily adopted a modernist stance.[8]

Modernism is not a style in and of itself in the sense that the Renaissance and Baroque were styles with unifying principles. It can be regarded as a succession of attempts to redefine the syntax and the grammar of artistic composition (the poems of Mallarmé, the stream of consciousness of Joyce and Woolf; the buildings of Mies van der Rohe and Le Corbusier). As a result, and rather perversely, to the extent that it has deliberately been made difficult and inaccessible, artistic production has also shown itself to be modernist. In some cases, there has been an effort to go beyond issues of syntax and grammar and to seek to establish new form languages which, because they are not culturally based (that is, familiar), are by necessity personal or self-referential.[9]

Modernism does not accept the appearance of things as they are in nature and in the man-made world; it seeks always to take them apart in order to discover their hidden and presumably essential character. Modernism seeks to close and ultimately to eliminate the distance between the object perceived and the person perceiving the object. It seeks to do this in two ways: by insisting that all experience and thereby all art exists in the present — Giedion's phrase was the *'eternal present'* — and by insisting that each work of art and each act of artistic production is a personal act.[10] This presentism and the self-referential aspect of artistic production are fundamental to any examination of the nature of modernism in relationship to the issue of an on-going culture which we call the Western Humanist tradition.

It has been argued that modernism can never be a part of any tradition, that it is a thing apart, a parallel tradition to Western Humanism. This issue of modernism as a sensibility apart from the Modern has resulted in that plethora of modernist styles or *isms* which has made the history of the literature and art of the last 125 years seem so confusing and troubled.

While the term 'Modern' as in the phrase 'the Modern period', is a term of historical description (like 'the Middle Ages'), it is also a term of sensibility and style. It can be used as the term Baroque is used — with and without a capital 'B'. One can exhibit a baroque or modern turn of mind while acting outside the Baroque or Modern period.

As a term describing a style, the use of the word 'modern' opens up a veritable Pandora's box of confusion: for example, 'L'Art Nouveau', for a while known as 'Le Style Moderne', is a style in the Modern period and, more specifically, it was a 'modernist' style in that it sought to stand free of the *historical continuum*. At the same time, insofar as it is the 'fine art' manifestation of the bohemianism of the *fin de siècle* it also represents a sensibility.

Another meaning for 'modern' is up-to-date or 'contemporary'. The term contemporary cannot be used to describe a stylistic sensibility because it signifies merely the absence of any strongly defined period features. Thus, actually all current production is modern: in fact, *'the great claim of modernism ... that it at last was free of style — fianlly and forever open to direct experience'*[11] is rendered preposterous by the history of the Modern Movement.

As Susan Sontag has observed, this *'notion of a style-less transparent art is one of the most tenacious fantasies of modern culture. Artists and critics pretend to believe that it is no more possible to get the artifice out of art than it is for a person to lose his personality. Yet the aspiration lingers — a permanent dissent from Modern art with its dizzying velocity of style* changes'.[12] Harry Levin articulates what I believe to be a fundamental characteristic of the modernist era: *'Now we are all contemporaries; about that we have no option, so long as we stay alive. But we may choose whether or not we wish to be modern'*[13] (by which I think Levin means modernist).

Thus, one must be wary of the use of the term 'modern' in architecture, as in most of the arts and in literature. It is not really a description of a style but, as Irving Howe has observed, a term of critical placement and judgement.[14]

Contemporary historians and critics of Modern architecture, perhaps even more than their counterparts in literature and the fine arts, seem to confuse the broad historical definition of the Modern period with related but distinct ideas pertaining to modernism and to use the terms interchangably. While the issue of historiography critically affects the seeming confusion of the current situation, it is too long and too complex to be dealt with effectively in this essay. Suffice it to say that until the impact of Hegelian and Marxist thought came to dominate the developing discipline of art and architectural history in Germany in the second half of the nineteenth century, historians undertook to define modern architectural history in broad terms and to regard the Renaissance as the first of a sequence of modern styles. Even as late as 1929, Henry-Russell Hitchcock in his *Modern Architecture: Romanticism and Reintegration*, embraced a chronologically broad and relatively inclusive definition of Modern architecture. Nonetheless, perhaps under the impact of his subsequent collaboration with the more polemical Philip Johnson on the book *The International Style*, and perhaps as a result of his subsequent contact with European modernist historians such as Giedion and Pevsner, Hitchcock has since drawn back from his earlier and more inclusive position.

In *Modern Architecture*, Hitchcock traces the origins of the Modern period to the breakup of the Gothic style, regarding each phase since that time not as an 'independent style' like the Greek or the Egyptian, but rather as a subsidiary manner of one Modern style. Yet, even in *Modern Architecture*, Hitchcock was already under the sway not only of the emerging polemic of the International Style but also of the historical determinism which pervades so much German art historical writing of the period. In *Modern Architecture* Hitchcock claimed that a fundamental characteristic of the Modern style is a *'preference for formal experimentation'*, as if Egyptian and Greek architects in Antiquity were never interested in trying anything new.[15] In his later books, by inference, and explicitly in an essay 'Modern Architecture — A Memoir', Hitchcock has altered his original position, claiming that had he followed his initial plan to cover *'...the whole range of time from the Late Gothic to the present it would have been more or less analogous to the books of the nineteenth century architectural historians such as James Ferguson (who) ... dealing with the "modern styles" ... interpreted "modern" in the old sense as the third portion of the relevant past: "Modern times", that is, the period from the Renaissance onward, in distinction to "antiquity" and the "Middle Ages".'*

Hitchcock goes on to observe that *'...what is, at any given point, accepted more broadly as "modern architecture" can have no fixed beginning — various historians and critics have set its start all the way from the early fifteenth century to the early twentieth. Nor, even more obviously, can it have a fixed ending. What is still properly considered modern architecure began, according to my present view, in the 1880s, not way back in 1750, nor yet in 1900 or in 1920; it will be over when we or the next generation have another name for it.'*[16]

Thus Hitchcock brings us to a fundamental issue of the moment: although at first glance it seems difficult to sustain as the broadest definition of Modern architecture all the production of the Post-Medieval period, upon further reflection such a definition seems more workable than those later attempts to link the historical definition of the Modern period in architecture too closely with specific economic, political, or cultural events that have occurred since the middle of the eighteenth century — that is, with the Industrial Revolution, and the political revolutions in the United States and France — or with prior positions taken on behalf of any particular manifestation of current or contemporary production that might seem more 'advanced', 'innovative' or 'progressive'. Such a broad view opens up the definition of Modern architecture, enabling it to be understood not as a humanistic pursuit involving a continuous interweaving of diverse and often contradictory formal tendencies assembled, discovered, sometimes even invented through various processes including eclecticism, modernism, and technological as well as functional determinism. Such a view would hold out 1750 as an important marker in time, as it would also note the decisive shifts that took place in period 1870-1890 (emergence of a dominant post-modernism). But this view, as I hope to demonstrate later, would not see decisive reasons why any of these phases should mark the conclusions of the Modern period's larger themes, or their replacements by themes not already present in the formative stages of the Modern period.

It is not Hitchcock, but Giedion, Pevsner and J.M.Richards who have exerted the greatest influence on the profession's and the public's view of what Modern Architecture was and should have been during the past forty years: much of the confusion about the character and chronology of the Modern period in architecture can be attributed to their tendency to present the history of the architecture of the past two hundred years as a series of morality tales involving heroic struggles between pragmatic materialism and high ideals, 'good guys' and 'bad guys', 'progressives' and 'reactionaries', 'constituent' and 'transitory' facts. Whole careers and aesthetic movements have been cut off from the so-called 'main stream' of historical flow: Giedion's *Space, Time and Architecture* and Pevsner's *Pioneers of the Modern Movement* have been the most influential in the architectural profession and therefore the most troublesome. In these works, as Hitchcock has observed, much of the architecture of the nineteenth century has been treated *'as constituent premonitions of (the) modern architecture'* of the 1920s and 30s and not as legitimate artistic production in its own right.[17]

Outside the architectural profession, most educated people now in their 40s and 50s were exposed to this point of view in introductory courses in college, sometimes in the original text of Giedion and Pevsner, but more often in such popularising work as Richard's *Introduction to Modern Architecture* in which *'the words "Modern Architecture" are used here to mean something more particular than contemporary architecture. They are used to mean the new kind of architecture that is growing up with this century as this century's own contribution to the art of architecture; the work of those people, whose number is happily increasing, who understand that architecture is a social art related to the life of the people it serves, not an academic exercise in applied ornament. The question that immediately arises is whether there is in fact enough difference between people's lives as they are lived in this century and as they were lived in previous centuries to justify a truly "modern" architecture being very different from that of the past — and indeed whether "modern" architecture is quite as revolutionary as it is supposed to be...*

*'For whatever reason, modern architecture has been passing through a sort of "puritan" phase, in which the negative virtues of simplicity and efficiency have been allowed to dominate, and since 1939 a concentration on the essentials has also been necessitated in most countries by the overriding need to build cheaply.'*[18]

The revisionist architectural history of the 1950s and 60s, which owes a considerable debt to the example of Hitchcock's comprehensive *Architecture: Nineteenth and Twentieth Centuries*, sought to develop a broader characterisation of the Modern period which would include the stylistic revivalism of the late eighteenth and nineteenth centuries as well as the self-referential modernism of the twentieth. But despite Hitchcock's influence, the deterministic view of history typified by Giedion's *Space, Time and Architecture* seems to have prevented the revisionists, in their search for a broader view, from considering events earlier than the mid-eighteenth century. Thus, even the very important redefinition of Modern architecture which Scully offered in 1954 and refined in 1961, though the first to free the stylistic analysis of architectural production from the futurist polemic of the Modernist Movement of the 1920s, is not free from political determinism and is not, in the final analysis, sufficiently broad in its historical scope. Acknowledging a debt to Frank Lloyd Wright, Scully offered a definition of Modern architecture as the *'architecture of democracy'*, an *'image of ourselves'* emerging *'precisely at the beginning of industrialism and mass democracy (where) we find it, in terms of fragmentation, mass scale, and new, unfocused continuity'*.[19] In this sense Scully, seeking to reconcile the views of such early twentieth century historians as Fiske Kimball with those of Giedion and Pevsner, brings us to the threshold of our current perception of the distinctions between the Modern tradition and modernism.[20] As a result it is now possible to see the Modern Movement as an episode in the broad history of Modern Architecture itself.

Similarly, one can see modernism not as style but as a strategy, one of a number of *isms* which have emerged in the Modern era to help the artist express his attitudes toward the present in relation to his sense of the past and/or the future: in architecture 'eclecticism', 'associationalism', and 'technological determinism' are other attitudes which interact with modernism to help organise a theory upon which to base work. Thus, though modernism has had its period of hegemony, resulting in a univalent style whose abstraction rendered it difficult and uncommunicative from the first, it should not be seen as a style in and of itself. The International Style was the great modernist style, and modernism itself remains a Modern sensibility. Yet there are those who would argue that it is a sensibility parallel to Western humanism and thereby outside it, that is not at all part of the tradition that began with the Renaissance, and it is this issue which constitues the crux of the current debate.

The idea of a Post-Modern age was introduced by Arnold Toynbee in his *A Study of History*,[21] and has been developed by a number of historians, most notably Geoffrey Barraclough.[22] The post-Modern Age is discussed by Toynbee and Barraclough as one in which there is increasing recognition that co-existence is the *modus vivendi* of the pluralist condition of our time. This pluralism in turn forces a close examination of the validity of the proposition that the distinction between a single standard and competing standards sets the contemporary of the Post-Modern period apart from the Modern period as a whole. If, as Toynbee and Barraclough argue, the Modern period began at the end of the fifteenth century, when Western European culture began to exert its hegemony over vast land areas and cultures not its own (and Westen European man found himself having to deal not only with the pluralist politics of European nationalism in its formative stages but also with the pluralism brought about by encounters with the 'native' populations of the 'New World'), then it perhaps can be argued that the Post-Modern or contemporary phase they describe is really just another stage in Modern history, a 'global' or 'Post-Industrial' Age following a 'National' or 'Industrial' Age, an era of 'relativism' that at once accepts the inherent diversity of the present while seeking order and meaning through a connection with the past, especially with the Romantic era.

Post-modernism should not be seen as a reaction against modernism; it seeks to develop modernism's themes by attempting to examine them in relationship to the wider framework of the Modern period as a whole.

The divided nature of modernism complicates our understanding of the Post-Modern devolution. At the beginning of this essay, I defined two kinds of Post-Modern sensibilities which can now be seen as related to modernism: a traditional one and a schismatic one. But the complex nature of modernism itself, with its two distinct conditions or types united by an apocalyptic view of history — not to mention the claims that are sometimes made for modernism as a sensibility completely independent of Western Humanism — complicate the situation with regard to post-modernism. As a result, it can be argued that there are not one but two sets of Post-Modern doubles: that there are *two types of traditional post-modernism* and *two types of schismatic post-modernism*.

The first type of traditional post-modernism — and the one which I would argue is the more viable of the two — argues for a break with modernism (where modernism is itself seen as a *break with* Western Humanism) and a reintegration with a view of Western Humanism which includes modernism among its many and sometimes conflicting conditions. The second type sees itself as a continuation of modernism (in which modernism is itself seen as a successor to the Baroque and Rococo), a sensibility and style that is contradictorily and inexplicably, in its presentism, a contradiction of the very notion of style.

This second type of traditional post-modernism is somewhat dubious: at the very least it fails to account for the stylistic complexity of the Romantic era, and it leads us to a question of whether such a post-modernism is really different from modernism itself. For if traditional modernism is a condition in which all art is seen as being in the present, though not breaking with the values and symbols of Western Humanism, then where can this second type of post-modernism stand in time? Is there a place beyond the present?

The first type of schismatic post-modernism — and the one which I would argue is the more viable of the two — is the one which argues for a *continuity with* modernism (in which modernism is itself seen as a *break with* Western Humanism). This kind of schismatic post-modernism, like the second type of traditional post-modernism, is a continuing modernism, but the use of the prefix 'post' has meaning because it permits the designation of a condition which is distinct from modernism because it breaks with the Western-Humanist tradition. Schismatic post-modernism of this type marks the full flowering of a sensibility which has its origins in modernism's aspiration toward a clean break with the Western Humanist tradition.

The second type of schismatic post-modernism is itself seen as a *continuing* tradition. This is the so-called *'post-modern breakthrough to post-modernity'*,[23] in which a totally new state of consciousness is achieved that insists on the obsolescence of modernism as well as the entire Western Humanist tradition. Attractive though such an image seems to those who view the current situation as unnecessarily confusing, it is difficult to make clear just exactly how this new condition will emerge. As Richard E. Palmer has written:

*'Post-modernity raises the question of a transition and transformation so radical as to change the fundamental view of language, history, truth, time and matter — so radical that "understanding" becomes a quite different process. It raises the possibility, in other words, of a "new hermeneutics".*

*'The hermeneutical problem of bridging the gap between modern and post-modern sets-of-mind goes in both directions: the problem of understanding a post-modern way of thinking when the assumptions and furniture of our thinking are themselves given by modernity, and the problem of a person who, having achieved a post-modern, post-spatialized, post-perspectual, or holistic framework, must then communicate it to someone who has not reached it."*[24]

Thus, though there are four conditions of post-modernism, it would seem that in the case of two, questions of considerable complexity remain unanswered at the present moment, thereby limiting the effectiveness of these conditions for artistic production if not for discourse. The difficulties raised by the second type of traditional post-modernism — that is, the notion of a continuing modernism — simultaneously claiming a position within Humanism and apart from history, seem hopelessly contradictory. It seems to be a condition which, despite the Post-Modern label that might be applied to it, is no more or no less than that of the traditional modernism of Marcel Proust, of the James Joyce of *Ulysses*, of Picasso, and of Le Corbusier.

The difficulties of the second type of schismatic post-modernism — the post-modernist breakthrough — have already been discussed. It takes as its point of departure the work of such writers as James Joyce but, as yet, it has not found a truly convincing voice. Such critics as William Spanos and Ihab Hassan are attempting to articulate the nature of the post-modernist breakthrough.[25] Because this type of schismatic post-modernism is only schismatic, it doubles back on itself and reaches a dead end.

Thus it becomes clear that the second type of schismatic post-modernism is not just a shift of emphasis within modernism; its relationship to modernism is not comparable to that which post-impressionism had to impressionism; schismatic post-modernism is radical in the extreme. In an essay on 'Joyce, Beckett and the Post-modern Imagination', Ihab Hassan observes that though *'one might be inclined to conclude that modernism is simply the earlier movement ... and that post-modernism is the later movement, which began to dominate Western literature after World War II'*, one must finally see that *'however jagged or ironic modernism allowed itself to be it retained its faith in art, in the imaginative act, even at the end of cultural dissolution ... Post-modernism on the other hand, is essentially* subversive *in form and* anarchic *in its cultural spirit. It dramatizes its lack of faith in art even as it produces new works of art intended to hasten* both *cultural and artistic dissolution.'*[26]

The two conditions of the Post-Modern that are at this moment important, and the ones I should like to consider in some detail in the remaining pages of this essay, are: 1) the schismatic post-modernism that argues for a clean break with Western Humanism and a continuity with modernism and 2) the traditional post-modernism that argues for a break with modernism and a reintegration with the broader condition of Western Humanism, especially with the Romantic tradition. These seem the only possible categories because they are the only ones that contain in them the 'double' sensibilities of continuity and change which are necessary to sustain generative cycles of creation.

The emergence of the Post-Modern sensibility can be seen as a logical result of the opposition between the Romantic and Modernist sensibilities, the former revelling in diversity, the latter struggling to find a universal cultural voice. Post-modernism is not revolutionary in either the political or artistic sense; in fact, it reinforces the effort of the technocratic and bureaucratic society in which we live — traditional post-modernism by accepting conditions and trying to modify them, schismatic post-modernism by proposing a condition *outside* Western Humanism, thereby permitting Western Humanist culture to proceed uninterrupted though not necessarily unaffected.

Post-modernism, though a reaction to modernism, is not a revolutionary movement seeking to overthrow modernism. Modernism cannot be ignored. We cannot pretend that it never existed and that we can return to a pre-modernist condition (such is the folly of such neo-traditionalist architects as John Barrington Bayley or the theorist Conrad Jameson). Post-modernism is especially affected by that aspect of modernism which derived from romanticism itself, particularly the romantic belief in the religious aspect of art. Most importantly, the Post-Modern condition arises out of the need to account for, and to continue to condition action in this last third of our century. Thus it must be seen that post-modernism is a Modern sensibility that includes modernism by virtue of its reaction to it; it is the manifestation of what Irving Howe describes as *'the radical breakdown of the modernist impulse'*, which came as a result of the experience of the Holocaust, of World War II, of the use of the atomic bomb. At its root lies existentialism, an attitude toward history and the idea of time which has extended beyond our thought processes to the very mode of our consciousness.

Schismatic post-modernism can be seen as an outgrowth of the anti-intellectualism of the modernism of the 1920s and 30s. In philosophy and literature it is represented by such writers as Norman Brown, Herbert Marcuse, Marshall McLuhan, Donald Barthelme, Samuel Beckett, and William S. Burroughs. In architecture, Peter Eisenman is its leading advocate. It rejects the Western Humanist tradition and, in the realm of aesthetics, it rejects Aristotelian composition. Though very much related to modernism, schismatic post-modernism is nonetheless a distinct sensibility. And it adopts the post modernist label to differentiate itself from the modernist tradition.

Schismatic post-modernism separates itself from traditionalist post-modernism by suggesting that it is not simply the crises of mid-century life that have irreparably changed the relationship of men to each other and to their ideas, but that these events have rendered untenable that relationship between men, objects, nature, and the sense of the ideal (the deity) which has been accepted since the Renaissance. Schismatic post-modernism sees the relationship between men and objects as a competitive one, and God as dead or, at least, removed from the fray.

It is in this context that Eisenman's position can best be understood. His proposal to make architecture autonomous is anti-historical and anti-symbolic; his endeavours to produce an architecture that is autonomous and self-referential — that is hermetically sealed from all concerns except the process of its own fabrication and fabulation — make his works virtually impenetrable. Eisenman's houses become symbolic of their own process of conception, but that process is so cut off from contemporary culture, history, and pragmatism that in the end, the effectiveness of the symbolic gesture ceases to be symbolic of anything outside itself; the building runs the danger of becoming merely an object which can, at best, make its appeal on a sensuous and hedonistic level. Although it struggles to free itself from all cultural references, by its very physicality it cannot but remind the viewer of some object previously seen or experienced.

Despite his belief in an autonomous architecture, Eisenman's ideology is culturally based. It draws extensively from the linguistic theories of Noam Chomsky and from the work of such literary critics as Roland Barthes and William Gass, who has himself written about one of Eisenman's buildings, House VI.[27] In basing his argument for an autonomous architecture on theories developed in relation to others in parallel but not necessarily related artistic disciplines — and in making comparisons with discoveries in the sciences, especially mathematics and physics — Eisenman seems caught up in a contradiction not unlike the one which characterised the justifications devised for modernist architecture by historians and polemicists such as Giedion, who sought to justify architectural modernism by connecting it with Einsteinian physics.[28] Schismatic post-modernist architecture, as represented by Eisenman (and I can think of no other architect who might be included with him in this category) buoys itself up with analogies to literary and linguistic theory.[29] But where modernism's connection to physics was *ex post facto*, schismatic post-modernism's connections have been established the other way around. As a result there seems to be in Eisenman's work what John Gardner has observed in the work of such schismatic post-modernists as John Cage and William Gass: a sense of 'art which is all thought ... art too obviously constructed to fit a theory.'[30]

To sum up: Eisenman's work, in its dazzling extremism, brings into focus the fundamental dilemma of schismatic post-modernism which, to paraphrase Kermode, is based on an inherent contradiction that can be seen in modernism itself: can one reconcile a cult of self-referential form-making with a denial of the existence of form itself? Schismatic post-modernism leaves us little choice: with all of previous culture removed in theory, at least, we are left with an aesthetic of unparalleled abstraction and hermeticism and without, as yet, even a hope for the emergence of an atavistic mythology to help crack the code. Eisenman leaves us terribly alone, naked.

John Gardner has written that the problem with the idea of art as pure language — which it seems to me is the basic concept of Eisenman's position as it is basic to Cage's and Gass' — is *'that it shows ... a lack of concern'* on the artist's part for *'people who care about events and ideas and thus, necessarily, about the clear and efficient statements of both'*.

*'Linguistic opacity'*, a phrase of Gardner's, suggests that the need to communicate is not a primary function of art. One might ask what can this seeming *'search for opacity'* do for us? What are we to make of these *'linguistic sculptures'* which at best make, as Gardner writes, *'only the affirmation sandcastles make, that it is pleasant to make things or look at things made, better to be alive than dead?'*[31]

It may well be that the extreme position which Eisenman represents in architecture, Cage in music, and Gass in literature, marks an end part in a cycle, and that a viable post-modernism must be one that opens up possibilities for a new production rather than describes a situation that can be seen as ultimately futile and nihilistic.

Irving Howe has argued that although there is in modernist literature a *'major impulse'* to express *'a choking nausea before the idea of culture...'* there is also *'another in which the writer takes upon himself the enormous ambition not to re-invent the terms of reality'*.[32] It is this 'realistic', 'accepting' aspect of modernism that is carried over in the second, traditional or 'inclusive' post-modernist reactions.

Howe regards Saul Bellow, William Styron, and Bernard Malamud as 'traditional' Post-Modern writers, in the sense that in their books, the action of individuals takes place in relationship to specific cultural conditions. Robert Gillespie, writing about the younger American novelists of the 1960s, states that the work of a considerable group, among them Wendell Berry, Scott Momaday, Larry McMurty, Wright Morris and the Ken Keysey of *Sometimes a Great Notion*, shares a traditional post-modernist point of view. These writers accept *'responsibility for the world's conditions, and therefore of authority in managing it. Consciousness for them is less a curse than it is an act of conscience. They are eager to locate themselves in "a place on earth" (the title of one of Berry's novels) and to merge their lives with that place. From such felt relation comes sustenance ... so a region has its own mythology which may offer the only sustaining relation between the past and the future'*.[33]

Traditional post-modernism is simultaneously inside contemporary society and critically detached from it; it uses art to comment on everyday life; it is at once 'satiric' and accepting in its view of culture; in this sense it seeks to make telling interpretations of everyday life. Such a post-modernism begins to *'restore that state of balance between unchecked fabulation and objective social realism'* necessary to prevent artistic production from degenerating into trivial self-indulgence.[34]

In painting and in architecture, traditional post-modernism relies increasingly on representational as opposed to abstract or conceptual modes. Rackstraw Downes equates traditional post-modernism with a revived realism in painting. Critical of what he describes as modernism's *'pictorial narcissism — it became a painting capable only of admiring its own nature'*, Downe's argument against modernist abstraction and in favour of pre-modernist representation hinges on his criticism of modernism's exclusivist principle of selectivity:

*'While Old Master painting had allowed emphasis of the different aspects of form, its nature was holistic and embracing, whereas Modernist styles were partial. As were their means, so was their grasp on reality. Expressionism, Dada and Surrealism were associational styles which dealt respectively with emotions, ideas and fantasies. Hedonistic Impressionism, Cubism — a still life style — and Purism which dealt in Utopian absolutes, concentrated on particular properties of form. Modernism, then, constituted a rapid succession of specialized styles, each one supplying some deficiency of the rest; what they gained in intensity and concentration they lost in comprehensiveness and range.*

*'Modernism was ... to excel in uncompromisingly personal triumphs and, likewise, fail to produce a syntax sufficiently limber and resourceful to be widely shared and passed along. In fact, that was one of its rules, that no manner should develop into an available language; because if it did so it would become transparent and the Modernist purpose would be lost.'*[35]

Downes notes that while the modernist looks to the examples of the past in a search *'for lessons which it would not have known it could reach'*, the post-modernist looks back on history *'in a spirit of emphathy for its ostensible purposes'*. Nonetheless, traditional post-modernism does not advocate stylistic revival, though it does support the concept of emulation. Traditional post-modernism looks back to history to see how things were done and to remind itself that many good ways of doing things which were cast aside for ideological reasons can be usefully rediscovered. Thus, for example, inclusive post-modernism can employ recognisable imagery in an abstract way — it can be at once pre-modernist and modernist.[36]

Traditional post-modernism opens up artistic production to a public role which modernism, by virtue of its self-referential formal strategies, had denied itself. In painting, as William Rubin has observed, *'one characteristic of the modern period* seems *to be ending. That is the tradition of the private picture — private in its character and subject matter as well as in its destination — that is, for the small circle of collectors and friends of the artists, who sympathize with vanguard art'*.[37] In this sense, the current interest in photography should be seen as a last-gasp modernist stance.

Architecture, of course, is by definition a public art. Yet in its modernist phase, it often spoke the private language of painting — one need only recall the arguments advanced in Henry-Russell Hitchcock's book *Painting Toward Architecture*.[38] More importantly, as Suzannah Lessard points out:

*'between the abstract beauty of technological principles and the underpinning of intricate solutions to innumerable problems, there is a kind of middle ground which was overlooked in the exuberant rush to modernity. Between man's desire to expand his ego and the needs of man as ant — I can think of no better way to express the dual preoccupation of the age of technology — the question of what human life would be in the new world, floated unasked, unnoticed.'*[39]

It is this aspect of social and cultural responsibility — not in the narrowly simplistic sense of architectural do-goodism but in a broader and more profound sense of a genuine and unsentimental humanism — that characterised traditional post-modernism's distinction from the abstract, self-referential schismatic post-modernism which we have already discussed.

Traditional post-modernism rejects the anti-historical biases of modernism; influences from history are no longer seen as constraints on either personal growth or artistic excellence. History, no longer viewed as the dead hand of the past, now seems at the very least a standard of excellence in a continuing struggle to deal effectively with the present. Modernism looked toward the future as an escape from the past; traditional post-modernism struggles with the legacy of that attitude, a world filled with objects whose principal artistic impetus often came from a belief that in order to be 'Modern' they must look and function as little as possible like anything that had been seen in the world before. The traditional post-modernist struggle then, is not to free itself from the past, but to relax what has been characterised as *'the stubborn grip of the values created by the rebellion against the past'*.[40]

Traditional post-modernism rejects what Charles Moore has described as the *'obsessive normalization of the recent past, where we have drawn our expressive elegance out of poverty ... (and) our process out of crisis'*.[41] It argues that it is proper and sufficient to struggle with the problems of the present viewed in relation to the values continuing from the past while leaving the future to those who will inherit it.

Traditional post-modernism recognises that the public has lost confidence in architects (though it still believes in the symbolic power of architect ure). Modernist architecture offered very little in the way of joy or visual pleasure; its conceptual basis was limited and disconcertingly materialistic. By once again recognising the common assumptions a culture inherits from its past, traditional post-modernism is not only an announcement that Modern architecture has emerged from its puritan revolution, its catharsis at last behind it, but it is also an avowal of self-confidence in contemporary architecture's ability and willingness to re-estblish itself on a basis which can not only deal with the past but also match it, value for value, building for building.

Traditional post-modernism seeks to look backward in order to go forward. It should not be regarded as a jettisoning of Modern architecture itself, but as an attempt to pick up the threads of a theory and style which were cut by the pioneers of the Modern Movement, especially the concerns for architectural history and for visually comprehensible relationships between old and new buildings. In its inclusiveness, traditional post-modernism does not propose an independent style; it is a sensibility dependent on forms and strategies drawn from the modernist and the pre-modernist work that preceded it, though it declares the obsolescence of both. It is *a* Modern style but not *the* Modern style. In its recognition of the transience and multiplicity of styles within the historical epoch we call Modern, it rejects the emphasis on unity of expression that was so central to modernism itself. Traditional post-modernism recognises both the discursive and expressive meaning of formal language. It recognises the language of form as communicating sign as well as infra-referential symbol: that is to say, it deals with both physical and associational experience, with the work of art as an act of 'presentation' and 'representation'. It rejects the idea of a single style in favour of a view that acknowledges the existence of many styles (and the likely emergence of even more) each with its own meanings, sometimes permanently established, but more often shifting in relation to other events in the culture.

In architecture, Robert Venturi and Charles Moore can be seen as the leading advocates among an older generation of traditional post-modernists; Michael Graves and myself, among others, from the point of view of age, though not from one of ideology, occupy a middle ground (that is, we are young enough to have been students of Venturi and Moore); and an even younger generation, including Stuart Cohen, Thomas Gordon Smith and the Arquitectonica group, is beginning to make its position felt as well.

Venturi and Moore are in many ways transitional figures: their theoretical positions are more 'advanced' in the movement toward a position which includes modernist and pre-modernist values than is their built work, which as often as not tends to be abstract and non-representational (Venturi's Oberlin Museum and his Hartford Stage; Moore's own house in Los Angeles) as it is representative of ideas that are contextually based (Venturi's three Brant houses, and his Benjamin Franklin house 'restoration'; Moore's Burns House and his Piazza d'Italia). This is not surprising since their education was modernist, and until recently theirs has been a virtually solitary struggle to integrate its ideals with the wider body of architectural culture.

The work of the other traditional post-modernists who have been cited can be characterised by a struggle to use traditional languages without falling into the presumed trap of revivalism. The heritage of modernism remains a problem for all: its impulse to *'make it new'*, as Ezra Pound put it seventy years ago, conflicts with the sensibility to make it legible and make it appropriate; the preoccupation with traditional languages is often at the expense of the languages of modernism, which, no matter how abstract, have come to mean certain things in the culture at large and the recognition of stylistic diversity can be viewed as *laissez-faire* permissiveness. Thus, in some traditional post-modernist work the grammar of architectural composition has not been explored with the same care as have the individual elements or the overall meanings; in other words some traditional post-modernist work has become 'picturesque'.

Everywhere there are signs of an emerging cultural resynthesis: Richard Gilam sees a *'new naturalism'* in the drama; John Gardner pleads for a *'moral fiction'* based on a belief in an art dedicated to the *'preservation of the word of gods and men'*; Daniel Bell states that the *'problem then is whether culture can regain coherence, a coherence of substance and experience not only of form'*. Signs of the shift in sensibility in art and architecture abound. All this seems clear enough, and I hope that what I have written has shed some light on the nature of these shifts. If what I have written has any value, it is as a reminder that all which glitters in a new or different way is not necessarily golden, that the ranks of the avant garde may not any longer be the exclusive defenders of the holy grail of insight: that a shift in sensibility need have very little if anything to do with progress. The fact of the matter is that the reaction to modernism is not only a vote of 'no confidence' in its ideology but also a recognition that its forms are exhausted. As Gardener observes:

*'When modes of art change, the change need not imply philosophical progress; it usually means only that the hunter has exhausted one part of the woods and has moved to a new part, or to a part exhausted earlier, to which the prey have doubled back...*

*'Aesthetic styles — patterns for communicating feeling and thought — become dull with use, like carving knives, and since dullness is the chief enemy of art, each generation must find new ways of slicing the fat off reality.'*[42]

The fundamental nature of this shift to post-modernism has to do with the reawakening of artists in every field to the public responsibilities of art. Once again art is being regarded as an act of communication as opposed to one of production or revelation (of the artist's ego and/or of his intentions for the building or his process of design). Though art is based on personal invention it requires public acceptance to achieve real value — to communicate meaning. An artist may choose to speak a private language, but a viewer must be willing and able to 'read' the work, whether it be a book, a painting, or a building, for the work to have any kind of public life at all. To the extent that contemporary artists care about the public life of art, they are post-modernists (modernist artists make things only for themselves and/or for the gods); to the extent that an artist believes in the communicative role of form but is not willing to accept that such a role necessarily carries with it cultural meanings that are not inherent to the form, his is a schismatic post-modernism.

Modernism in architecture was premised on a dialectic between things as they are and things as they ought to be; post-modernism seeks a resolution between — or at least a recognition of — things as they were and as they are. Modernism imagined architecture to be the product of purely rational and scientific process; post-modernism sees it as a resolution of social and technological processes with cultural concerns.

Post-modernism seeks to regain the public role that modernism denied architecture. The Post-Modern struggle is the struggle for cultural coherence that is not falsely monolithic, as was attempted in the International Style in architecture or National Socialism in the politics of the 1920s and 30s, but one whose coherence is based on the heterogeneous substance and nature of modern society: post-modernism takes as its basis things as they are, *and* things as they were. Architecture is no longer an image of the world as architects wish it to be or as it will be, but as it is.

**Notes**

1 Kenneth Clark, 'Boredom Blamed', *Art Digest*, Vol X (November 15, 1943) 3. I am indebted to Peter Eisenman, Kenneth Frampton and Vincent Scully for reading and commenting on portions of this manuscript in a much earlier stage of development; Suzanne Stephens has read it more recently. What is written here is much the better for their advice. Nonetheless, I am sure they will be relieved to learn, I take full responsibility for the final product.

2 Portions of this text are based on material introduced by me on previous occasions. See 'Postcript at the Edge of 'Modernism', in my *New Directions in American Architecture*, 2nd edition revised (New York: Braziller, 1977) 117-136; 'Five Houses', *G A Houses*, 1(1976) pp 36-41; *Architectural Design*, 47, no.4 (May 1977); 'Something Borrowed, Something New', *Horizon*, 20 no.4 (December 1977) pp 50-57.

3 Charles Jencks, *The Language of Post-Modern Architecture* (London: Academy Editions, 1977); see also, Jencks, 'Post-Modern History', *Architectural Design*, 48, no.1 (January 1978) pp 11-62.

4 The term seems to have been initiated by Joseph Hudnut in his essay 'The post-modern house', *Architectural Record*, 97 (May 1945) pp 70-75, which was reprinted as Chapter 9 in Hudnut's *Architecture and the Spirit of Man*, (Cambridge, MA: Harvard, 1949) pp 109-119.
Its earliest influential use was in Arnold J. Toynbee's *A Study in History*, 8 (New York: Oxford, 1954-59) p 338.
Peter Eisenman and I discussed the term and its probable definitions at considerable length in the summer of 1975. I first 'went public' with a definition for the term in relationship to architecture in 1976, using it to characterise a shift in mood represented by an event — the Beaux Arts exhibition at the Museum of Modern Art — and a shifting of alliances among the architects who constitued the 'White' and 'Gray' groups of the mid-1970s. See my 'Possibly, the Beaux-Arts Exhibit means something after all (with apology to Clement Greenberg, Rosalind Kraus and the month of October)', a paper delivered at the 'Oppositions Forum', Institute for Architecture and Urban Studies, 22 January 1976, and published in William Ellis, editor, 'Forum of the Beaux-Arts Exhibition', *Oppositions* 8 (Spring 1977) pp 169-171; see also my 'Gray Architecture as Post-Modernism or Up and Down from Orthodoxy' (Gray Architecture: *Quelques Variations Post-Modernistes autour de L'Orthodoxie*), *L'Architecture d'Aujourd'hui, 186. (Septembre 1976) p 83.*

5 Renato Poggioli, *The Theory of the Avant Garde* (Cambridge, MA: Harvard 1968) translated by Gerald Fitzgerald, p217; see also, Daniel Bell, *The Cultural Contradictions of Capitalism* (New York: Basic Books, 1976) p 34; Frank Kermode, *Continuities*, (London: Routledge and Kegan Paul, 1968) 8.

6 See Stephen Spender, *The Struggle of the Modern* (Berkeley: University of California, 1963) passim.

7 Kermode, *op cit*, pp 27-28.

8 See Kermode, *op cit*, pp 8, 13; Kermode observes that 'the fact that defining the modern is a task that now imposes itself on many distinguished scholars may be a sign that the modern period is over', p 28.

9 See Clement Greenberg, 'Modernist Painting' in Gregory Battcock, editor, *The New Art* (New York: Dutton, 1973, revised edition) pp 100-110; William Jordy, 'The Symbolic Essence of Modern European Architecture of the Twenties and its Continuing Influence', *JSAH, XXII, no.3* (October 1973) p 117.

10 David Watkin writes that 'an art historical belief in the all dominating *Zeitgeist*, combined with a historicist emphasis on progress and the necessary superiority of novelty, has come dangerously close to undermining, on the one hand, our appreciation of the genius of the individual and, on the other, the importance of artistic tradition', *Morality and Architecture* (London: Oxford, 1977) p 115. See also, John Alford, 'Modern Architecture and the Symbolism of the Creative Process', *College Art Journal, XIV, no.2* (1955) pp 102-33; see also, Bell, *op cit*, pp 13, 20, 46-52.

11 David Antin, 'Modernism and Post-Modernism: Approaching the Present in American Poetry', *Boundary 2*.

12 Susan Sontag, *Against Interpretation* (New York: Delta, 1966) p 17.

13 Harry Levin, 'What Was Modernism', in Levin, *Refractions: Essays in Comparative Literature* (New York: Oxford, 1966) pp 271-295;

14 Irving Howe, *Decline of the New* (New York: Harcourt, Brace, 1970) p 3.

15 Henry-Russell Hitchcock, *Modern Architecture: Romanticism and Reintegration* (New York: Payson and Clarke, 1929) p xvi.

16 Henry-Russell Hitchcock, 'Modern Architecture — A Memoir', *JSAH*, 27, no.4 (December 1968) pp 227-33; the broad view was taken by Montgomery Schuyler, for example, who stated that 'modern architecture, like modern literature, had its origin in the revival of learning. The Italian Renaissance in architecture was inextricably connected with the awakening of the human spirit which was the beginning of modern civilization'. 'Modern Architecture', *Architectural Record IV* (July-September 1894).

17 Hitchcock, 'Modern Architecture — A Memoir', passim; Robert Venturi and Denise Scott-Brown first used the good-guy, bad-guy analogy in their 'Learning from Lutyens or the Case of the Shifting Zeitgeist', *RIBA Journal*, 76 (August 1969) pp 353-54.

18 J.M. Richards, *Introduction to Modern Architecture* (Hammondsworth: Penguin, 1960) pp 9, 13; see Watkin, *op cit*, passim; also Peter Collins, *Changing Ideals in Modern Architecture* (London: Faber and Faber, 1965) passim.

19 Vincent J. Scully, 'Modern Architecture: Toward a Redefinition of Style', *College Art Journal VII*, no.2 (Winter 1958) pp 140-59; see also Scully's *Modern Architecture* (New York: Braziller) passim.

20 Fiske Kimball and George H. Edgell, *A History of Architecture* (New York: Harper, 1918); Chapter XII, 'Modern Architecture' was written by Kimball; see also, James D. Kornwolf, *M.H. Baillie Scott and the Arts and Crafts Traditions* (Baltimore: Johns Hopkins, 1972), XXLV.

21 Toynbee, *op cit*; see also, Toynbee, *The Present Day Experiment in Western Civilization* (London: Oxford, 1962) pp 26-37.

22 Geoffrey Barraclough, *An Introduction to Contemporary History* (New York: Basic Books, 1965).

23 Gerald Graff, 'The Myth of the Postmodernist Breakthrough', *Tri Quarterly* no. 26 (Winter, 1973) pp383-417; see also, Bell, *op cit*.

24 Richard E. Palmer, 'Postmodernity and Hermeneutics', *Boundary* 22, (Winter 1977) pp 363-393.

25 William Spanos, 'The Detective and the Boundary: Some Notes on the Post-Modern Literary Imagination', *Boundary 2*, 1 (Fall 1972) pp 147-68.

26 Ihab Hassan, 'Joyce, Beckett, and the postmodern imagination', *Tri Quarterly*, XXXIV (Fall 1975) pp 179-200; see also Hassan, *Paracriticisms, Seven Speculations of the Times*, (Urbana, Illinois: University of Illinois, 1975) pp 55-56.

27 William Gass, 'House VI', *Progressive Architecture*, 58, No.6 (June 1977) pp 57-67.

28 Siegfried Giedion, *Space, Time and Architecture* (Cambridge, MA: Harvard, 1941) passim.

29 Mario Gandelsonas, 'On Reading Architecture', *Progressive Architecture*, 53, no.3 (March 1972) pp68-88.

30 John Gardner, *On Moral Fiction* (New York: Basic Books, 1978-9).

31 *Ibid*, pp 69, 71

32 Howe, *op cit*, p 5.

33 Robert Gillespie, 'Beyond the Wasteland: The American Novel in the Nineteen Sixties', *Boundary 2*, III, no.2 (Windsor, 1975) pp 473-81.

34 Gerald Graff, 'Babbitt at the Abyss: The Social Context of Postmodern American Fiction', *Tri Quarterly* no.33 (Spring 1976) pp307-337

35 Rackstraw Downes, 'Post-Modernist Painting', *Tracks* (Fall 1976) pp70-73.

36 Traditional post-modernism should not be confused with the neo-traditionalism of Henry Hope Reed, John Barrington Bayley, Conrad Jameson. For Bayley and Reed, see Henry Hope Reed, *The Garden City* (New York: Doubleday, 1959) passim.

37 Rubin is quoted by Douglas Davis' 'Post-Modern for Stories Real and Imagined/ Toward a Theory', in his *Art Culture — Essays on the Postmodern* (New York: Harper & Row, 1977). See also the 'Post-Modernist Dilemma', a dialogue between Davis and Suzi Gablik, *Village Voice*, March 24, April 3 and April 10, 1978.

38 Henry-Russell Hitchcock, *Painting Toward Architecture* (New York: Duell, Sloan and Pearce, 1948) passim.

39 Suzannah Lessard, 'The Towers of Light', *The New Yorker*, 54 (July 10, 1978) pp 32-36, 41-44, 49, 52, 58.

40 Lessard, *op cit*; James D. Kornwolf makes the interesting observation that 'Le Corbusier's generation was misguided not to recognize that the nineteenth century's struggle with the past was also its struggle, and that a new understanding of the past, not a denial of it, was what was needed'. *op cit*, p 513.
Peter Collins observes that 'the idea of an "International Style" was a product of the Renaissance. In fact, the so-called "battle of the styles" might be more reasonably and meaningfully interpreted as an attempt to refute the concept of an "International Style" rather than as a conflict between "Gothicists" and "Classicists". This was certainly the essence of the position taken by Viollet-le-Duc and Ferguson.' *op cit*, pp 171-72.

41 Charles Moore, 'Foreward', in Sam Davis, editor, *The Form of Housing* (New York: Van Nostrand Reinhold, 1977) p 6.

42 Gardner, *op cit*.

Robert A. M. Stern

# Models for Reality: Some Observations

I do not design in model form, I draw (often — but not always — a key elevation first and then work on the plans and sections). My initial drawings are crude; others refine them and contribute to their meaning (for me, architecture can never be a solitary pursuit). This process of initiation and refinement continues until a set of ideas has been sufficiently crystalised so that my colleagues and I are convinced that it is time to build a model.

Small scale models usually come first — frequently in quick succession as massing and gross relationships of interior spaces and fenestration are explored and established. Then, at a critical time (usually after the scheme is set and has met with the client's preliminary approval), a 'big' model is built, as much to include the client into the exact nature of the design as into the process of its making (both of which are usually too abstract for the non-architect to grasp at this stage) and to 'double-check' what has been done to date.

The big model shows only a portion of the building: it focuses our attentions on the shapes of the interior spaces which in our work we increasingly aim to make in such a way that they are sufficiently defined in three dimensions to be worthy of the name 'room', even though they may be combined in unexpected and even ambiguous ways. The big model affords an opportunity for all parties concerned to 'poke around' in what is a fairly close approximation of the future building: big size helps all concerned to *see* relationships rather than to imagine them. A big model can simulate and stimulate reality to an astonishing degree, especially when combined with photography. But it is a cumbersome tool, limited in its usefulness by problems of transportation not to mention cost. Most of the big models that have been made in our offices are scaled at 1″-1′. They are built of foam core board pinned together, rather than glued and often constructed episodically as design issues arise. The pins permit change as new thoughts occur.

Architects have become accustomed to use the word 'model' in a very different way from its traditional usage: once it conveyed a sense of action (to model a space); now it conveys a static noun-or-object-like quality (a spatial model). Even though the theory of Modern architecture is changing dramatically, so far this shift has had little effect on the day-to-day working habits of architects: the dependence on models goes hand-in-hand with the 'weightless' cubism of the canonical International Style. The miniaturised object quality of models not only focused virtually all design energies on the formal problems raised by buildings-in-the-round (as opposed to buildings as fragments), but also diminished the potential for expression that a single wall plane, a 'facade' might have in its own right. Similarly, when the traditional, expressive elaboration of detail based in part on construction was jettisoned by the form givers of the International Style, in favour of the smooth, rendered stucco surfaces, the impetus for making elaborate drawings evaporated. Only in the 1950s when Mies, and later Kahn, began to think of structure as decoration did the big-scale drawing began to re-establish its role in the design process; but it only achieved a tentative position, supplementary to the great models of structural details which merged from Mies' and, to a lesser extent, Kahn's offices.

But it is not only the nature of one kind or size of model as opposed to another but our very dependence on the model as a design tool which need to be examined as our architecture is redefined. The dependence on models which has characterised practice in the last thirty years is perfectly understandable given the formal premises of the International Style. Not for no reason does Reyner Banham describe Walter Gropius as the 'great gray visage of the white cardboard style'. Models, much more than drawings, tend to foster surface simplification; their inherent miniaturisation and their limitations arising from the point of view of craft, tend to lull the designer into a false security about the nature of the building fabric. After all, why think about mouldings and corner beads when straight pins and glue will do?

On the other hand, a large scale drawing (an elevation, or a cross-section), such as those produced as a matter of course at the Ecole des Beaux Arts, demands that the designer think through every inch of the building's surface that is depicted: if an empty drawing is visually boring, is it not the same for the building it purports to represent? And if one draws a wall of brick at large scale, is not one obliged to depict each brick and the mortar joints between, while if one makes a model of the same in foam core...?

The changing definition of architecture and the changing tide of our intentions seem to call for new models in every sense of that term. As I write this, four major exhibitions stressing contemporary architectural drawings are being held in two important cities. I think their message is clear: because drawing as such was so long a dead issue, architects seeking clear ground to say new, or at least different things are concentrating on drawing their way toward a more modern architecture — at least until such time as they can conceive of modelling it in more subtle ways or even, perhaps, getting to build their new visions whole, leaving them out in the rain to take their chances, which is after all what its really all about, isn't it?

First published in *Great Models*, the student publication North Carolina State University, no. 27 (1978) pp 72-75.

# Catalogue of Works

**Residence for Mr. & Mrs. Samuel U. Wiseman, Montauk, New York 1967 (●003)**
A year-round vacation house for a growing family, this house sits on a high wooded site overlooking the ocean and the beach as it stretches toward Amagansett. Within the overall discipline of the gable shape, a variety of spaces surrounds a two and one half floor high entrance hall. Living areas are raised for the view. A roof deck above the tree tops provides a sweeping vista of ocean and bay. The contrast between the front and rear elevations is a direct response to the orientation, the view, and the character of the site, which is visible from a great distance and calls for a big scale on the south.

**Residence, East Hampton, New York, built 1900; remodelled 1969 (●005)**
**Robert A.M. Stern & John S. Hagmann architects**
The house is a late example of the 'Shingle Style' of seaside architecture. As such, it is characterised by a clear spatial organisation of interrelated rooms giving off an ample stair hall. The existing house was restored with almost no structural changes undertaken within the plan. The furnishings, wherever possible, are modern equivalents of traditional design elements. The armoire in the master bedroom is massive and assertive in the space, yet simply detailed and laquered white to match the wall, while the living room chairs were selected because they are appropriately solid and comfortable while modular and therefore capable of a variety of arrangements in space.

A new screeened porch was added to the garden facade of the house. An old-fashioned and uniquely American phenomenon, this porch acts by day as a room-sized bay window for the house and at night as a lantern for the garden. Its double height yields a real sense of space and airiness, while the elevation of the floor and the faceted curve reinforce the sense of enclosure and separation from the garden. It is, then, an exedral/transitional space, a meeting point between outside and inside; in short, a garden pavilion which, because of the arcuated plan (not a semicircle), the use of material, and general proportions, complements the scale of the house and imposes a compositional unity not previously there.

The porch replaces a glassed-in dining room, which had been built in 1955 for a previous owner of the house. This addition, built of wood, though detailed in a manner reminiscent of Mies van der Rohe's work in steel at I.I.T. or Philip Johnson's Glass House of 1949, straddles the 'joint' between the two wings of the existing house and seeks to unite them by introducing a third, dissimilar element. In this sense, its composition seems to recall the insistent asymmetries so often associated with Bauhaus painting and design, and quite unrelated to the grand and confident accretions of the house to which it is appended.

**Showroom and ofices for Tiffeau-Bush Ltd., New York, New York, 1969 (●006)**

**Showrooms for Helen Harper, Inc. (Hang Ten and Charlie's Girls), New York, New York 1969-70 (●009)**

**Two projects for an office addition on the ground floor of a house in Long Island 1969-1970 (●010)**
**Robert A.M. Stern & John S. Hagmann Architects**
This was intended to house expanded office facilities for a dentist in a small town. The existing house was a Victorian relic which had been badly remodelled in the past to make apartments and offices and had recently been clad in white asphalt shingles. Our strategy was to leave the existing shell alone and to add on to it a new frontispiece, which would contain a double-height waiting room, a receptionist's area, and a dental operating room. The differences between the two schemes are largely ones of shape; the client didn't like the round space of the first scheme. The second scheme was built, but not fully in accord with the architects' intentions.

**Residence for Mr. and Mrs. John W.R. Jenkins, East Hampton, New York, 1969-1970 (project) (●012)**
This house was designed for an interior lot in a wooded subdivision. The house represents a development in terms of complexity of programme and shape-making beyond the bow-fronted porch addition to the Stern house which preceded it.

The plan configuration is bent to form a motor court, which receives the thrust of the driveway as it gently meanders down the panhandle of land which gives access to the public road. Two doorways give off the motor court. One, a square-arched opening, leads under the bedroom wing to a shaded terrace and swimming pool beyond. The other is a more ambitiously conceived doorway, replete with scale-enhancing mouldings. This leads into a 'vestigial' stair hall space, which is part of the living room. The living room is set back under the overhang of the master bedroom as a protection against the southern sun; it is sheltered on the east by the screened porch. The space of the living room is kept low to focus the viewer's attention out to the south, where a small *allée* is cut in the woods in an effort to give a greater illusion of distance.

Upstairs, greenhouse glazing is introduced in the corridor in an attempt to expand the apparent space and to make of it a kind of 'porch' that is part of the outdoors but protected from the elements. The articulation of the exterior wall surfaces reflects an attempt to express certain particularities of the spatial organisation (stair, seating bench in kitchen) and, at the same time, to give the house a big scale. Thus, the handling of the screen porch, the use of the crossed window/central pier, the bridge of bedrooms, the bent plan with motor court, all give the house a greater presence than its modest size might otherwise suggest.

**Apartment for Mr. William White Jr., New York, New York, 1969-71 (●014)**

**Travelling exhibition, 'Another Chance for Cities', originated at the Whitney Museum of American Art, New York, New York, 1970-71 (●016)**

**Poolhouse and related facilities for Mr. and Mrs. Richard Danziger, Purchase, New York, 1970-71 (●019)**

**010**

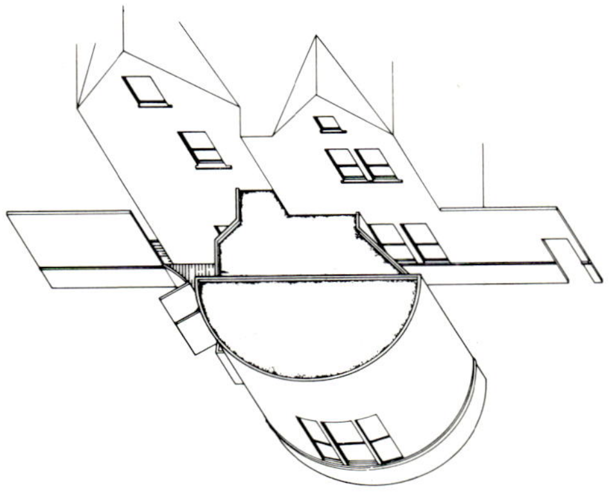

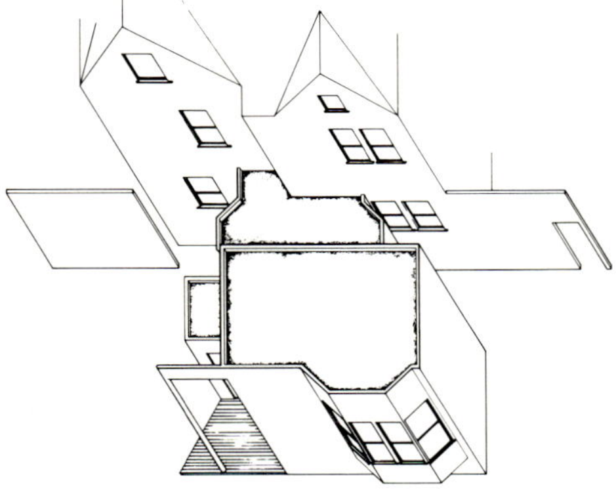

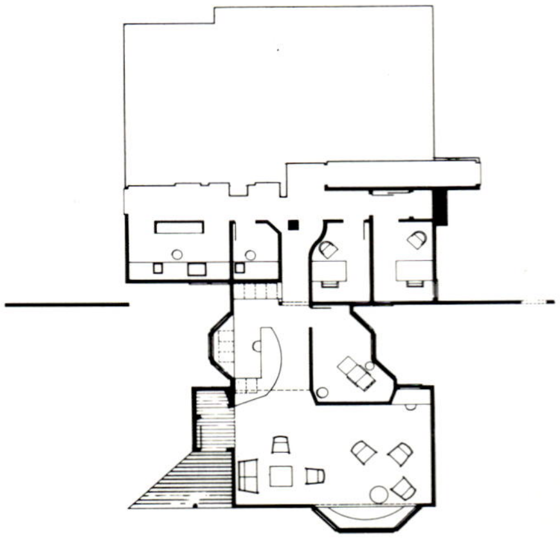

019

**Guest house, house, and cabana for Mr. and Mrs. Frederick Beebe, Montauk, New York, 1972 (●023)**

An integrated complex of three buildings winding down a sixty foot cliff, this project effects a direct response to the client's requirements for an architecture appropriate to the scale of the landscape, the beach and the sea. The spirit of the client's programme was imbued with a love of the place on which the houses were built and a desire to build well and in harmony with the climate and site. Though the houses are suitable for year round use, summer life is their special focus. The scheme is therefore based on desire to maximise a sense of site, and to take advantage of the prevailing breezes. To this end, in the main house, a system of monitors with sliding glass doors at their tops brings air and light into the centre of the house. The double height spaces, the changes of levels, and the strong interior geometry help to articulate the various spaces within the open plan.

In both houses, wainscoting is used for metaphorical as well as practical reasons: the inner walls form a lining that at once reflects the ruggedness of the outside shingles while being more luminescent and lighter in texture. Lighting is located in the monitors, coves, and cabinets. Pierced ceiling planes are avoided. The ambience at night therefore, complements the daytime lighting without imitating it.

The architects assumed complete control of the interior furnishings as well as the landscape design.

**Apartment for Commissioner and Mrs. Jerome Kretchmer, New York, New York, 1971-1972 (●024)**

**Residence, Gladwynne, Pennsylvania, 1972 (●026)**

**Danziger apartment, New York City, 1973 (●029)**

This long and narrow 50-year-old duplex apartment has been completely renovated in accord with the lifestyle of a young family that has particular interests in art. A chopped-up plan of many small rooms strung out along rather long gloomy

023

coridors has been considerably simplified, providing for three master bedrooms and reading and entertaining spaces for both adults and children. Two new staircases connect the floors: one leads from the kitchen to the children's bedrooms, and the other connects the major living spaces on the lower floor with the master bedroom and sitting room. This main staircase provides the major statement of verticality in the scheme and its impact is extended through the use of cabinetwork connecting the library, living and dining rooms. Two gentle curves relieve the severity of the rectilinear organisation and shorten the apparent length of the apartment.

The architects also designed the furnishing scheme which combines French and English antiques with well designed modern pieces; built-in cabinetwork is subdued in its overall effect in order to avoid clutter and to focus maximum attention on the people in the space.

**Apartment for Mr. and Mrs Lester Eisner Jr., New York, New York, 1973 (●033)**

A three bedroom rooftop apartment has been remodelled with three aims in mind: first of all, to maximise the impact of a spectacular view south toward mid-town; secondly, to relieve the oppressive nature of the low ceilings by breaking through the room to gain light from above; and thirdly, to clarify the organisation of space thus giving the illusion of greater size. Standard pre-fabricated units (sliding doors, greenhouse, ceramic tile) are used in combination with refined materials (brass, laquered wood cabinets, antique furniture) to provide an atmosphere that is at once a response to the established lifestyle of the owners and to the contextual demands of a unique rooftop location.

In order to adapt the greenhouse to the particular demands of the situation — a small scale manifestation of the kind of typological transformation which is characteristic of the post-industrial age architecture - the following moves were necessary:

1 the standard greenhouse module was extended in length; the bright green aluminium tube provides necessary support at the critical juncture between the extension and the basic

037

module;

2 overhead outdoor electric lighting was devised which automatically rotates over the opaque roof area when not in use. In designing this feature, the idea of swivelling television antennae was used as the prototype;

3 the standard exterior aluminium greenhouse blinds, necessary to control heat and glare before they affect the glass and metal structure itself, were motorised for the first time; to achieve this, our office designed a complex system of pulleys, gears, and tapes on two shafts that rotate at different speeds operated through relays and a limit switch to permit the blinds to negotiate the curving section of the greenhouse while moving up or down, and to stop anywhere on route.

*Illustrated in colour on page 6*

**Mercer House, East Hampton, New York, 1973-1975 (●037)**

**Robert A.M. Stern architects with Alfred De Vido**

The house incorporates parts of the foundations, platform, and partitioning system of a 1950s ranch house. Major contextual factors in forming the design include the problems of noise and privacy, which are generated by the property's frontage along the main road leading to the ocean beach, by the shift in axes between the platting of the property and the most desirable orientation to the view and to the sun, and by the long axis of that view across the pond to the ocean beyond. For these reasons, the house is conceived of as a wall against the street, with principal living spaces and the master bedroom situated on the second floor. The introduction of the diagonal plan is a response to the questions of orientation.

The outside is sheathed in two kinds of shingles: on the roof hand-split shingles are used to yield increased scale through coarser texture; on the walls the shingles are machine-cut to provide a more delicate and lighter coloured surface. Inside, bleached wooden columns and mouldings are introduced to enrich the palette. There is no air-conditioning; large panes of fixed glass are confined to emphasise major views, while French doors are used for ventilation. Where

026

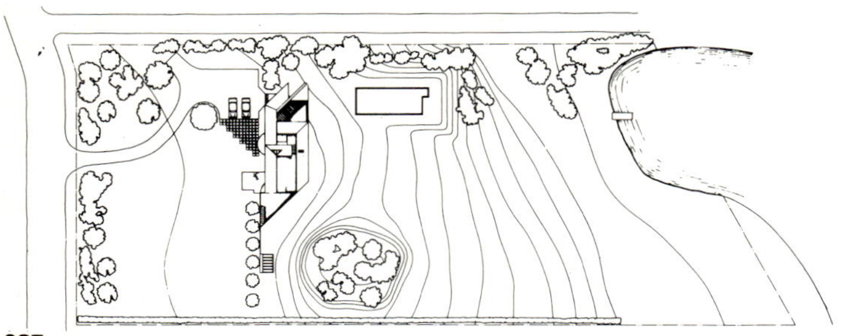

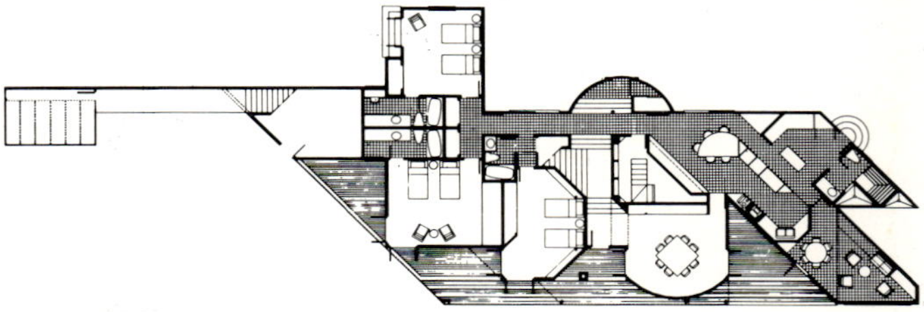

037

the French doors occur on the second floor, brass railings are projected to make each opening into a miniature balcony.

**New York 'Greystone', New York, New York, 1972-1979 (●038)**
This renovation involved the relocation of access ways to the upper apartments in order to make feasible a more open plan for the owner's triplex apartment at the bottom. The design solution involves a complex layering of major and minor spaces along the longitudinal axis, using exaggerated structure to define rooms and circulation routes. The structural frame continues out into the rear court in response to engineering requirements and to the need to heighten the impact of the spatial ordering of the design without getting in the way of routine use.

The new facade for the house expresses at the ground floor the dual nature of the space allocation of the townhouse: owner's apartment; three floors of rental apartments. The grey stucco finish, divided into panels, recalls the coursing and colour of the masonry of the grander Edwardian townhouse which abuts our project on the east, while the obvious thinness of the finish is more in keeping with the typical brown-stone facades on the west.

The interior is all white to serve as a background for the owners' growing collection of Pop and colour field art.

**Residence for Mr. and Mrs. Paul Henry Lang, Washington, Connecticut, 1973-1974 (●047)**
The design of this house represents both a development of and a considerable shift in the specific formal direction of our work. A year-round residence, it responds to conditions of programme, site, and cultural context quite different from those of many of our previous houses, which have been vacation 'cottages' on or near the south shore beaches of Long Island. The house was designed to be economically competitive with the customised prefabricated houses on the market. We were successful in reaching this goal because we only fine-tuned the design of certain parts — the facade, the spaces for entertaining, the stair hall — while bedrooms, kitchen, and service spaces were kept very simple.

The transverse axis of the house is shifted to form an outdoor vestibule. The shift intensifies the perception of the plan's axiality, heightens one's sense of the layering of spaces. The vestibule buffers the house from the wind and at the same time gives the house big scale. A double-height light monitor stretches across the garden front, backwashing the living and dining spaces with warm south light. A second monitor introduces light at the rear end of the living room. The curve of the principal monitor and its extended screen wall give the house a big scale in the landscape and also frame the views from the inside.

The exuberance of the swelling curve of the garden facade, with its high oval oculus, is in severe contrast with the entrance facade, where decoration is introduced to obscure and intensify the scale. The decoration also enables us to indulge, in a witty way, in overt recollection of older modes of architectural expression. Is this a neo-Palladian Regency Art Deco farmhouse?

Beyond questions of image are those of taste and artistic intervention. The house is intended as a capsule for a fully developed way of life: it enables its owners to see the familiar objects of their daily life differently; it does not, however, demand that they discard all of these possessions for different ones simply because their new house is different from their previous house. As a work of architecture, it aims toward an acceptance of the idiosyncracies of its inhabitants. At the same time, it is not without idiosyncracies of its own.

**Poolhouse for Mr. and Mrs. Frederic A. Bourke, Greenwich, Connecticut, 1973-1974 (●048)**
Though physically attached to the main house by means of walls as well as an enclosed service passageway, this pavilion and its bath house wing seem completeley separate. The desire for a sculptural solution free of the constraints of everyday functional accommodation is mediated by a desire to work within the same family of forms which governs the design of the main house.

From the outside the bath house wing seems little more than a wall; once inside, however, the bounding surfaces of the various spaces combine with the natural light that is introduced from overhead sources and the use of dazzling colour to produce a freewheeling series of spaces that seem virtually free of contextual constraint. Not only are these spaces unpredictable from the outside, but they also suggest the freshness of summer all year round and thereby invite the suspension of belief so necessary to a good-time place.

To an extent, the same can be said for the pavilion itself, which is conceived of as a billowing shingled tent, washed with light from above, cooled by natural breezes (in the appropriate seasons), and inflected toward principal views. With the exception of the screened porch at the east end, the pavilion is heated in winter. In summer, glazed doors slide back into pockets, permitting the porch and big room to be combined into one continuous space for entertaining, living, dining, and cooking.

*Illustrated in colour on page 7*

**Cullman House, North Stanford, Connecticut, 1975 (●050)**

**House, North Stamford, Connecticut, 1975 (●050)**
**Assistant in charge: Jeremy Lang**
**Assistant: Ronne Fisher**
This house, which began life seventy years ago as a Sears Roebuck log cabin, has been altered many times over. Our task was to infuse it with a clear sense of functional and ceremonial order without compromising its pleasant informality. The siting of the house on the downslope of a hill facing northward toward a view presented unusual challenges. Because of drainage and subsurface conditions, a new motor court is set above the level of the front door which is on the service side of the house. A continuous skylight was introduced along the hallway to introduce direct sun into the very deep cross section; this is especially effective at the rear of the dining room.

The plan is not only very thick, but also strung out. Therefore, a double curve was introduced to make one gentle shift in axis that would enhance the sense of privacy in the bedroom wing. A screened porch was added to the west to provide a shaded daytime sitting area and a place to dine outdoors protected from insects. Its curving wall and its somewhat tenuous connections to older parts of the house make explicit the strategy devised for the unification of the exterior in

053

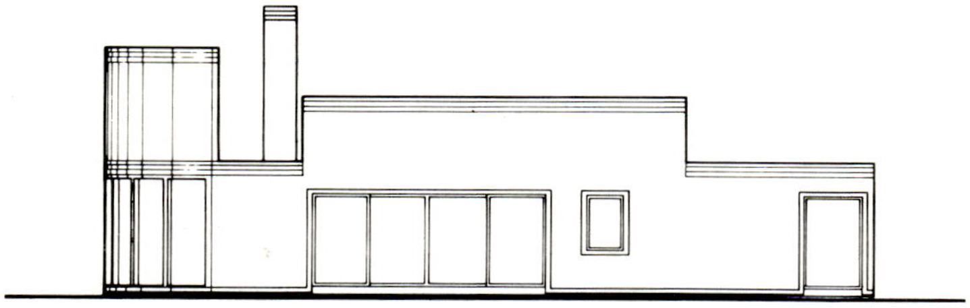

general — which is to handle the walls as thin shingled skins drawn across the idiosyncratic complexities of an aggregated and somewhat ad hoc composition.

**Apartment renovation, Elkins Park, Pennsylvania, 1975 (●051)**
A long and narrow dwelling space in a new, rather indifferently conceived and executed apartment house in suburban Philadelphia has been completely reorganised. The original builder's plan of box-like rooms has given way to layered spaces that recede in symbolic importance in direct proportion to their distance from the natural light; the principal rooms are arranged *en filade* along the window wall, which overlooks a swimming pool and woods beyond. Natural light is introduced into the glass block wall; the wall, which boldly curves in plan, articulates the living space into formal and informal places for sitting and dining. Manipulation of the intensity of the artificial lighting conceals or reveals the activities in the servantless kitchen. The limited palette of finish materials provides a sympathetic background for the classic, modern and antique furniture and the *objets d'art*.

**Residence, gardener's residence and utility building for Mrs. Frederick L. Ehrman, Armonk, New York, 1976 (●053)**
This complex of houses is reached by a new one-half-mile-long road. The site is at the top of a steep hill; a magnificent hemlock grove and superb views of the neighbouring countryside are its principal features. The driveway follows a number of switch-back curves up the hill, then straightens out, passing between the utility building/greenhouse and the gardener's house and leading to a motorcourt at the entrance facade of the main house, 300 feet beyond. The house is placed at a diagonal to the axis of the driveway to minimise the impact of its length. This diagonal axis is reiterated in the placement of the fireplace mass and by the focus of the living room through its glazed southwestern corner and to the view beyond.

A curving screen wall is introduced at the entrance which provides for a covered entry, allows for the development of a private outdoor space for the servants, and facilitates the resolution of the diagonal driveway axis with the othogonal planning of the house itself. On the rear or garden facade, a bowed screen wall in combination with landscaping serves to reduce the apparent length of the garden elevation, provide integral sun protection, and focus views from the principal interior spaces.

*Illustrated in colour on page 7 and back cover*

**New York townhouse, 1975 (●055)**
A complete reconstruction of a townhouse structure squeezed between large apartment house blocks facing one of New York City's most fashionable avenues, this design deals with issues of privacy, light and orientation within a constrained urban context. In response to the problems of scale created by the larger neighbouring buildings, several strategies are employed: reference on the facade to the real sizes and positions of the elements in the plan and section is obscured, and an abstract gridding is introduced alluding to the base/shaft/capital schema of taller buildings. There are intimations of pilasters at the edges and a gradual progression in the vertical plane from solid to void, capped by a cornice which appears to be suspended from above. All these connect our facade with the form language of its neighbours and evoke images of traditional, classicising townhouse design.

Inside, the major living and entertaining spaces are linked by a sucession of stair runs and passage spaces which describe a *promenade architecturale* extending from the front entrance hall up to the master bedroom suite at the top. A circular stairway toward the rear of the building offers a more functionally direct vertical linkage, while an elevator provides a third means of circulation, and allows access to the basement playroom and service areas. Because of the exceptional depth of the house and the undesirable views that might be obtained along the North and South walls, a four-storey high atrium is introduced to bring light from monitor windows above and to give an internal focus to the plan and section.

Rich polychromy characterises the interior design. Bold saturations of colour are employed in individual spaces such as the childrens bedrooms, the circular stair and the spaces of arrival, while delicate shades such as lavender and peach are used to emphasise the sensuous curves of cabinetry. In addition, wall planes are themselves used as decoration: the South wall — which functions as an inner lining of the building, concealing storage and mechanical equipment — is articulated with deep reveals set between panelled areas, thus giving the wall a sense of materiality while also modulating its scale in relation to the sizes and proportions of the rooms it abuts.

*Illustrated in colour on pages 2, 6 and 10*

**Library, community museum and civic square, Biloxi, Mississippi, 1974 (●057)**
**Robert A.M. Stern & John S. Hagmann architects**
This proposal combines new construction with recycled space in a former, grandiloquently designed Elks Hall. The site, facing the City Hall, is at the edge of downtown and surrounded in equal measure by small wood-frame houses, low warehouse buildings, and parking lots. Elk Hall is treated as the frontispiece of our scheme. Its lower floors are removed to expose the brick supporting piers and to provide a shaded outdoor exhibition area. The Community Museum is accommodated in the double height space of the former ballroom. The library is housed in new infill construction which conects with existing commercial building on the site and defines a mid-block pedestrian walkway leading from downtown.

**Housing for Roosevelt Island, national competition, first place award, 1975 (●059)**
In November 1974, the New York State Urban Development Corporation announced an open competition for housing on a parcel of land on Roosevelt Island in New York City. The housing is intended for one thousand upper, middle, and lower income families on an 8.8 acre site which completes the Northtown portion of the island's development. The competition had approximately 750 registrants from all over the country; 250 submissions were received; this office's submission was awarded first prize.

Our solution introduces a pedestrian street running longitudinally through the site and continuing the diagonal offsets of the street pattern established in earlier stages of the island's development. Our street, which we have called 'Octagon Way', gives access to the thousand apartments in the development as well as to the various community functions, such as meeting rooms, a day care centre, two public schools, laundry rooms, and an amphitheatre. It provides the principal pedestrian gateway to Octagon Park, a major park and recreational area planned for the island.

The three apartment towers are placed at the water's edge to take advantage of river views and to minimise their apparent bulk and the effect of their shadows on the usable open spaces. Almost all apartments have two exposures, and throughout the project there is a wide variety of apartment types. More than one-half of the apartments are accommodated in six- and eight-storey buildings which provide residents with a comfortable relationship to the ground plane. All apartment buildings enter directly from Octagon Way and all townhouse apartments have direct access to it, enhancing the sense of identity and privacy for the individual apartment dweller.

The individual apartment plans themselves are worked out in relationship to overall size and social conditions, with the majority of large family units placed at ground level or near to it to facilitate child supervision. Many of the larger units are duplexes; many of the apartments have additional unprogrammed living spaces and private gardens, terraces, or balconies. Other issues addressed in the scheme include those of around-the-clock ground level security, design and maintenance of public and semi-public open space, preservation of existing trees, and orientation to sunlight and to the principal river views.

We believe our decision to create in Octagon Way a vital, active pedestrian street as the focus of the development strategies makes it possible to provide for the accommodation of a large number of families living in close proximity within a strong

**059**

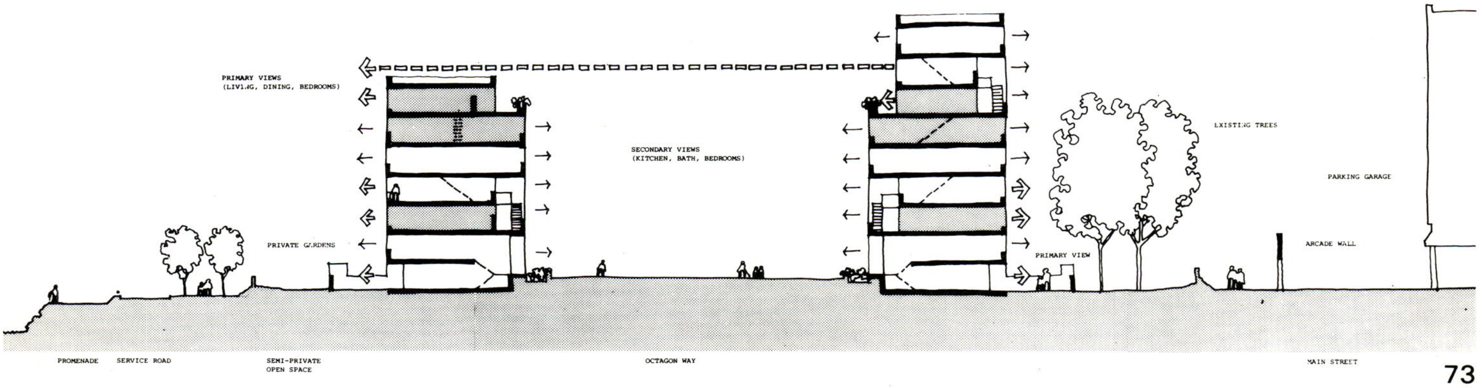

architectural framework that is at once socially responsive, lively, and humane.

### Jerome Green Hall, School of Law, Columbia University 1975 (●060)
### 'Some things borrowed/Some things new'

The programme at Jerome Greene Hall called for the conversion of the technologically antiquated and aesthetically vandalised facilities of the former Women's Faculty Club into a student centre for the School of Law. Along with a variety of lounge spaces, Greene Hall includes offices, seminar and conference rooms as well as a new bridge to connect with the adjacent Faculty House.

Our design is intended to counterbalance the impersonal abstraction of the principal Law School facility, a building of the late 1950s. It is intended not only to recapture as much as possible of the original character of the club rooms — which were designed in a style best described as etiolated Adam via last-gasp posthumous McKim, Mead and White — but also to extend, revitalise and thereby revive the original vocabulary. The new work at Greene Hall tries to speak the language of the old; ours has been a process of restoration, renovation, and recycling — but not one of remodelling in the literal sense. In short, we see ourselves as architectural re-weavers using deliberately inconspicuous (but elegant) new stitches to repair the old. If our efforts are successful it is because the finished product, which is largely new, seems as though it has always been there.

This emphasis on continuity extends to the interior furnishings in the public rooms which were selected with one eye cocked toward heavy-duty performance and the other toward that of appropriate character. The principal public room is conceived of as a club lounge for law students: deep, comfortable, enveloping couches and armchairs covered in red and brown look-like-leather vinyl suggest characteristic anglo-american club decor; wall sconces, table and floor lamps, make atmospheric pools of light; an elaborately patterned oriental-style carpet completes what we believe to be a familiar and appropriate ensemble.

### Downtown Urban Development Plan, Regina, Saskatchewan, Canada, competition scheme, 1975 (●061)

This design constitutes a proposal for the development of a parcel of land that will soon be cleared near the downtown centre of Regina. Our solution seeks to reinforce and revitalise the existing use patterns that occur in areas bordering the redevelopment area. The central portion of the site lies at the head of Regina's major commercial strip, Scarth Street, which the city intends to turn into a pedestrian mall. Our development plan reinforces this idea by proposing that Hamilton Street, another parallel shopping street, also become a mall and that they meet at a newly created hub of downtown activity called Station Square. From Station Square, pedestrian circulation flows out in an interconnected system that runs through all of the new commercial and residential areas of the site. Immediately adjacent to Station Square is a commercial area with an internal heated and air conditioned Galleria connecting stores, offices, a cinema, a hotel, parking and a bus transportation centre. Angling off diagonally from the square in Scarth Way, a pedestrian street which is lined with housing and shops and is intended to create a lively atmosphere that is the most 'city like' of any of the areas of the plan. From the ends of the Galleria and Scarth Way pedestrian and bicycle routes branch out even further in the east and west to two new wholly residential districts, the Elphinstone neighbourhood and the Arcola neighbourhood. The former neighbourhood has a series of garden apartments on cul-de-sac streets, with parking areas and landscaped foot paths. It is laid out to utilise the geometry of the existing city street grid. The Arcola housing is denser and more urban but has a pedestrian walkway system extending from the town centre. Existing vehicular circulation has been cut off in areas where it would interfere with pedestrian activity and has been routed to the periphery of the site, where it feeds into parking areas to accommodate people driving into downtown Regina from outlying districts. The planning recognises the importance of the automobile in a place such as Regina and provides access for it to the redeveloped downtown. Once the automobile is parked, the opportunities for easy and comfortable pedestrian circulation present themselves, and the vitality of a new downtown centre grows as more and more people discover it on foot.

### Points of View, Mount Desert Island, Maine 1975-76 (●062)

This year-round vacation house is intended to capture the spirit of holiday pleasure that one usually associates with the rambling shingled cottages that are so characteristic of the island community on which it is built. The modestly sized site, made available as the result of a fire which took a previous house, is exposed to the water on three sides. The house attempts to take advantage of the views, providing upper level decks for viewing sailboat races in the harbour. The attempt to evoke traditional shingle style and local vernacular precedents can be seen in the covered entry porch that suggests a *porte-cochère*, a stair to the second floor that marks outs its own landscape for sitting on as well as walking, and a schedule of interior finishes and details that are based on established formal precedents and time-honoured construction techniques.

### Ferrin House, Eastern Long Island, 1975-77 (●064)

Though technically an alteration, this project might more accurately be described as a recreation of a 1906 carriage house which had been virtually lost in a fire. Mouldings and columns are newly designed in emulation of traditional architectural ornament; the traditional and subtle colour scheme reinforces the patterns of the ornamental detail and articulates the lofty cubic proportions of the downstairs rooms. A grand stair hall, like those in the Shingle Style houses of the 1880s, leads to the bedrooms in what was once the hay loft on the second floor. A new screened porch, a pool and pavilions clearly conform to, and expand upon, the vocabulary of the older structure.

### 'Seaside Suburb': Riviera Beach competition, Singer Island, Florida, 1976 (●065)

Singer Island, which for years was little more than a sand bar on the East Coast of Florida, has developed as a result of the recent boom in Florida real estate into a resort and residential community, organised along a vehicular spine. Its natural features, the sun, the sea, the flat topography, and the lush vegetation are so typical of the region that the man-made environment creates the particular identity and character of the island. In effect, the architecture of the highway strip, the high-rise residential towers, and the motels, shops and residential subdivisions which have developed along the highway have become the only elements capable of establishing an identity for the island at a scale appropriate to its size and to the speed of the automobile. At present, most of the architecture on the island is devoid of symbolic intention: it is watered down International Style, modern in form, and deriving its only associative connotations from the similarity of its forms to those used in the gloss-glamour resorts of the 1930s and 1940s in Miami, Acapulco and Rio.

The rapid development of Singer Island has tended to inhibit the evolution of local character and a sense of place. Its growth has shown an obsessive concern for the requirements of vehicular traffic, and yet it has failed to adapt to, or exploit, the possibilities inherent in the particular form of suburbanism that the automobile creates. In our proposal for Singer Island, methods and strategies are outlined for the evolution of a sense of place that is unique to the island, and based on an imagery that is at once integral to the architectural growth of the island and responsive to the problems of scale and speed that the vehicular 'strip' involves. Energies are concentrated on the entrance to the island from the mainland, on the shopping strip, and on a plaza created at the principal public access to the beach. This plaza acts as a hub of pedestrian activity on the island; located at a critical bend of the state highway, it forms the gateway to the municipal parking lot and to the public bathing beach. The symbolic sailfish gate should become a favourite place for photographs; and the raised level of the plaza provides a clear view of the sand and sea from downtown.

*Illustrated in colour on page 14*

**061**

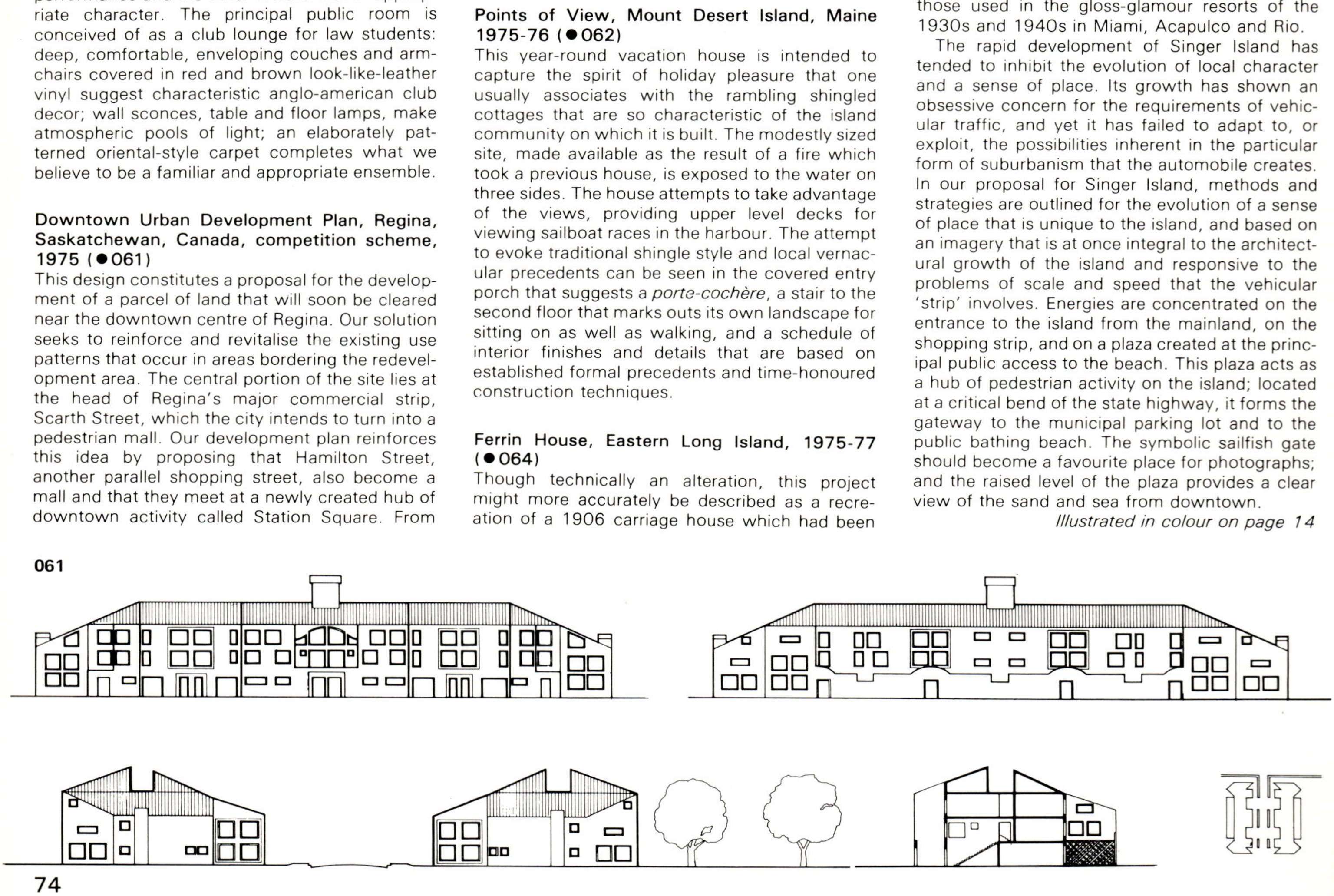

065

**Redtop, residence at Dublin, New Hampshire, 1979 (● 068)**

**'Subway Suburb': Venice Biennale, official entry representing the United States, 1976 (● 069)**
In a project prepared for the Venice Biennale, an attempt is made to define a new kind of suburb to be built within the legal confines of the city, relatively close to its centre, utilising urban land that has been abandoned, and has no apparent higher value. Though purely speculative in origins, this project suggests uncharacteristic ways to develop the land in burned out, marginal areas of the city, that will utilise existing street and utility grids to offset development costs, and take advantage of existing rapid transit services while also accommodating the automobile within the new development. To provide housing in the city at the densities of new moderate-priced suburban development in the outlying area, it accepts known functional paradigms and confines its invention to the realm of shape and symbol, re-introducing historical and cultural allusion into the design process; Regency Crescents, the University of Virginia, the small-town American porch, Forest Hills Gardens are all consciously evoked. The basic housing type devised for Subway Suburb is based on the free standing cottage of the American small town, circa 1900. Incentives to individual proprietorship of open space are provided through the reintroduction of identifiable front yards of substantial size, places which by their nature will mark out a clearly definable turf maintained by the private citizen for the benefit of the community.

**Ski Lodge for Killington, Vermont, national competition, honourable mention, 1976 (● 070)**
The proposal for a ski lodge, which is intended to be the focal point for the expansion of an existing ski resort, involves a four-phase development. The first phase incorporates the major facilities of the lodge (main lobby and reception, dining, bar, shops, lounge spaces, and related support functions) as well as 27 bedrooms and suites. The remaining three phases (for which only a generalised concept of design and siting were required) add approximately 150 rooms to the complex, as well as secondary support and recreational facilities.

Our solution develops a linear 'street' that links the major facilities on the main floor and integrates the connections to future phases of development. The building is articulated to follow the contours of the hillside, a configuration which also resulted from a desire to reduce the apparent bulk of the structure, and permit the development of a principal facade related to the approach road and the view to the ski mountain. Additionally, this creates a semi-enclosed sheltered area for the terrace and pool, where a secondary facade (its axis shifted slightly from the primary facade) overlooks the golf course. The facades and massing of the Phase I development recall grand resort hotels such as Mohonk in the Catskills, as well as the Shingle Style casinos and hotels of the last century, with their casually articulated facades, integrated by the unified massing of the pitched roofs. Similarly, the design of the main lobby, which rises through three floors, utilises an interplay of columns, screen walls, balconies and alcoves reminiscent of the relaxed grandeur of the large hotels which were developed at the turn of the century for national parks such as Glacier and Yellowstone.

**St. Joseph's Village, housing for the elderly, Brookhaven, Long Island, New York, competition 1976 (● 071)**
Set in a scrub oak forest at the outer fringe of suburban development, this proposal includes an explicit critique of prevailing formal and organisational paradigms for low-density housing. It also comments on the continuing validity of such pre-modernist American models as Radburn and the University of Virginia. Relationships between public and private open space, wild and controlled natural landscape, car, house and street, are considered in an attempt to provide a variety of useful places to live in within a context that is recognisably 'American/suburban' and not an evocation of a Mediterranean village. The proposal is intended to foster a sense of community despite the inherent limitations of a project which isolates old people from young and discourages their natural interaction.

**Minnesota II — State Capitol Building Annex, design competition, 1976 (● 72)**

**Park Avenue apartment, New York, New York, 1977 (● 076)**
The principal feature of this apartment is the free-standing screen-wall arcade. This device links the dining and living rooms at either end of the long entry foyer and articulates important features of the plan. It provides an ambiguous reading of closure to the rooms along its length, increasing their apparent size. The inherent nature of the screen wall, that is its arcade-like aspect, suggests exterior space and heightens the sense of openness. The somewhat Mediterranean colour palette reinforces this effect while maximising the impact of the brightly lit windows at either end.

**Residence, Fairfield County, project, 1977-78 (● 077)**
**Assistant in charge: Clair A. Martin III**
**Assistant: Ethelind Coblin**
This project for a residence in a new subdivision in suburban-Connecticut uses a traditional parti and traditional forms to create a house which aspires to formality without being rigid. Certain details, as for example the entrance porch, recall the traditions of the region as well as their innumerable subsequent revivals. The interior consists of discrete spaces which are interrelated axially.

**Erbun Fabrics Showroom, New York, New York, 1978 (● 081)**
This fabric showroom occupies an awkward space in the Design and Decoration Building. The mirrored lattice walls are arranged like the leaves of a traditional folding screen to create multiple reflections and lead customers past the fabric carousels. Despite the extensive use of mirrors, the lattice and other woodwork give the bounding walls a sense of permanence and scale. The neutral colour scheme of white, grey and black complements the colourful fabrics.

**First Avenue Squash Club, New York, New York, 1978-79 (● 082)**
This small three-court squash facility occupies space initially intended for twin cinemas in the basement of a recently completed apartment

071

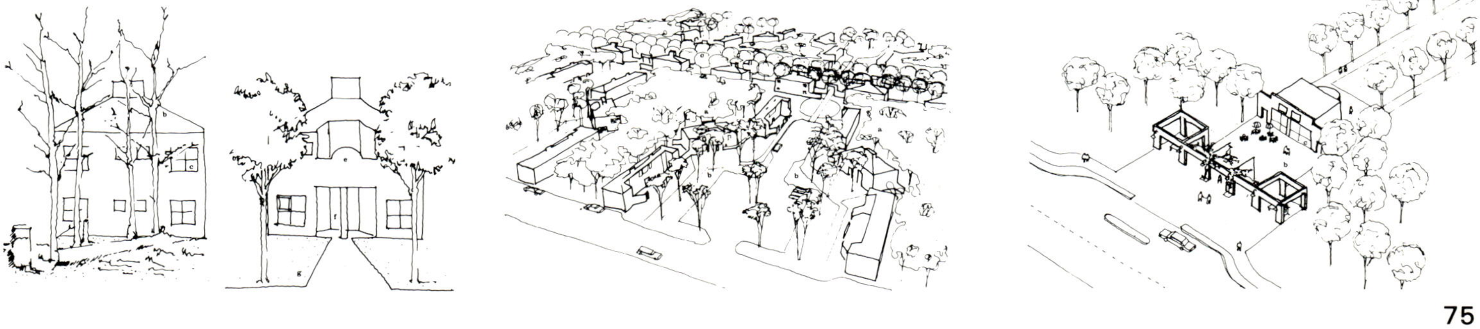

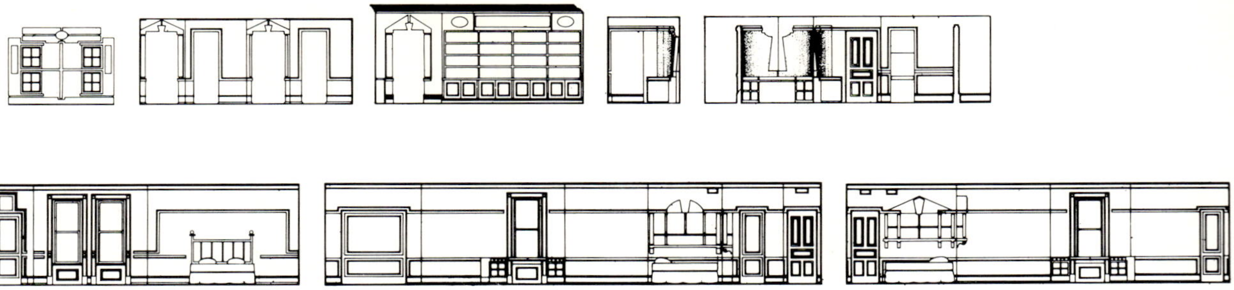

088

building. A variety of strategies were employed to brighten and lighten the character of the subterranean space without compromising its essential nature as an artificially lit and ventilated environment. Thus, while the stepped profile of the pilasters suggests columns supporting great weight, their comparative thinness combines with the mirrored ceiling to dematerialise the building mass and to suggest a spacious airiness that is not really there.

Similarly, a game of reversals is played between the club lounge conceived of as a 'veranda' or 'terrace' located between the club 'house' containing the service desk (set behind the screen wall) and the glass walled squash courts themselves which are intended to be seen as 'outside'. This allusion to the out-of-doors, and to country club life, is carried further through the use of slate gray carpeting which evokes bluestone terracing and sky blue painted walls which are particularly effective as seen reflected in the ceiling.

**Fresh café, 1978-79 (●084)**
This proposal for a new type of café selling light sandwiches, fruit drinks, exotic coffees and fine pastries, was to have occupied a store-front in a typically banal speculative apartment building on First Avenue. Colour and the highly articulated entrance vestibule are intended to evoke a subtropical atmosphere that is associated with citrus groves, jasmine and starry night skies, all combining to reinforce the owner's conception of gastronomic purity and the need to establish a sense of place in an absolutely banal context.

**Residence, studio and outbuilding for Mr. and Mrs. Joe Brooks, East Hampton, Long Island, New York, 1978-79 (●087)**
**Assistant-in-charge: Roger H. Seifter**
This complex of buildings includes a spacious residence and a separate studio for the owner who is a musician and composer. The formal impetus of the scheme comes from the local architectural context — the Shingle Style of the 1880s and 1890s — and from the generic character of suburban estate planning in the early part of this century. The main house employs traditional compositional strategies to produce a suite of rooms across the garden front which are at once discrete and centred yet opened to each other, to the grass terrace and to the formal garden beyond.

The studio is conceived of as a converted barn or carriage house. The ornamental treatment of the gable ends reflects the shifted centre of the double-height work room with respect to the overall composition. The studio is closed on three sides to provide privacy from family activities; on the fourth it opens to a small, walled garden.

**Hitzig apartment, 1979-80 (●088)**
Our work in this flat, located in New York's second oldest apartment house, involved the reconfiguration of one half of the available space (that devoted to sleeping, bathing and cooking) in order to more comfortably accommodate a family of four and in order to attempt to bring that space up to a level of artistic excellence commensurate with the rest which consists of two magnificently configured and interestingly detailed Edwardian rooms.

**Renovations to International House, New York, New York, staged renovation, 1979 (●089)**
International House is a residence and social facility for five hundred foreign and American students enrolled at any one of the universities and academies in New York. Since its construction in 1924, the main building has been renovated several times on a piece-meal basis, often at the expense of the stylistic consistency of its neo-Georgian interiors. By the mid-1950s a radically altered neigbourhood situation had forced the House to close its principal entrance, which led axially from the building onto a public park, and to open in its place a securely guarded but inconveniently located and overtly modest doorway at the Claremont Avenue basement level.

Now nearing completion, the first phase of our work at International House represents an attempt to infuse the mundane spaces of the Claremont Avenue entrance with some of the original character of the largely unused public rooms of the House. For the sake of ease in maintenance as well as rather strict budgetary control, the older Georgian vocabulary here has been abstracted so as to suggest what is further within the House to those entering off the street. A proposal for the facade of this entrance, awaiting funding, attempts to build up the scale of the tiny doorway and to provide a large sign to identify the house to the general community. The use of the canvas canopy is not only a convenience in inclement weather, but also, by virtue of its association with entrances to hotels and apartment houses downtown, contributes to the efforts of the House to free itself from the negative image of a 'dormitory'.

The second phase of construction, also nearing completion, deals with the more ceremonial, less heavily used entrance to the House from Riverside Drive. As this area leads directly to the still intact formal public rooms, the original detailing has been restored, maintained, and played upon in a quite traditional fashion.

**Smetana loft, New York City, under construction (●090)**
Located in a converted loft building in the Soho district, the design proposition of this combined residence and consultation facility for two doctors grows out of a need to adjust the vast size of the principal space to a more comfortably human scale without sacrificing the pleasures inherent in possessing so much cubage in which to live and work. To this end, the big room is treated as an exterior space trapped between the brick walls of other buildings, the lamps as *torchères* or perhaps even street lights, the kitchen and balcony enclosures as walls of other adjacent buildings, the latter in a state of semi-decay represented by the tear along one wall which reveals the wooden structural frame behind.

**Maynard Residence, East Hampton, New York, 1979 (●092)**
**Assistant-in-charge: Gregory Bader**
This renovation of a shingle style house represents an attempt to combine scholarship with spatial invention. A new sense of openness is achieved though the traditional vocabulary of the original is maintained. New windows introduced in the large gambrels, and a continuous wall of glazed doors flood the interior with light; a portion of the second floor has been removed to form a double height sun room, partially ringed by a second floor balcony sitting room.

**Residence for Mr. and Mrs. Albert Cohn, Llewellyn Park, New Jersey, under construction (●094)**
This project consists of two components: the renovation of a Georgian house designed in 1929 by Edgar Williams; and the addition of alterations to the terraces and garden to accommodate a new tennis court and a new structure housing an indoor swimming pool. The renovation of the original structure responds to the owners' needs for more living space and less servants' quarters and to a feeling that the character of the original interior space was pompous. In reordering the interiors a syncopated counterpoint emerges between what appears to be, though is not necessarily, old and new. This is particularly vivid on the first floor where a new classically composed columnar order is introduced to counterpoint the free curves of the screen wall that encloses the living room. It can also be seen on the second floor where a sweeping diagonal ties together space in the principal part of the house with that in what was formerly the servants' wing.

The pool house is deliberately complex in its formal references — a good-time place cloaked in an envelope that responds to the character of the original house while at the same time taking on the character of a landscape feature: it is a kind of grotto or nymphaeum that marks a transition between the house, its terraces, and the garden. The palm tree columns that carry the terrace recall John Nash's at the Brighton Pavilion. These columns are used in a way similar to that used by Hans Hollein in a travel office in Vienna — to trigger appropriate and pleasant thoughts of sun-filled tropical islands. The tile walls induce a subaqueous character to the room. The use of faux-marble pilasters of almost archaic character are a complement to the various high-tech strategies employed to capture solar heat and natural light and to open the pool to the garden.

*Illustrated in colour on page 11*

**Residence for Mr. and Mrs. Albert Cohn, Chilmark, Martha's Vineyard, Masssachusetts, under construction (●095)**
Set on one of the highest sites on Martha's Vineyard, commanding views of water in three directions, this shingled house, with its gently

096

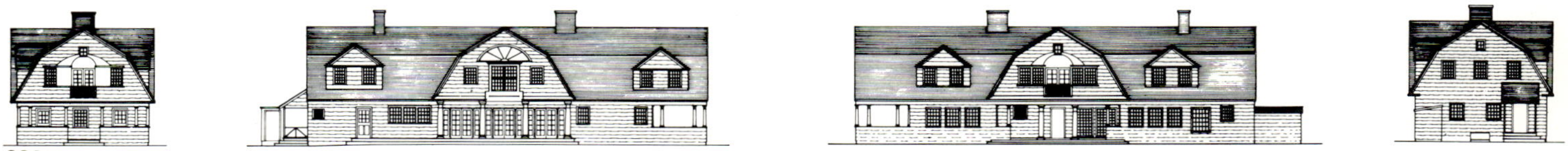

092

hipped gable roof, dormers, bay windows, subsumed porches and inglenook continues the language of traditional sea-side house architecture that emerged in the 1870s and which for many has virtually ever since defined pleasant summertime living along the New England shore. At the entrance, the roofline is interrupted by a large gable containing the asymmetrically located front door and a circular window which illumlnates the generously proportioned stair behind. On the opposite side, the hipped gables are gently distended to provide a second storey balcony overlooking the principal water view.

**Best Products Facade, 1979 (●096)**
**'The Earth, the Temple, and the Goods'**
**Design: Robert A.M. Stern architects; Gavin Macrae-Gibson, assistant-in-charge**
**Model: John Ike, Mark Albert**
**Perspective: Gavin Macrae-Gibson, Charles Warren**

The standard BEST Products building is a box whose purpose is to supply the objects that are demanded by and in part define the lives of those who live out a version of the American Dream — a version in which material possessions, once the objects of religious sacrifice, now serve to mark out rituals of daily life. To a considerable extent our household goods have become our household gods, our markets, temples of consumerism. In designing a facade for BEST, we have undertaken to tell the story of this transformation of values in a witty way, and to describe the cycle of life to which it bears witness.

It has been observed that shopping has become a cultural act for many Americans. For this reason, the temple front, with its widely recognised associations in high culture, seems appropriate. The bold scale of the pediment silhouetted against the sky, and of the stoa-arcade gives the showroom enough 'skyline' and enough 'mass' to be seen by motorists howling along the highway. The attention of the motorist is first held by the letters within the pediment, which have replaced the sculpture of antiquity, while at closer range, the introduction of column-like cut-outs within the arcade brings the scale down to one that is sympathetic to the parked car and the pedestrian.

The columns have been squashed by the great weight of the pediment and record the changes that have taken place in the anatomy of the temple, yet they can also be read as table-legs, the canopies as table tops, supporting the goods as if in a residential setting. The gold colour refers to the sacrificial instruments of archaic rites, while suggesting the affluence of contemporary American society. The stoa-arcade and its heroically scaled metopes are the guardians of the temple, with its treasures within, standing upright, braces with outstretched arms against the enormous space of the parking lot.

The facade is intended to be read in a number of specific ways. The classical language transforms the catalogue showroom into a temple of consumerism, the columns of the stoa-arcade carry out the historical theme of consumerism and support metopes whose silhouetted images depict typical products sold by BEST. The placement of each metope-image corresponds to the approximate location of the product depicted in the showroom; at the same time the arrangement of the metopes on the facade can be read from left to right documenting an idealised cycle of contemporary life: courtship leading to engagement; marriage with its wedding gifts and attendant photographically recorded hoppla; the wedding trip followed by the routine of married life, with hours spent watching television; the passage of time leading to childbirth and the repetition of the cycle.

The front door penetrates the cycle in the centre. What was the opening in the inside wall of the temple becomes solid and comes forward, and the column that would have stood in front of it becomes the void through which the portal is entered. The huge void column 'supports' the letter 'T' above, and is thus related to the smaller void columns on either side, but at the scale of the landscape rather than at the scale of the cars in the parking lot. The column beyond the silhouette is the last vestige of the real columns that once existed, but it is made of glass, the material of museum cases, and it is thorugh this object that the temple with its affordable treasures is entered.

The facade is to be built of porcelain enameled steel and anodised aluminium panels; the former assembled in such a way as to suggest the rusticated masonry of the enclosing cella wall of traditional temples, the latter serving as the cladding of the elements in the stoa-arcade including the metopes that carry out the programme of narrative decoration.

In the drawing, a larger cycle of time is superimposed on the life-cycle portrayed in the facade. The catalogue showroom is shown in its typical setting along a roadside strip, taking a position in relation to the natural landscape and to the present man-made and man-manipulated environment. The siting of the BEST temple, like that of examples from ancient Greece, tells a story of men and the forces of nature, of hubris, and of reverence for things as they are.

*Illustrated in colour on pages 3, 14 and 15*

**Super Spa for *House Beautiful* and the Kohler Company, 1979 (●097)**

Super Spa was intended to showcase new plumbing fixtures and new ideas about the sybaritic potential of the bathroom in American life. The pavilion functions as an oasis. After ascending onto the platform containing a hot tub at its centre and flanking sheltered banquettes, one enters a high central room in which a combination tub-shower takes on the characteristics of a baldachino; to the left and right of this are rooms containing sinks and toilets, an exercise room and a chamber in which various climatic conditions can be simulated. The overall character of the Super Spa is related to *fin de sicle* Art Nouveau and Viennese Secessionist experiments, the former because of its suggestion of subaqueous life, the latter for its progressive classicism employing flat areas of colour, often in tile, to render the exterior surfaces grand yet not oppressively monumental.

**Lawson House, Quogue, New York, under construction (●098)**

Set along the ocean beach on a typical, narrow seaside lot, this design seeks to connect with the traditions of the Shingle Style and more particularly with the kinds of 'beach cottages' that

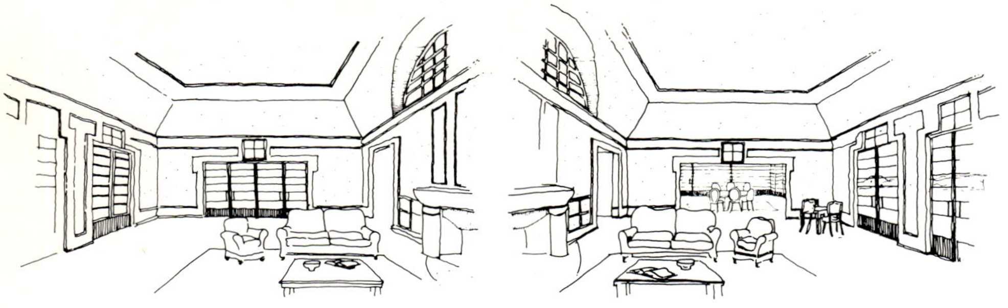

SOUTH LIVING ROOM NORTH

FRONT HALL

104

proliferated along the East Coast in the 1910s and 20s, cottages whose astylar simplicity and direct use of materials surely grew out of the writings and designs of Gustave Stickley. The position of the house at the edge of a high dune made it possible to duck three small guest bedrooms at grade behind the dune. Thus, the oversealed stoop leads up to the principal floor just below the level of the dune. It also provides an inviting porch from which to observe the sunset across the bay. The master bedroom is located in the attic, lit by a boldly arched window at the sea side that gives the house big scale and connects it with the high architecture of classicism just as the eyelid dormer in the master bath pays its respects to Richardson. Though the eroded configuration of the principal floor responds to particular considerations of site, view and solar orientation, the fundamentally symmetrical organisation of the mass is intended to give the house a dignity and iconic clarity of its own — an object of calm amidst the helter skelter.

**Residence, King's Point, New York (● 104)**
**Assistant in charge: John Averitt**
**Assistant: Terry Brown**

This new house in an established residential neighbourhood evokes the traditional architectural language of the Regency Style while satisfying the particular demands of site and use. Commissioned by an older couple, the programme required good views of the bays from all rooms, ample outdoor spaces for entertaining and a plan which avoided the use of stairs. To satisfy these requirements the house necessarily became long and low. Two symmetrical wings were employed to order the facade and plan, one for the kitchen and garage and another for the two master bedrooms. Two guest bedrooms and the maid's quarters were located on the second floor to give the house scale, modulate the silhouette and achieve a double height section in the living room. The front, with its nearly unpunctured brick walls flanking the entrance court, is a quiet, horizontal facade that orients itself about the large green. On the back the pavilion form of the wings is emphasised, making a more vertical and active composition that gives a sense of place to the various outdoor spaces. Here, the necessity of views dictates a more transparent facade, the bricks and columns parting to make way for a glass and steel skin which weaves its way along the perimeter.

We believe that this design demonstrates that the single-family house remains a testing ground for ideas in architecture and that traditional languages continue to have meaning for both owner and architect and therefore can be used in new ways in our time.

**Modern Architecture after Modernism — A pavilion in the Forum Design Exhibition at Linz, Austria, 1980 (● 106)**
**Assistant-in-charge: Gavin Macrae-Gibson**
**Assistant: Mark Albert**

What is commonly called Modern architecture is in reality merely a phase of a broad, ongoing tradition that extends back to the Renaissance. Modern in the broad sense, combines three things: firstly, a search for iconographically appropriate form based on a sense of meaning derived from history, especially that of the classical past; secondly, a recognition of the unique characteristics of the present as expressed through technological innovation; and lastly, a certain continuing cultural *malaise* which takes its most powerful expression in the conviction that the vernacular forms of architecture represent a purer form of cultural expression. Modernism, on the other hand, is a phase which seeks to establish a new language of architecture by overthrowing Modern architecture's roots in the classical past and in the vernacular in favour of a set of forms based solely on the processes of production. As a result, the function of the building and the way it is constructed are particularly emphasised at the expense of any symbolic means derived from the past or from everyday life. In the 1970s, it became widely apparent that after fifty years modernism had run its course; the post-modernism which succeeds it is not a new, anti-modern, avant-garde style, but a reintegration with the broad stream of Modern architecture. It is an attempt to resynthesise current production with its natural roots in classical and vernacular form while at the same time making appropriate use of the advanced technological processes of the present. Hence the title of the pavilion: 'Modern Architecture after Modernism'.

The central element of the pavilion is a polychromed Greek temple front, an icon representing the search that has been made recently into the past. The temple front recalls, in a relatively literal manner, early Greek temples such as those at Paestum, Selinus and Segesta, but with the columns rendered as voids, and the spaces between the columns as solids. Since the void columns are the means by which one enters the temple it is as if one is in fact walking through history into the past. The six columns that have been removed from the temple front have a double life; they are the objects that populate the forecourt as well as those that populate the enclosed space within. These columns are humanistic embodiments of architects whose work is of special interest today, whether they are from the past, as outside, or the present, as inside.

In the forecourt, across which one approaches the temple, is a field of six columns each one representative of a Modern architect from the past. Each column is covered with black and white photographs of the work of one of these architects. The columns are arranged to present a ruin, enhancing the Greek ambience, emphasising the central importance of the classical tradition and portraying the state of the past after the harsh neglect of Modernism. It is from these ruins that strength can be drawn today for a continuation of the Modern tradition after the unfortunate impoverishment of form that was brought about by the modernist period. The upright columns within the temple embody the work of six contemporary architects whose work demonstrates the richness of form that can be achieved through the rediscovery of the past and through a conscious attempt to reestablish the continuity of Modern architecture. Illuminated from within to provide the only light in the darkened space, the columns of post modernism are covered with colour transparencies of the work of each architect and are ar-

109

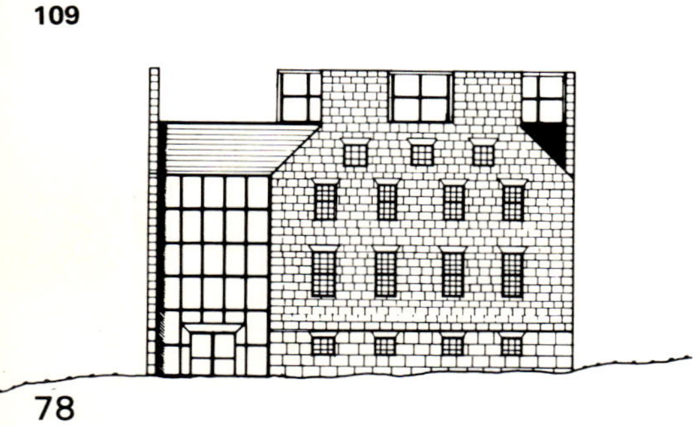

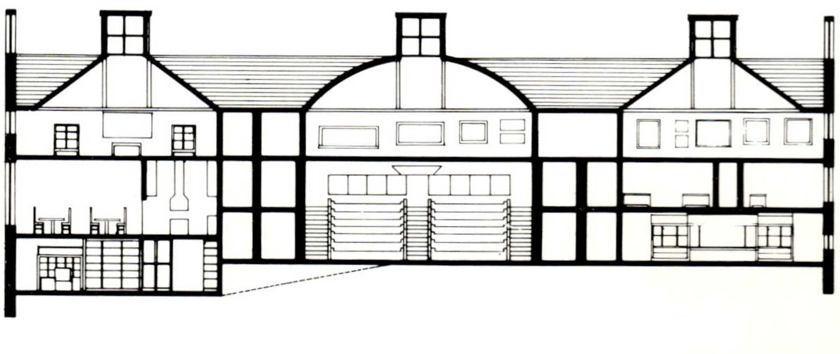

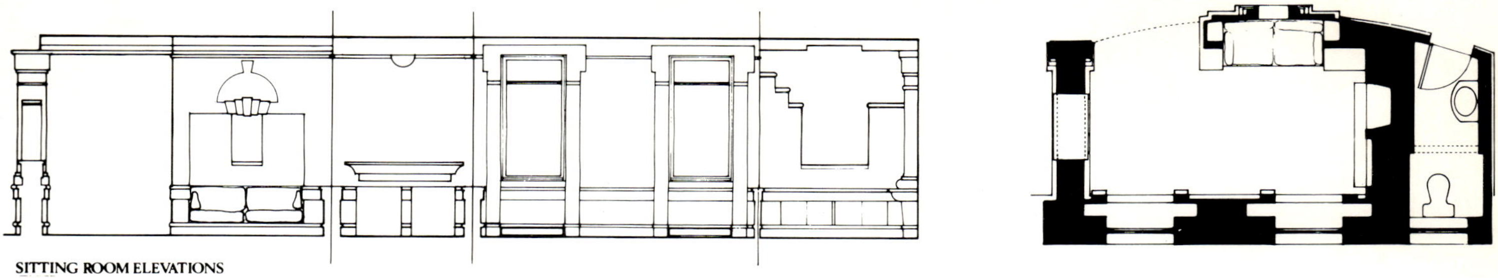

SITTING ROOM ELEVATIONS
113

ranged as if engaged in debate over the issues raised by the pavilion.

**The Chicago Tribune Tower, 1980 (● 107)**
**Design: Robert A.M. Stern Architects**
**Assistant-in-charge: Gavin Macrae-Gibson**
**Perspective drawing: Mark Albert, Charles Warren**

Our project for the new Chicago Tribune Tower takes as its primary reference, Adolf Loos' entry in the original 1921-1922 competition, and attempts to marry that project to the Miesian prism. To build a classical tower out of glass, we have used architectural elements rooted in the culture of the past though executed in the technology of the present.

The flat pilaster is used as opposed to the round column employed by Loos in order to retain the shape of the standard office building box. These pilasters are tripled on each face in the manner of Michelangelo's third storey of the Palazzo Farnese, to increase the sense of verticality of the tower, provide multiple corners that add interest to the interior, and increase the opportunities for reflections on the exterior. The corners of the block are quoined in a striped pattern of black spandrel glass and white frosted glass: this pattern makes reference to Loos' house for Josephine Baker, with its striped articulation, and to the black and white lines of the newspaper itself.

The signboard at the top refers to the cultural conditions of the Mid-West which in earlier days gave rise to the urbanism of the false front, and whose nostalgia for the somehow grander things from other places gave rise also to the name 'Chicago Tribune' with its self-righteous overtones of Roman morality. The Tuscan order of the pilasters best approached the nostalgia for the moral austerity and rectitude of the ancient Roman tribunes, while the red and gold colour scheme best recalled that period.

The word 'Tribune' on the south face of the building is directed to those across the Chicago River in the Loop and announces that in crossing the river one is entering the land where the Chicago Tribune pioneered large scale development. In the same way, recalling Henri Labrouste's 'Bridge connecting France and Italy', the word 'Chicago' on the north face announces that one will soon be entering the 'real' Chicago of the Loop area — the frame and infill architecture of William Le Baron Jenny beloved by Siegfried Giedion, and leaving behind that other Chicago of suburbs and styles, the cultural complexities of Frank Lloyd Wright, Howard Shaw, and David Adler.

**Venice Biennale — 1980 (● 108)**
**Assistant-in-charge: Gavin Macrae-Gibson**
**Assistant: Mark Albert**

*'We didn't need sound. We had faces...*
(Gloria Swanson as Norma Desmond, extolling the methods of the silent film in Billy Wilder's *Sunset Boulevard* (1951).

The single most positive aspect of the current exploration of traditional values in contemporary architecture is the recuperation of the concept of the facade. No longer, as in the canonical modernism of the past seventy years, is the facade merely a representation of the syntactical aspects of architecture — that is, the building's plan and section — or merely a revelation of the processes of its own production. The facade has been unbound and its blindfold and gag untied. Like the silent faces, the facade offers revelations of things as they are, while representing things as one might want them to be.

Our proposal for 'La Strada Nuovissima' is a discussion of the reality and illusion of the past. The past is treated both as recent past — addressing the work of our office, and as distant past — addressing the history of architecture. The elements of the facade connect these two levels, while also addressing the pavilion's location in a street of ambiguous scale and in a coastal city that was once a great sea power. Thus the abstracted curtain/columns with their suggestion of a proscenium not only tell of a 'show' of office work that lies within ready to be seen by the audience at La Biennale but also of a more enduring drama acted out by players upon a stage of infinite dimensions. While the 'show' is a reality in the present, the greater drama is a constantly changing flow of illusions, interpreted differently at different times by different people. Noble among the players in this shadow play is the Greek temple, an abstraction of which appears as a void upon the silent face of the figure that stands before the curtain of history. This image — at once literal and abstract — inhabits the new street, a Venetian trader dressed in gold and red damask before a backdrop of maritime colours. Yet the temple, like the overscaled moulding which adorns the proscenium above it, refers also to office projects that have marked important stages in our stylistic direction: the former refers to the Best Products facade of 1979 and the latter to the Lang House of 1975.

The illusions of the past become the reality of the present on the interior where the temple form becomes more explicit and is used as a framework to display the work. The threshold of this transition is a void, rusticated column, an icon from another recent project, the house at Llewellyn Park, emphasising the importance of entering the past in order to fully experience the richness of which the present is capable.

**Shaker Village, Pleasant Hill, Kentucky, competition, 1979 (● 109)**

**Capasso Residence, Fifth Avenue apartment, New York City, 1980 (● 113)**

**Cincinatti City Hall Annex, competition, 1980 (● 120)**

**Residence at Farm Neck, Oak Bluffs, Massachusetts, 1980 (● 121)**

**'Human scale at the end of the age of modernism': Architectural League Collaborative, 1981 (● 122)**
**Sculpture: Robert Graham**
**Base Design: Robert A.M. Stern Architects**
**Assistant-in-charge: Charles Warren**

There are no stale subjects, only stale artists...

120

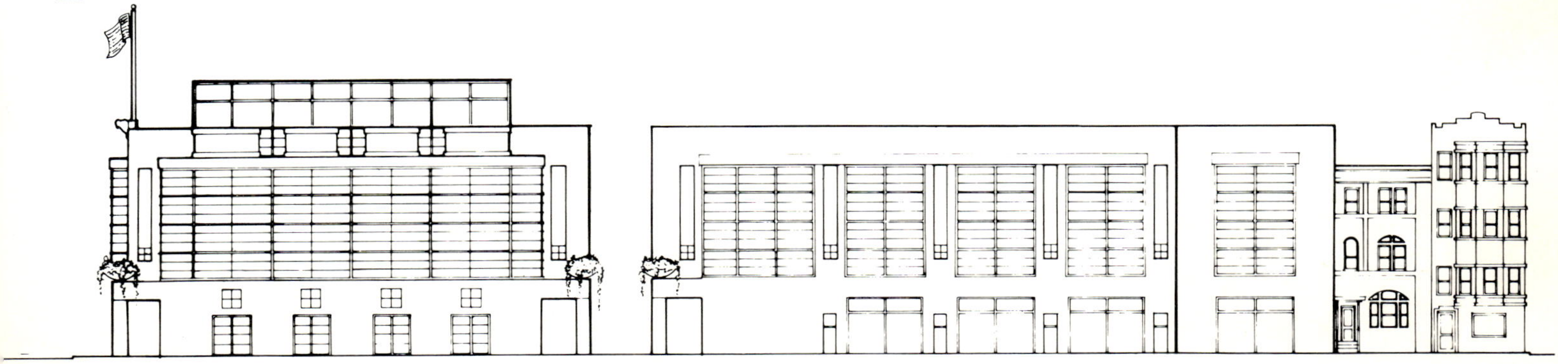

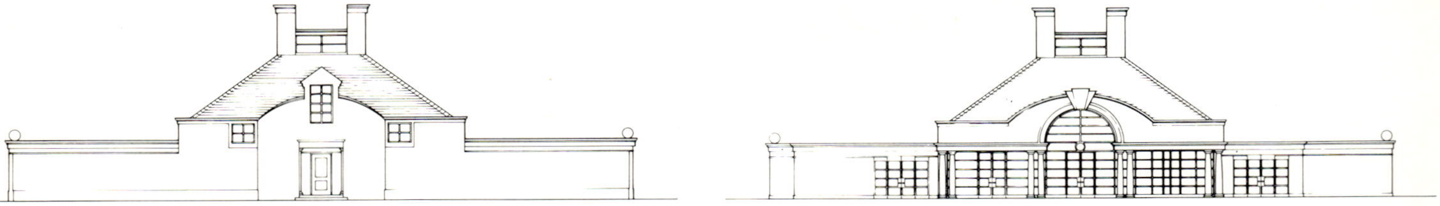

129

Our collaboration attempts a rich and meaningful allegory for the current condition in the arts. This condition, frequently labelled as post-modernist, seeks to recuperate traditional form in order to go beyond the impasse of late modernism with its belligerently anti-symblic stance, extreme abstraction and reductionism.

The female figure is cast in bronze; the naturalism of its modelling is a clear representation of our continued confidence in the expressive capacity of the Western humanist tradition. The figure surmounts an Ionic column raised on a plinth, both executed in faux marble. Further investigation reveals that the column and base are only partially modelled and appear to be emerging from an asymmetrically composed, scaleless mass sheathed in mirror glass in emulation of the current stage in the evolution of the high-rise office block. The contrast between the two systems of composition in the base — the classicist and the modernist — is an explicit representation of the disjunction that currently characterises the arts in general, and architecture in particular.

The triumph of mechanomorphology over humanism, so long and so impatiently awaited by the purveyors of the modern movement has not come to pass, while its artistic impact as something 'new', free of history and of style, has diminished with the years. The art historical clock cannot be turned back. The 'new' has become old, or at least traditional, and pre-modernist modes of perception have not disappeared (but have merely been eclipsed). Modernism and classicism now co-exist in an uneasy proximity, no longer colliding as opposites but struggling towards a new synthesis.

*Illustrated on front cover*

**DOM Headquarters Competition, Bruhl, Germany 1980 (● 124)**

Our proposal intends to be a jewel and a strong box at once, a building of diamond-like objectivity set apart from the rough industrial landscape, a working monument that incorporates in steel and refletive glass those qualities of precision that one associates with the products of the DOM corporation.

The proposal consists of an office tower sitting upon a base housing the entrance hall, cafeteria and training facilities. The base relates in height to the low mass of the adjacent factory; its shape, that of two superimposed squares (set at a diagonal to one another) seeks to enhance the frontality of the tower on the entrance side while permitting it to be read more sculpturally in the round from the motor highway. The tower and the base are sheathed in tinted glass; the colours, green, black and silver are selected to further enhance the desired image of cool mechanical perfection.

While the design seeks to be forward-looking through its precise use of advance construction technology, it also draws upon a rich tradition of modern classicism to place itself within a broad cultural and architectural context. Thus the design seeks to continue and expand upon the tradition of technically advanced and classically composed buildings established by Otto Wagner, Gropius and Meyer. In its interior spaces the headquarters draws upon lessons from the commercial buildings of Frank Lloyd Wright. His Johnson Wax Headquarters is specifically invoked in the great reception hall/product presentation room at the top, a room that can become a major public space for DOM.

The tower is designed to be impressive by day and by night. Its principal feature is the stepped dome at its top which by day admits natural light to the product presentation room at the top and, when artificially illuminated, acts as a symbolic beacon blazing across the night sky an image of the DOM company.

**Garibaldi Meucci Museum, Staten Island, New York, 1980 (● 125)**
**Assistant in charge: Charles Warren**
**Assistant: Tony Cohn**

The primary concern in this project is to maintain the character of the existing house — where the Italian patriot Giuseppe Garibaldi lived for several years, as did Antonio Meucci, the true inventor of the telephone — while adding a large amount of space to serve as a museum of Italian-American culture. It was our concern that the spirit of the place with its informally landscaped front yard and its Gothic revival simplicity should not be overwhelmed by a new building unrelated in style or intention.

Most of the building is below grade, the roof forming a series of terraces to display statues and artifacts which are at present rather randomly placed around the site. The stepping of the terraces allows variation in the section of the new museum space. The porch and arbour at the back provide shelter for outdoor activities while screening from view the house on the adjoining property. The terrace is also designed to take advantage of the large trees and elliptical pond in the park next door. A small pavilion at the front sympathetically echoes the style of the existing house while providing entry control, a guard house and a connection between museum and terrace levels.

**Residence in Glen Cove, Long Island, New York, 1980 (● 129)**

**San Juan Capistrano Library Competition, California, 1980 (● 133)**
**Assistants-in-charge: J Averitt, R Seifter**
**Assistants: Terry Brown, Anthony Cohn, John Ike, Erica Millar, Charles Warren**

Our goal in designing the public library at San Juan Capistrano is a building that responds gently to its context while at the same time providing operational efficiency. Such a combination can go a long way towards nurturing the activities that a library shelters and the quality of life of the town as a whole. While the new building responds directly to its programme and to its immediate physical situation, it also reflects the larger stylistic current from which these surroundings are derived; in so doing, it 'speaks' the traditional language of the place without using all the same words.

In organising the library we have employed an L-shaped plan that separates and at the same time links the three principal programmatic zones of public reading, assembly and service. The information area terminates this gallery at the east and provides a formal and observational focus for the main reading and lounging areas extending southwards and parallel to El Camino Real. Organised on a symmetrical open plan basis to promote planning flexibility, the reading areas are in turn flanked by separate spaces for study, book storage, and quiet refuge. A separate wing for the quiet reading room leads to a fountain courtyard open to the public and to a walled reading patio which is accessible only from the library.

The library is constructed of materials sympathetic to the local technology and to the Spanish Colonial style: stucco-covered concrete block walls; clay tiled roofs. The major public spaces of the interior are sheltered under the exposed roof structure of wood trusses, purlins, and decking. The interior is suffused with a soft light coming from operable hopper and fixed clerestory sash windows which reduce direct sunlight while providing cross ventilation and a comfortable degree of ambient daylight.

**Ram Island Residence, Shelter Island, New York, 1981 (● 140)**

140

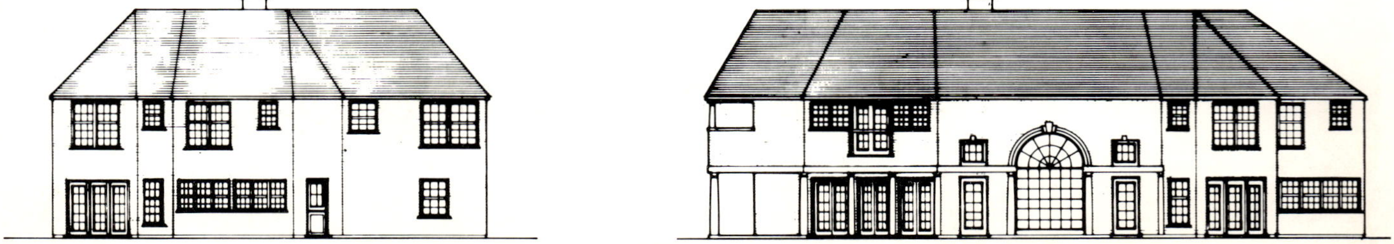